THE SCOPE

OF

PHILOSOPHY

THE SCOPE

OF

PHILOSOPHY

John Young

GRACEWING

First published in 2008 by Warrane College,
University of New South Wales, Australia

This edition published 2010

Gracewing
2 Southern Avenue, Leominster
Herefordshire, HR6 0QF

ISBN 978 085244 733 8

CONTENTS

INTRODUCTION

He was a University lecturer in philosophy, and he was telling us of the sentiments of undergraduates as they approach this subject for the first time. Many of them, he said, are full of eagerness, expecting to find answers to the ultimate questions. Now they will learn the truth about the nature of reality, God's existence, the way of life they should follow. These problems will be rationally explored and the truth revealed. They get quite a jolt when they find what philosophy is really about: for example, painstaking analyses of language which leave the big questions just as remote as before. In fact, the lecturer stated, much recent philosophy has had the effect of pushing ultimate questions off the board, of ruling them out.

Glancing around the small group of us listening to him, he asked: "What's your opinion? Do you feel like the disappointed undergraduates when you hear that recent philosophy is mainly analysis? Do you think it should tackle these ultimate questions?"

A short silence followed. Then I answered that I considered questions such as the nature of reality and the existence of God to be proper ones for philosophy.

The lecturer smiled and said: "If you were to write a book dealing with these questions, and published it, philosophers would read it and say, 'If Mr. Young intends his system as a set of definitions with conclusions drawn from them, it is an interesting arrangement, although probably of not much practical value. On the other hand, if he means that this is true, he's wrong!'"

I was writing this book at the time, but he did not know that. The incident is instructive in a number of ways.

It illustrates the extent to which much philosophy today is severed from the efforts of great thinkers of the past. I say much philosophy, because the situation is not as clear-cut as the lecturer depicted it – many philosophers still regard metaphysical questions as valid. But many do not, and are therefore forced to leave out of account ideas of some of the most renowned thinkers of the ages. Again, this incident illustrates the radical change which has occurred, in many circles, in the notion of philosophy. It used to be regarded as the investigation of the ultimate questions human reason can ask; so once these questions are ruled out philosophy finds it has changed into something else. A third thought that arises from this incident concerns the intellectual confusion found in the world today. People are questioning positions and beliefs that were once regarded as basic. And questions are much more conspicuous than answers. Is not the confusion due in large measure to the lack of a well-grounded philosophy? Has man lost the key to the depths of life, so that he is condemned to stay on the surface and to restrict his understanding to the surface?

Consider two men with opposed outlooks. The first looks on man as a mere organism which has evolved by blind physical laws to its present state. Man has no intelligence distinct from his sense knowledge, no free will, no destiny beyond this life. There are no moral laws in the traditional sense. Nothing above the corporeal is knowable. The second individual believes man to transcend the purely physical, to have a spiritual power of intelligence above his sense knowledge, to have free will, to have a soul destined to live forever. He believes in a supreme being to whom human life is ordered.

If each of these men really tries to live out his conception of things, their lives are going to be very different: their opposite conceptions will influence their judgments, actions, manner of facing difficulties. It comes to this: each will strive to relate himself to what he sees as reality, and will consider himself to be acting realistically when he is thus related. But will he be right? That depends on whether his conception of reality is the right one. If it is not entirely right, he will be out of relation to reality to the extent that his conception of reality errs. And this maladjustment, if serious, will lead to distortion in his personality and in his relation to others. If there are sufficient maladjusted people, society itself will be distorted. It is not enough to have sincere intentions, necessary though they are. A doctor acting in ignorance of medical facts will harm his patients whether his intentions are good or not. A man acting in ignorance of more basic realities will harm himself and society in spite of good intentions.

When error about these matters is widespread in a society it is very hard for an individual to see the truth. The educative influence society should have is perverted into a process of indoctrination. We can see how this works by looking at errors in past ages which were believed without hesitation by extremely intelligent people – simply because they had become a part of the accepted culture.

How, then, are we to achieve a true and harmonious view of things, a view that will relate the various fields of knowledge to each other, will give us an insight into ultimate truths, will show us how we should live and what our goals should be?

I am convinced that philosophy – or more specifically, the philosophy whose greatest master is St. Thomas Aquinas – is an essential part of such an intellectual and personal integration. Without it, our understanding is dangerously incomplete and liable to become very warped. It would not be so bad if our culture were informed by healthy philosophy; we would tend to imbibe the philosophy with general culture, even though we did not make a special study of it. But that is not the actual state of affairs. Such philosophy is not even understood.

Some object to this approach on the grounds that religious faith should be our guide, not philosophy. Reason, they say, is sterile in these matters; it can give no certainty, no comfort, no life. It concerns itself with straw-splitting distinctions, with barren abstractions, with meaningless jargon, with a shadowy world of empty concepts.

In reply, I would point out that religious knowledge does not exist in a sealed compartment of our minds, but in contact with, and influenced by, a hundred other subjects. And truths harmonize; one cannot contradict another. Much theology today is in a state of bewilderment, and a major reason for this is the shattering impact various philosophical views have had upon it. Unless a theologian has a sound philosophical basis his theology will suffer; and the same applies to anyone who interests himself in theology. Even a man of "simple faith", who says theology is a waste of time, will be affected by current philosophical opinions – he will be affected far more than he realizes. But the above objection is partly a reaction against degenerations of true philosophy; and I have no wish to defend those.

Philosophy, historically and as it is conceived in the present work, is the discipline or science which investigates the basic nature and deepest principles of reality, under the light of reason. It does not concern itself with phenomena and their laws: that is the task of the physical sciences. Nor does it investigate or depend on divine revelation. It begins with evident principles and with facts we can see, hear or otherwise sense; and from these it proceeds, by reasoning, to a fundamental understanding of being. It does not appeal to faith or authority of any kind: it reasons out all its conclusions. To the extent that something is beyond reason it is beyond philosophy.

The early chapters of this work sketch philosophy's development from the ancient Greek cosmologists to the current postmodernists. In this way we see the great questions unfolding, and gain an insight into influences working on our culture today. It also becomes clear that philosophers must understand what knowledge is before they can advance very far – that is the key to understanding philosophy. Several chapters are devoted to that problem. Then we go on to examine a number of other major questions, including the nature of man, the existence and nature of God, the purpose of human life.

Chapter One

PHILOSOPHY BEGINS

It was in ancient Greece that the path to philosophic wisdom was first found. From that beginning have come the philosophies of the Western world.

1. The pre-Socratic period

From the first, Greek philosophy developed separately, on the whole, from the current religion. It started from observation of the world, striving to explain the nature of things; particularly, at first, the physical universe.

The Milesian School. According to Aristotle, the first philosopher was Thales of Miletus, one of the Seven Sages. Little is known of his life. He lived in the sixth century B.C.; had travelled in Egypt; became famous as an engineer and inventor, for his astronomical observations and as a statesman. Later writers exaggerated his knowledge, assuming that he possessed all the theory implied by his practical observations.

Aristotle says he thought water was the material cause of all things. And here we meet a question which occupied all the Greek philosophers, and has been debated ever since. The problem is this: things undergo change. Food is eaten and becomes flesh; a tree is burnt and becomes ashes; among lifeless things one substance is transmuted into another. But how is this possible? It is not a case of one complete thing being replaced by another, a tree being removed and a heap of ashes placed there instead. It is a real change of one into another, a transformation. But doesn't this require some underlying subject of change, something that will link the previous reality with the new one, the tree with the ashes? Otherwise we are not positing an inner change, but the total replacement of one thing by a completely different one.

Thales and others thought that what was required was one of the familiar elements, which would be the permanent base for all changes, and the element from which all things are made.

Anaximander, an associate of Thales, posited "the boundless" as the foundation of things, teaching that the elements we know – water,

9

fire, etc., – arise from this. By the boundless he probably meant the indeterminate, arguing that what can be all things must according to itself be quite indeterminate – if it were already something determinate, how could it become something else without losing itself?

An associate of Anaximander named Anaximenes gave a more elaborate explanation of nature than his predecessors had done. According to him, air is the underlying reality. The process of becoming is explained, ingeniously, through rarefaction and condensation. By rarefaction air becomes fire; by condensation it becomes, progressively as it is more condensed, wind, cloud, water, earth, stone. He applied his theory consistently, explaining the cosmos by means of it: the earth arose from air; the heavenly bodies, which are fiery, arose from moisture from the earth, which became rarefied; the human soul is air, and thus holds us together.

The Milesian school – Thales, Anaximander, Anaximenes – set the Greek intellect on the path to be followed in succeeding centuries. Their approach and views may seem crude to us.

But if it were not for them, our civilization might never have existed. In striving to learn the nature of things, and to do so by observation and thought applied to uncovering the basic causes, the most universal and comprehensive explanations, they initiated the scientific spirit. They stimulated others by their ideas: not only in cosmology, but also in politics and in regard to practical inventions.

Pythagoras. Untold influence on later thought was exercised by Pythagoras of Samos (sixth century B.C.), who founded a religious fraternity at Kroton in Southern Italy which became the chief scientific school of the Greek world. Because he left no writings, his teachings are uncertain, but he is diversely represented as a religious teacher, as a man of science, and as a statesman and reformer. Apparently he taught reincarnation and the kinship of men and beasts. He regarded philosophy as a purification which will release man from the "wheel of birth": that is, his soul, ennobled by philosophic contemplation, will no longer need to be united with a body, but will lead a separate existence. He helped found the science of mathematics, and emphasized the mathematical harmony of things – proportion and harmony in music, for example. His tendency to explain reality in mathematical terms, to reduce physical things to mathematics, was to have a marked influence on Plato and others. It is a tendency found in much modern thought.

Heraclitus and Parmenides. In the fifth century there arose two opposite explanations of the world, one proposed by Heraclitus of Ephesus, the other by Parmenides of Elea, in Southern Italy.

Heraclitus was fascinated by the fact of change. Wherever we look we find things undergoing movement or change; this constant process is ceaselessly altering things. Heraclitus illustrated it by a flowing stream: "You cannot step twice into the same river; for fresh waters are ever flowing in upon you." [1]

By the time you have stepped into the river, it is no longer the river you started to step into, because *that* water has moved downstream, to be replaced by completely different water. He says in another place: "We step and do not step into the same river; we are and are not."[2] He means by this that a thing which is ever altering lacks any permanent identity: it both is and is not – it is not what it was an instant before. Nothing in our experience is being (in the sense of something stable); everything changes continually. These changes, in his opinion, are not merely superficial, leaving a stable core; they are utterly radical, leaving nothing the same.

Reacting against the teaching of Heraclitus, Parmenides went to the other extreme. He taught that reality is so permanent that it is not subject to any change at all. He argued that being either is or is not: there is no room for anything in between. Now, if something is not (is non-existent) it doesn't explain or affect anything. But if something *is*, it is not in a state of becoming. To say a thing is changing is to imply that it both is and is not – that it is non-identical with itself, for it is becoming something else. But it is contradictory to say that a thing both is and is not itself.

Parmenides took as his first principle: it is. By "it" he meant being or reality. Then he drew the conclusions that seemed to follow from his principle. What *is* must be one. From whence would diversity come to it? Not from nothingness, since nothingness is not the cause of anything. So *what is* has utter unity. Apart from what is there is nothing, so there is no source from which anything could be added to it. Therefore it is complete. It did not begin to exist, for to do so it would have had to arise from nothingness. It cannot be deprived of anything, for there is nothing outside to attack it. It cannot change in any way. In short, reality is uncreated, indestructible, complete, indivisible, immovable. He regarded it as corporeal: he speaks of it as a sphere; and Aristotle tells us Parmenides believed only in a sensible reality.[3]

The source of the opposite positions of Heraclitus and Parmenides lies in their starting points. In a true understanding of reality, it is necessary to reconcile being with becoming, unity with plurality, the principles of reason with the testimony of the senses. The method of Parmenides concentrates on being, unity, the principles of reason. If his solution does not square with sense experience, so much the worse for the senses. As he himself says: "All these are but names given by mortals who believe them to be true: coming into being and passing away, being and non-being, change of place and alteration of bright colour."[4] Heraclitus accepts what the senses reveal, a world of change and multiplicity. But if change went as deep as he supposes, being, unity and rational principles would be destroyed. However, it should be added that Heraclitus certainly did not see the full implications of his theory.

Empedocles. A citizen of Akragas in Sicily, Empedocles is famed for many things besides philosophy. He probably had early associations with the Pythagoreans, and their influence appears in his religious teachings, which are hardly compatible with his philosophy. He believed in reincarnation and kinship with the lower animals. He also claimed to be a god. He was a democratic politician. Aristotle ascribes to him the invention of rhetoric. According to Galen he was the founder of the very influential Italian school of medicine.

In philosophy, he started from the principle of Parmenides: what is, *is*. But he understood it in his own way. He wished to account for the obvious fact of change. Now, change cannot be accepted if all being is one in the Parmenidean sense. So Empedocles taught that there are four substances, each indivisible and immutable like the Parmenidean *one*, except that they undergo movement from place to place. They are earth, air, fire and water, the four elements which were regarded, for many centuries, as the basis of all bodies, although not with the immutable substantial character Empedocles gave them. He taught that these four alone are real natures or substances, that all the other things we call substances are combinations of these. A tree, for example, has not a real nature of its own, but is just a collection of primary elements united in a certain way. Combinations and dissolutions of these elements are brought about by love and strife – or attraction and repulsion, as we might say. The world's present state is accounted for by evolution: creatures arose in a variety of combinations – he speaks of "offspring of oxen with the faces of men, while others arose as offspring of men with the heads of oxen"[5] – and those combinations survived which were fitted to do so.

Anaxagoras. Born c. 500 B.C., Anaxagoras lived first in Clazomenae in Asia Minor, then in Athens – from which he was exiled – finally in Lampsacus, a colony of Miletus. He had probably studied in the Milesian school; he was a teacher of Pericles. He held that all corporeal things contain all others. The meaning of this, apparently, is that each thing contains tiny portions of all the others: that each piece of bread we eat, for example, contains tiny portions of blood, flesh, bone, etc. His reason for holding this extraordinary view was his acceptance of Parmenides' thesis that being neither comes into, nor passes out of, existence. Yet Anaxagoras wanted to admit change. So he reasoned that the world is made up of innumerable basic elements which never change into anything else, but which combine in different proportions. And we name different "substances" from the elements that predominate in them.

Anaxagoras went beyond the other early philosophers in maintaining that an intelligent cause is necessary to account for the universe. He speaks of this as Nous (Mind), and says Nous has knowledge of everything, power over all, moves all and orders all.

Leucippus of Miletus. The difficulties inherent in these various theories of the nature of bodies helped to originate philosophical atomism. Leucippus seems to have been the real originator of this theory. He taught the existence of innumerable and ever-moving elements, the atoms, moving in the void, which also has real existence. He probably taught that all atoms are alike in kind and that differences in things must therefore be accounted for by the shape, size and arrangement of atoms.

2. Socrates

By the time of Socrates (469–399 B.C.) thought had reached an impasse. There were conflicting theories in cosmology, psychology, ethics, politics.

In the previous section we have sketched the various explanations of matter. None was satisfactory; each explained some aspects of things by neglecting other aspects. Conflicting explanations of the human soul were proposed: it was thought of as composed of air or of the four elements; or else it was thought to be a subsistent something that would survive bodily death. In ethics, some regarded social convention as the guide, while others despised such popular morality. In politics, everything from democracy to tyranny was advocated.

Politically, it was a turbulent and exciting period into which Socrates came, the age of Pericles and of the expansion of Athens. In literature, it was the golden age that begot Aeschylus, Sophocles and Euripides.

Philosophic thought was at a stage where it could either degenerate or make a new thrust upwards. Socrates was to prepare the way for that new thrust, and in this lies his immense importance for later Greek thought and indirectly for all later thought.

He left no writings, so what we know of his life and ideas comes from others, particularly Plato. The writings of Plato are mainly in the form of dialogues with Socrates as the chief speaker; and it is difficult to know how far the teachings given are those of the historical Socrates and how far they are original to Plato, and merely put in the mouth of Socrates. A judicious comparison of Plato's accounts with those of others, especially Xenophon – who was a disciple of Socrates – and Aristotle, can bring us nearer the real Socrates, but haziness still remains.[6]

In his early life Socrates was engrossed in cosmological speculation, hoping to learn the truth of things from that source. But he was disappointed there, for the explanations offered seemed too superficial, and he became convinced one had to go deeper to uncover the ultimate truths. It was always ultimates Socrates sought, especially in the moral order. What is knowledge? What is virtue? What are prudence, justice, temperance and fortitude, and how are they related? What is goodness? What is beauty?

In the *Symposium*, Plato represents Socrates as recalling what he was taught, as a young man in search of wisdom, by a certain priestess, Diotima of Mantinea. Whether historical or not, the account illustrates the truth that the whole activity of Socrates is dominated and illuminated by his devotion to supreme goodness and beauty. Diotima says to him: "But if it were given to man to gaze on beauty's very self – unsullied, unalloyed, and freed from the mortal taint that haunts the frailer loveliness of flesh and blood – if, I say, it were given to man to see the heavenly beauty face to face, would you call *his* an unenviable life, whose eyes had been opened to the vision, and who had gazed upon it in true contemplation until it had become his own forever?"[7]

The attraction of this vision inspired Socrates as he pursued his chosen mission: to seek wisdom and goodness, and lead others to do the same. He used to spend his days in the streets and gymnasia of Athens, talking to anyone who would listen to him, disputing questions of philosophy. Always his aim was to reach the essences or natures of things, and express these in precise definitions. He detested glib explanations and shallow thinking – and there were plenty of these, for they were practiced by the professional Sophists. The Sophists responded to the need for higher education felt by many rich young men. They offered, for a price, an all-round education in everything worth knowing. They would teach politics and ethics, science, grammar, rhetoric. Some, such as Protagoras, were at least well-intentioned; others were not. Socrates objected to them because they claimed knowledge is easily attained, whereas he knew its attainment to be an arduous task; because they dispensed superficial cleverness, not deep wisdom; because they pandered to popular beliefs, instead of proclaiming unpopular truths; because they produced slick debaters, not honest dialecticians.

Socrates regarded himself as ignorant of most things, but as a seeker of wisdom. He developed a dialectical method that would aid him in his search and destroy the pretensions to knowledge of the Sophists and their disciples. It worked like this. Socrates would propose a question, such as, What is justice? His interlocutor would give some quick and superficial answer. Socrates would follow up with further questions, all designed to reveal the inadequacy of the other's answers.

Finally the opponent would be reduced to utter confusion, finding he knew nothing of the subject he had thought he knew quite well. The questions would continue, but now with the object of leading the other to a true understanding. Socrates did not believe in doing anyone's thinking for them, but in helping them to do their own.

He had an ardent following, principally of young men. While his method could have the great advantage of leading them to think realistically, it sometimes had unfortunate results. It could easily lead a youth to rebel against the status quo without being able to suggest anything to replace it; it could breed sceptics and rebels. This was far from the intention of Socrates, who faithfully observed the laws, had a great love for Athens and was a man of admirable moral integrity. But he was always in search of truth, not in possession of it; and his questionings and difficulties and doubts had a bad effect on some of his disciples. This was one reason why he was regarded as a menace to Athenian society. Another was political enmity engendered by his unsparing opposition to the hypocrisy and double-dealing of current politics.

In the year 399 he was brought to trial on two charges: impiety and corruption of the minds of youth. He denied the charges, but was condemned to death. The *Phaedo* of Plato gives a magnificent account of his last day. His friends were allowed to spend the day with him in his prison cell, and he followed the pattern established over the years: he discussed philosophy.

He talked about the duty of obedience to the laws; about the superiority of the soul to the body; about the goodness of philosophic contemplation; about the immortality of the soul. As sunset drew near and it was nearly time for him to die, Plato quotes him as saying: "To feel confident about the fate of his soul is the right of any man who during life has turned his back upon the pleasures and adornments of the body, looking upon them as alien to him and more likely to do him harm than good; who has been anxious to enjoy the delights of learning; and who, after adorning his soul with no alien trinkets but with the true ornaments of self-restraint, justice, courage, freedom and truth, awaits his departure to the other world, ready to march whenever fate may call."[8]

The prison officer prepared the hemlock, and Socrates calmly drank it. He walked up and down the cell until his legs became heavy; and he said a few last words to his friends. Then he lay on his bed, while a spreading numbness neared his heart. He gave a convulsive movement, and his friends saw that he was dead.

3. Plato

Plato (427-347 B.C.) was born into one of the most distinguished families of Athens. They closely participated in the politics of the time, and he believed his vocation to be a political one. But as he saw practical politics in action, whether oligarchy or democracy, he rapidly became disillusioned. His disillusionment was completed by the unjust condemnation of Socrates, his friend and guide. He says: "The result was that I, at first full of zeal for a public career, when I saw all this happening and everything going to pieces, fell at last into bewilderment."[9]

He resolved to clarify his own ideas and to continue the work of Socrates. So he began his famous dialogues, expounding and developing the amazingly fruitful, but incomplete and exploratory, concepts of the old philosopher. When he was about forty years old, he established his Academy, named from the grove of the hero Academus in the garden where it was built. The Academy was really the world's first university, and it lasted nearly a thousand years, until closed by the Emperor Justinian in A.D. 529. Mathematics, physical science and philosophy – especially moral and political philosophy – were taught. Lectures were given to which the public were admitted, but the teaching method for the regular students was an adaptation of the conversational method of Socrates.

Plato did not work out a complete system of philosophy, nor did he put his deepest thoughts into writing.[10] His dialogues were intended for the educated public as well as for philosophers; and the deepest and most technical considerations were mainly reserved for the students at the Academy. Nevertheless, we can form a fairly clear idea of his philosophy from the writings. Fortunately, they seem to have come down to us complete: Plato is the one voluminous author of classical antiquity of whom this can be said.[11] Plato was a great literary artist as well as a philosopher, and his dialogues have been read as literature down to the present day. His dramatic genius adds a warmth, vividness and persuasiveness to the expositions of his teachings, but at times leaves him open to misunderstanding and to being taken more literally than he intended.

The Ideas. Fundamental to his philosophy is his doctrine of ideas. He saw that thought far transcends the corporeal things of our sensible experience. We see things that are to some extent beautiful or good, we compare things that are approximately equal. But what of absolute beauty or goodness, what of absolute equality? Do these exist? Suppose I see two pieces of wood of about equal length. They will not be *exactly* equal, yet from them I somehow derive the idea of absolute equality. Everything we experience is a deficient partaker of the absolute ideas we derive from it: it may be somewhat beautiful or good, and so on with other perfections, but it always falls short of the standard.

These absolutes are greater than the physical things of sense experience. Beauty, according to itself, is uniform and complete, admitting of no alteration; if the very essence of beauty were altered, it would become something else, just as, if a side were removed from the triangle, it would become another figure. Similarly, absolute equality admits of no deviation – it admits nothing of the unequal.[12]

We never experience absolutes in this world. Are we to conclude that they are nothing but mental fictions – that they have no reality outside our own minds? Plato would not allow this. On the contrary, absolutes are more real than the deficient imitations of them revealed by our sense-experience. They do not exist in the world of sense, but they certainly exist elsewhere; and they deserve to be called reality far more than do the fleeting objects of sense.

So Plato conceives the physical world as an inferior likeness of an immeasurably more magnificent reality, a reality we cannot sense, but of which we can gain some understanding by philosophic contemplation. He uses the terms ideas or forms to signify true being such as equality, beauty, truth. In reading his dialogues we must not equate idea (or form) with a mere concept in the mind. It means a supra-sensible reality. The exact meaning of the theory of forms was never set down in writing by Plato, and scholars give differing interpretations. Obscurities probably remained in his own mind about it. But it would be very naive on our part to imagine him teaching the existence of another world. which would be a replica (except spiritual and perfect) of the world we live in, and existing in some heavenly space. The forms are intelligible and immaterial, and consequently not localized in a place. Plato speaks pictorially of them in his myths, but even there he says that the real existence seen by the separated soul is "colourless, without shape and intangible, visible only to the intelligence which sits at the helm of the soul."[13]

How do we understand absolutes when we experience only deficient imitations of them? These imitations are not a proportionate cause of the ideas in our intellect. In other words, if I see two pieces of wood *approximately* equal, that sight, of itself, does not convey to me absolute equality. Plato concluded that these deficient imitations are but reminders of the forms or ideas. Even if a thing only vaguely resembles something else, it may remind us of that other thing. It is the same, he thought, with all physical things in relation to intelligible reality: they remind us.

An experiment to establish this conclusion is conducted in the *Meno*. Socrates asks geometrical questions of a boy slave who had learned no mathematics. Drawing figures and asking appropriate questions, he elicits from the boy the properties of these figures. He taught the boy nothing, he insists; he just put questions to him. But the boy had not previously learned mathematics in this life. Therefore he must have recalled knowledge he had prior to this life.[14]

So forms or ideas such as goodness, beauty, equality really exist, although not in this world. The human soul is an immaterial substance and existed before its union with the body. In that previous state it beheld the pure forms, the intelligible principles, and the memory of that vision lies dormant within it. The vision can to some extent be recovered through the process of recollection.[15]

The Soul. "A soul using a body"[16] is a definition of man given in the Academy shortly after Plato's time (unless *Alcibiades I* was written by Plato)[17] and it expresses his teaching. Seeing the soul as immensely superior to the body, he thought of the human body as a hindrance rather than a help in leading a noble and happy life. The soul's superiority is seen by various considerations: it can exist independently of the body, and originally did so; it is true being, while the body belongs to the shadowy world of becoming; it is incorruptible and everlasting, while the body is corruptible and temporal; it tends to the contemplation of reality, but the body drags it down to sensible appearances.[18] Although he stresses this aspect, in other passages he acknowledges the help the body can give the soul; in fact, he insists on a balanced development of body and soul.[19]

Being and Becoming. Plato wanted a middle way between the extremes taught by Heraclitus and Parmenides. Heraclitus had said the whole world is continually and radically changing. This Plato rejected. Such a concept was intellectually repugnant. Parmenides had taught the existence of one immutable being. This also was unacceptable, for it reduced to illusion the changeable things of sense. Either teaching was quite unliveable. Plato reasoned that "what is" must be divided into two spheres, a spiritual world and a material. That which is, without diminution of the meaning of *is*, must be pure, independent, unchangeable. To the degree that a thing has some impurity mingled with it, to that degree it falls short of what *is* means. It is, yet it is not. The things of which "it is" can be said without qualification are true being, reality without qualification.[20] But this cannot be said of anything corporeal, for the corporeal is a mingling of opposites, undergoing continuous changes. So "it is" can be said of a body only with qualification, and a body is becoming rather than being.

Since sensible things are in a state of becoming, and that which becomes requires some cause, there is a cause or maker of the things we experience. After saying it would be hard to discover the maker of the universe and impossible to declare him to all men, he goes on to speak of a Demiurge as fashioning the world. It is disputed whether he means God, or the Divine Reason, or a lesser being than God. The Demiurge looked to the eternal for an exemplar of the world, and made it in the likeness of this.[21]

An ingenious theory is put forward concerning the structure of bodies.[22] Plato accepts earth, air, fire and water as the primary elements of which all bodies are composed. He posits that each of these elements has a geometrical shape, assigning a figure according to the supposed properties of the body: earth is given a cubical shape because it is the most immobile and stable; fire is a pyramid because the pyramid has the sharpest cutting edges and the sharpest points in every direction. Each of the primary elements is so small individually that it is invisible, and only in combination are they seen. From such postulates he attempts to construct a system of physics and biology. The far-fetched nature of some of the conclusions is mitigated by his repeated insistence that these matters are too obscure for us to have certain knowledge of them, and we must be content with the likeliest hypothesis. His construction is interesting as showing an excessively mathematico-deductive approach to the understanding of physical reality.

The Purpose of Life. Plato vigorously combats doctrines that place the highest end in power or pleasure. Man's chief task in life is the "tendance of his soul". His life, harmonized by the moral virtues, must ascend to the contemplation of the highest things.

No one is voluntarily bad.[23] Badness is due either to a faulty bodily condition or to unenlightened upbringing, and these overtake a man against his will. But be must do his best by education to escape badness and become good. This doctrine implicitly denies free will, a denial Plato did not intend.

Plato makes "the Good" – or Beauty – supreme. His deepest thoughts on the Good were never committed to writing. But in the *Republic* he says this of it: "It is the cause of knowledge and truth; and so, while you may think of it as an object of knowledge, you will do well to regard it as something beyond truth and knowledge and, precious as both these are, of still higher worth."[24] And just as the sun gives existence, growth and nourishment to visible things, the objects of knowledge derive from the Good their very reality.

By the Good, does Plato mean God? The above text would later be very suggestive for the Neo-Platonists, and then for Christian theologians and philosophers.

Society. The individual is not solitary, but is a part of society. As such, he must serve society, putting it before his private interests; by doing so, he will achieve his own highest interests. But the evil effects of a badly regulated society are enormous, and only a rare individual, towering above his fellows in moral stamina and intellectual brilliance, will be able to resist such contamination. No existing community even approaches what society should be: corruption, selfishness, stupidity, laziness prevail everywhere.

In the *Republic*, Plato gives his famous delineation of the perfect society. He returns to this subject in his final dialogue, the *Laws*, where he goes into much more detail, and makes many changes from the earlier work. Reading him, one sees the shining grandeur of his ideals, the honesty of his aspirations. But this contrasts severely with the methods of implementation and with many of the things be wanted implemented. He saw that the vast majority, left to themselves – rulers and ruled – would never exercise the self-discipline necessary for the perfect society to exist. So his legislation imposes discipline on them from without, in the hope that they will see the goodness of it and co-operate. This is particularly evident in the *Laws*, for there the rules are worked out in detail, and are imposed on the whole citizen body; whereas in the *Republic* Plato is mainly concerned with the governing class, maintaining that if they are good, they will ensure a good society.

While there is much that can be objected to in his legislation, there is also a great deal of wisdom; and the jurisprudence emanating from the Academy had a deep and lasting, although usually indirect, influence on

Roman and later European law.

4. Aristotle

Aristotle (384-322 B.C.) brought Greek philosophy to its apex. Born at Stagira in Thrace, he went to Athens as a youth, and enrolled in Plato's Academy at the age of seventeen. He spent twenty years at the Academy, until Plato's death. After that he left Athens, but returned about 335 B.C. to found his school, the Lyceum, which he conducted until shortly before he died. That twelve year period as head of the Lyceum was a time of almost unbelievable labour: he composed most of his extant writings, gave technical lectures to his students and more popular lectures to larger audiences, and did an enormous amount of research work in the natural sciences and in the analysis of political systems. The sheer mental activity involved in constructing his philosophy must have been immense.

His method was to set out the questions to be solved, ponder the answers given by his predecessors, then reason out the solution, endeavouring to incorporate in his own thinking the truths grasped or glimpsed by others, while avoiding their errors. A genius in logic – he is rightly ranked as the founder of logic – much of his work comprises careful classifications designed to expose all the facets of the subject under consideration.

Aristotle composed treatises on logic, the philosophy of nature, metaphysics, ethics, politics, poetics, rhetoric. With these works philosophy reached a maturity and definiteness towards which it had been growing since the first efforts of Thales. Of course there remained gaps and weaknesses as well as serious errors; but these were not such as to vitiate the whole system and demand its replacement by something better. Thomas Aquinas was to show, so many centuries later, how keen were the insights and how fertile the truths set forth by the supreme philosopher of antiquity.

Let us look briefly at Aristotle's teaching about causes, man, and God.

The Four Causes.[25] A cause, for Aristotle, is whatever immediately contributes to the existence of a thing. He distinguishes four ways in which this occurs. Firstly, something may contribute to an effect in the way a block of marble contributes to the being of a statue. The marble is that from which the statue is made – the raw material, so to speak. It belongs to the reality of the statue. Yet marble is not from itself a statue, but requires that something happen to it to make it one. Originally it is potentially a statue, not actually one. This is what Aristotle calls the material cause, or the matter. It is that from which something is. Secondly, there is what Aristotle calls the form; which is the specifying element of a thing – that which determines it to be this rather than that, e.g., a man rather than a horse. In the case of a statue, this is the shape: the statue is that of a man and not a horse because of the imitation of human shape the sculptor gave it. In natural things the form is the basic intrinsic principle fixing the thing to be of *this kind*, not that. Think of a number of natural things: water, gold, a pine tree, a mouse, a man. All are bodily, yet each is different from the others. Aristotle rejected the idea that the differences arise merely from the way the same primary elements are organized; he taught that each kind of thing – each substance – is basically and intrinsically determined in its species. A mouse and a man are not just two collections of the same elements. Certainly the same elements are had by each, but this pertains to the material cause, the stuff from which they are constituted.

There is more to them than that: there is a determining principle which accounts for one being a man and the other a mouse. This principle is called the form – or in living things, the soul. Plato's mistake was in separating the forms from matter, giving them a spiritual existence. Thirdly, the agent which produces a thing is called its cause, e.g., the sculptor who makes the statue. The producer is termed the efficient cause. Unlike the two previous causes the efficient cause is extrinsic to, or other than, the reality produced. This usage of the term corresponds to what in everyday speech is usually signified by the word cause. Fourthly, the end or aim towards which the other causes are directed is a cause of the effect. The sculptor has some good in mind, some desire to be satisfied, in sculpting the statue: it may be the desire to produce a beautiful object, or desire for renown, or for money. Unless he had some compelling motive he would not act and the statue would not come into existence. Even in ordinary speech we sometimes refer to the purpose as a cause, as in saying: "Love of adventure caused him to climb the mountain."

Man. Aristotle applies his concepts of form and matter to man. Each bodily thing is a composite of form and matter. In the case of man, the life principle (or soul) is the form: it is what determines the matter to be that of a man, analogously to the way in which the shape is what determines the marble to be a statue of Pericles. Further, the statue is one thing: it is not marble plus shape, but shaped marble. And a man is not a body plus a soul; his soul actualises its matter to constitute with it a single entity. To ask whether the body and soul are one "is as meaningless as to ask whether the wax and the shape given to it by the stamp are one, or generally, the matter of a thing and that of which it is the matter."[26]

The soul does not simply make the human body alive, nor does it simply make it a human body; it makes it a body, and it does this by being its form.[27] Aristotle's position utterly rules out every concept of man which would posit him as two things – a soul and a body – joined in some kind of moral union.

Does this mean that the soul perishes with the dissolution of the body? Aristotle replies that it indubitably follows that, insofar as the soul is the actuality of certain bodily parts, it is inseparable from those parts. Yet some parts of the soul "may be separable because they are not the actualities of any body at all."[28] He had stated earlier in the same work, the *De Anima*, that the criterion of whether the soul is capable of separate existence is: does it do or receive anything in which the body has no share? If so, it can exist separately; otherwise it cannot.[29] Most of the activity exercised by living things is bound up with their matter. This is the case with the vegetative functions of nutrition, growth and generation; and also with sense perception and emotion.

But man's power of thought is different: that is, the power of knowing in an abstract and universal way, of understanding the meaning of things instead of merely seeing, touching, imagining, etc. Aristotle concludes, from a comparison of the sensitive and intellective faculties, that mind or the power of thinking is separable from the body.[30] It seems to be capable of eternal existence in isolation from all other psychic powers.[31]

Here a very difficult problem arises, one complicated by Aristotle's distinction between a passive intellect and an active intellect. What is this mind which is capable of separate existence? Is it the mind of each individual? If so, Aristotle is teaching personal survival after death. Or is it an intelligence transcending the individual, but in which he shares? We cannot go into the question here, but can simply note that interpreters disagree about Aristotle's meaning.[32]

In what does man's true happiness consist? Aristotle replies that it is contemplative activity. This activity is the best because: (a) reason is the best thing in us; (b) the objects of reason are the best of knowable objects; (c) it is the most continuous activity; (d) it is most self-sufficient; (e) it is loved for its own sake.[33] Man will live thus "insofar as something divine is present in him."[34] We must not confine ourselves to mortal things, but try our hardest to live in accordance with the best thing in us, namely, reason. And living thus we shall be living in harmony with our truest self, for reason is the thing most proper to man.

Metaphysics. The supreme part of philosophy, according to Aristotle, is first philosophy, or wisdom. It later came to be called metaphysics. This science is wisdom *par excellence*, because it deals with the deepest principles and explanations of reality. It embraces all things, studying them from the standpoint of being or reality as such, not from the more limited standpoint proper to, say, physics or mathematics. In his *Metaphysics* Aristotle discusses, among other things, substance and accidents, act and potency, the supreme substance: God.

Arguing that there must be an unmoved mover to account for the changes found in the universe, he goes on to deduce conclusions about the nature of the Prime Mover.[35] In God, precisely because he is the unmoved mover, there can be no alteration from one state to another. He is "a living being, eternal, most good, so that life and duration continuous and eternal belong to God; for this *is* God."[36] Thought is the most divine thing we know, so it must be possessed by God. But what object is fit for his contemplation? Only himself. In human knowledge there is a duality: the man who thinks is one thing, the object he thinks about is another; and even when he thinks about himself, the thought is not the thinker. But no duality exists in God. His thought is of himself, and is identical with himself.[37]

Aristotle has been criticized for making God too remote from man – of seeing him as the Prime Mover enclosed in self-contemplation and oblivious of man and his needs. Even his causality, for Aristotle, seems to be only final causality – he causes by being desired, not by acting on the world. However, although Aristotle's view of God is faulty, it contains profound truths (as St. Thomas was to show), truths whose implications correct the faults in the Philosopher's explicit opinions.

Concluding Remarks. In 2½ centuries – from Thales to Aristotle – Greek philosophy grew from its beginnings to the end of its formative stage. At first it was almost one with physical science, but its distinctive character became more manifest as it developed. With Plato and Aristotle it learned to handle questions that transcend the physical world. The differences between the two men have often been stressed, usually with a decided preference being expressed for one or the other. Aristotle's style is judged by some to be cold and forbidding. This criticism is unfair; his style is clear and very apt for the deep, intricate discussions he undertakes. The criticism arises partly from comparing his style with Plato's; but few writers indeed could survive that comparison. Besides, Plato aimed his works at a much wider public, reserving the deepest points for his oral teaching. Concerning doctrine, many differences exist between the two men; in particular, the Platonic theory of ideas was subjected to severe and detailed criticism by Aristotle. But the grave differences should not blind us to the many points of agreement, nor to the extent that Aristotle learnt from Plato.

1   Frags. 41, 42.
2   Frag. 81.
3   Aristotle, *De Caelo*, 298b 21.
4   Frag. 8.
5   Frag. 61.
6   Cf. Terence Irwin, *Classical Philosophy* (1999), pp. 10ff. for sources of the historical Socrates.
7   211e – 212a.
8   *Phaedo*, 114e – 115a.
9   *Ep.* VII, 325e.
10   Cf. *Ep.* VII, 343a.
11   Cf. A. E. Taylor, *Plato, the Man and His Work* (1955 printing), ch. 2, sec. 1.
12   Cf. *Phaedo*, 74 – 77.
13   *Phaedrus*, 247c.
14   *Meno*, 86; cf. *Phaedo*, 74, 75.
15   Cf. *Phaedrus*, 250.
16   *Alcibiades* I, 130c.
17   Terence Irwin, *Classical Philosophy*, p. 19, sees it as possibly authentic.
18   Cf. *Phaedo*, 80, 81.
19   Cf. *Republic*, 410 – 412.
20   Cf. ibid., 478 – 480.
21   *Timaeus*, 28, 29.
21   Ibid., 55d – 56c.
23   Ibid., 86e – 87b.
24   508e.
25   Cf. *Physics*, bk. II, ch. 3; *Metaphysics*, bk. V, ch. 2.
26   *De Anima*, bk. II, ch. I, 412b, 5 – 8.
27   412b, 10 – 413a, 3.
28   413a 6.
29   403a 10 – 15.
30   *De Anima*, bk. III, ch. 4.
31   Ibid., 413b 24 – 29.
32   Cf. Sir David Ross, *Aristotle* (1964 printing), ch. 5, final section.
33   *Nicomachean Ethics*, bk. X, ch. 7.
34   1177b, 27.
35   *Metaphysics*, bk. XII, ch. 6 and 7.
36   1072b 28 – 29.
37   Cf. XII, 9.

Chapter Two

DEVELOPMENTS TO THE RENAISSANCE

1. Epicureanism, Stoicism, Neo-Platonism

The achievement of Aristotle marks the high point of Greek philosophy. Geniuses like Plato and Aristotle are so nearly unique that a falling short by their successors is only to be expected. The teachings of the Academy and the Lyceum after the death of their founders varied greatly from one period to another, each being influenced by the Neo-Pythagoreanism, Stoicism, Epicureanism, scepticism, etc., of the times, and by the philosophical position of the current head of the school.

A general view of the philosophical world from the end of the fourth century BC until, say, the fifth century AD shows a great variety and conflict of viewpoints, and also an increasing eclecticism. The total culture of the ancient world became more and more cosmopolitan after Alexander the Great. The compact city-state was giving way to a larger whole – the Roman Empire was the culmination of this movement. The individual tended to feel lost and rootless in this immensity, and a craving developed for a goal worth pursuing and guidance in its pursuit. Philosophy reflected this by a tendency to concentrate on the practical, largely borrowing its speculative basis from previous ages. Some philosophers, for instance Epictetus, performed an office of moral and spiritual direction for their disciples. Philosophy often became a substitute for religion: the crude mythologies and the formalistic state religion were incapable of satisfying the yearnings of the human heart. The predominant schools in this period were Epicureanism, Stoicism and Neo-Platonism.

Epicureanism. The founder, Epicurus, was born at Samos in 342 BC. Settling in Athens in 307, he there opened his school.

His notion of the universe was materialistic, and derived largely from Leucippus and Democritus. Everything, man and the gods included, is composed of atoms. There is no design; the accidental collision of atoms caused the world as we know it. Following Democritus, the Epicureans explained knowledge by holding that images of things stream into the body through the sense organs and through the body's pores. Sense knowledge is the standard of truth, containing no error. Error arises when we judge falsely about the images.

We should not fear death, for at death the atoms are dispersed and we cease to exist. "Death is nothing to us, for that which is dissolved is devoid of sensation, and that which is devoid of sensation is nothing to us."[1] Nor should we fear the gods, for they are uninterested in man. The Roman Epicurean, Lucretius (c. 98 – c. 55 BC), in his philosophical poem *De Rerum Natura*, gives a clear and detailed account of the school's natural philosophy.

Epicurus' main concern was ethics, or the conduct of life. He held that pleasure is the highest good, to which all else should be subordinated. Pleasure is "the first good, being connate with us; and it is with reference to it that we begin every choice and avoidance."[2] This does not mean that one should plunge into a life of unbridled licentiousness. Pleasures differ qualitatively; for example, the pleasure of friendship is different from that of eating. The ideal to be aimed at is a life of tranquillity, a calm satisfaction of mind and body, an avoidance of inner turbulence. Intense bodily pleasures are a hindrance to the attainment of this end. Careful calculation is needed, pleasures and pains being balanced against each other, and a choice made in accordance with the aim – tranquillity – to be attained.

Two contrary misinterpretations of Epicurus' teaching are possible. One sees it as leading to an orgy of sensual self-indulgence. In fact, such a life would be a gross degeneration of Epicureanism. The ideal man in Epicurus' view would be one who, in his external behaviour, would hardly be distinguishable from a Stoic. He would be calm and gentle, with many friendships, a man who practiced the virtues of prudence, justice, temperance and fortitude, a man of iron resolve who had risen above the afflictions of life. Epicurus taught: "Though he is being tortured on the rack, the wise man is still happy."[3]

The other misinterpretation, deceived by externals, sees the Epicurean way of life as almost equivalent to Stoic ethics, which is based on the fitting and reasonable, not on pleasure. The truth is that the Epicurean ethic is self-centred and hedonistic. Each person lives for his own comfort, and all else is used to this end. Friendship is important *because* it brings him pleasure; virtue is important *because* it brings order and tranquillity into his life. In many respects the right behaviour is insisted upon; not, however, because of its intrinsic goodness, but because it will result in the most pleasure, overall, for the individual who practices it. For example, the wise man will keep out of politics, because participation in it would disturb his serenity. However, two exceptions are admitted, both concerned with his own enjoyment, not with the good of society: he should engage in political activity either because the defence of his security requires it, or because, owing to his temperament, political activity gives him a personal satisfaction that would be frustrated by a non-political life. It is only fair to say that in practice the Epicurean's life might be nobler than it theoretically should be.

Stoicism. Zeno (c. 336-264 BC) was born at Citium in Cyprus and came to Athens as a young man. His great admiration for Socrates, gained through the reading of Xenophon and Plato, turned him to the study of philosophy. He founded the Stoic school about 300 BC. The teaching was further developed by his two successors as head of the school, Cleanthes and Chrysippus, the latter of whom systematized Stoicism.

The Stoic conception of the world is materialistic, like that of the Epicureans, but is not a consistent materialism. God is thought of as an active fire, from which all else emanates and into which all is eventually absorbed, only to issue forth again; there is an endless cycle of births and deaths of the universe. This concept of a monistic-pantheistic flux is derived from Heraclitus. The whole universe is as a body of which God is the soul. This is reminiscent of the World-Soul of Plato's *Timaeus*. He directs all things, ordering all for the best; he is Fate or Providence. In this he resembles the Nous of Anaxagoras.

A famous Stoic maxim is: Live according to nature. This sums up their ethics. Nature means the whole of reality, including God as immanent in things. Each person is an integral part of that wonderful whole, a part with a share in the Divine Reason, and therefore capable of bringing his thoughts and his will into conformity with the all-embracing plan of the cosmos.[4]

Virtue is the supreme good: it is desirable for its own sake, not for the advantages to be gained thereby.[5] That is virtuous which is in accordance with human nature, rationally considered. And virtue is its own reward; there is no need for a system of rewards and punishments in a future life.

The emotions were viewed with suspicion; the wise person moderates, even eliminates, them. The story is told of Epictetus that, when he was a slave, his master began twisting his leg, and Epictetus said with a smile: "You'll break it." His master continued to twist the leg, and it broke. Epictetus remarked: "There, I told you so." The wise man should aspire to "stoicism" like this. He should seek freedom from passion and freedom from everything external: riches, honours, etc. All his striving should be to bring his interior dispositions into harmony with the workings of the cosmos. The cosmos is determined by inexorable laws, to which man is totally subject. He is no more free of the laws of nature than a dog tied behind a cart is free to run where it pleases. But man, through his reason, can follow fate willingly, loving the order of which he is part. The ethics of the Stoics is inconsistent with their determinism. But a similar inconsistency is inevitable in any determinist philosophy.

From their keen awareness of unity given them by their monism, and from their love of reason as something divine and participated in by all men, a view developed of man as a citizen of the world. All people, even slaves and enemies, have a claim to our benevolence. Seneca says: "Wherever there is a human being, there is room for benevolence."[6] And Marcus Aurelius gives us the famous sentence: "The poet says Dear City of Cecrops; and wilt thou not say, Dear City of Zeus?"[7] Sharing in God's divinity, man must love God's City, the universe, of which he is a part.

Such considerations produced, in some, a real benevolence towards their fellow-men, and a personal devotion to the divine principle of the world, a devotion which is evident in the beautiful hymn of Cleanthes and in many passages of the *Meditations* of Marcus Aurelius.

Whereas Epicureanism put pleasure first, Stoicism opted for virtue; Epicureanism was individualistic, Stoicism tended to the community; Epicureanism believed in chance as the underlying explanation, Stoicism accepted reason and order; Epicureanism considered the gods to be uninterested in human doings, Stoicism saw God as the father of all.

Neo-Platonism. With neo-Platonism, especially as represented by Plotinus, philosophy entered a quasi-mystical dimension.

Plotinus (c. AD 204-270) was born in Egypt. After searching for wisdom under various teachers in Alexandria, he became the disciple of Ammonius Saccas. Later he went to Rome and opened his school there. His life was ascetic and spiritual, his disposition kindly and affectionate.

Because of poor eye-sight, his writings, on his death, were left in a disordered and unrevised state. They were then edited and arranged by his great disciple, Porphyry.

The doctrine of God is central to the thought of Plotinus. He calls God "the One" and teaches that he is an immutable unity, a unity so perfect that every distinction is excluded. God does not think, because thought involves a distinction or duality between the thinker and the object in his mind. He does not will anything, for this would mean a distinction between him and the object in his will. Nor does he act, for this would imply change within him. The One is not even self-conscious. He is not below these attributes, but in his pure perfection is above them.[8]

In apparent contradiction of this doctrine of perfect unity and immutability, Plotinus conceives the world as emanating, in some way, from the One. But he never makes clear what he means by emanation. He has been accused of pantheism; however, this is at variance with his insistence that the One is not identified with anything else – in fact, so surpasses everything else that he is beyond being and beyond thought – and is not diminished by other things.[9] Other things are a reflection of the One; but the reflected is not diminished by its reflection.

To get from the pure unity of the One to the multiplicity found in the world, a hierarchy of intermediate beings is invoked. The first emanation from the One is a spirit whom Plotinus calls Nous (or mind). Nous is eternal and knows both himself and the One. From him proceeds an incorporeal World-Soul. This soul of the world links the spiritual world with the bodily. It is twofold, a higher soul and a lower, the latter being the soul of the phenomenal world.[10]

Plotinus held that each human soul existed before birth and will survive after death.[11] Man's highest calling is contemplation of the One. He prepares for this by freeing himself from sensual domination and by the practice of virtue; by studying science and philosophy; by going beyond discursive thought to union with Nous. The end – mystical union with the One – can be briefly experienced during this life, but can be consummated only after death.[12]

The need to see reality as orderly and displaying a gradual scale of being is prominent in Plotinus – and more prominent still in some of his followers, especially Iamblichus and Proclus, whose elaborate and intricately subdivided systems show a vast hierarchy of beings stretching between the supreme One and matter. Plotinus pictured the One as the sun: his radiance decreases as it goes further from him, becoming very obscure in bodies, and finally (in matter abstracting from form) reaching total darkness.

Plato's inspiration is strikingly clear; in many ways the system of Plotinus is an extension and interpretation of Plato's teachings. But it is much more than an interpretation; it is a new system, with tenets and emphases alien to those of Plato.

Neo-Platonism is by no means a single body of doctrine. While it finds its best representative in Plotinus, it was developed in various directions by other thinkers, and a number of Neo-Platonist schools sprang up – in Syria, Athens and other places. It was the last, and most religious, flowering of ancient philosophy.

2. St Augustine of Hippo

With the spread of Christianity the pagan philosophical schools declined. On the whole, philosophy ceased to be looked upon as a self-contained discipline: it tended to be merged with Christian doctrine as one all-embracing wisdom.

Attitudes among the early Christian writers towards the pagan philosophers varied from hostility and suspicion to admiration and efforts to synthesise the heritage of the philosophers and the doctrine of Christ. St Justin Martyr (AD c. 100-165), himself a philosopher and a convert to Christianity, thought of God as present to the pagan sages and leading them to elements of that truth which reached its fullness in Christianity. Origen (AD 185-253) attempted a mighty synthesis of Christian wisdom, drawing on the teachings of the philosophers.

The greatest of them all, St Augustine of Hippo (AD 354-430), while concerned with the elaboration of Christian wisdom and not with the construction of a system based simply on human reasoning, nevertheless made extensive use of philosophy. Neo-Platonism had helped free him from materialism and had enabled him to see that things can be real yet not corporeal; and it was mainly Platonism and Neo-Platonism that served him in developing his theology.

Tempted by scepticism as a young man, he resisted and worked out some elements of an epistemology.[13] He anticipated Descartes by maintaining that each person at least knows his own existence; even if deceived in other things, his act of doubting shows that he exists. "If you did not exist, you could not be deceived in anything."[14] But a person could not know he existed unless he were alive. So he is certain he exists, lives and understands.

Augustine expresses qualified confidence in sense knowledge, but (and here Plato's influence shows clearly) not only are the bodily senses mutable, but the corporeal world they sense is itself mutable and unstable, not providing apt objects of *knowledge* strictly so called. Rather, the soul must reflect upon itself, and attain the eternal truths of God and the spiritual world through this inner contemplation. Plato's influence is shown again in Augustine's teaching about the eternal standards the human mind applies to bodily things. Why is one thing judged to be better or more beautiful than another? Whence come our standards? Not from the relative and mutable things of our experience, for *they* are subjected to our absolute and immutable standards. One thing is judged more beautiful than another because we have an idea of beauty surpassing both of them – and surpassing anything we ever experience. Where did we get this idea? From God, answers Augustine. The Neo-Platonists had placed the exemplary ideas in Nous. For St Augustine they are in God. "The ideas are certain archetypal forms or stable and immutable essences of things, which have not themselves been formed but, existing eternally and without change, are contained in the divine intelligence."[15] To deny this and say instead that God lacked an eternal understanding of the world is to imply that he created it unintelligently.

So the ideal standards, the immutable essences, are in God. But how do we share in them? Augustine replies that God illuminates our minds, and in this light we see the eternal truths. The interpretation of this teaching is greatly disputed. Do we see the truths *in God*? This was Malebranche's interpretation, but seems opposed to St Augustine's meaning.[16] A more moderate interpretation is that God infuses ideas into our minds. Even this seems to be going too far.[17] The illumination in question appears rather to be an elevating and regulating of our understanding by God, so that, on the occasion of sense experience, we are able to grasp the absolute and immutable character of spiritual realities such as truth, a grasp that would exceed our weak minds if they were left unaided.

St Augustine knew from Revelation that God had created the world from nothing, and constantly maintains it in being. This gives his outlook a fundamentally existential awareness. "The power of the Creator...is to each and every creature the source of its continued existence."[18] He adds that if God were to cease conserving created things, they would wholly cease to exist. Some of us may have become accustomed to the concept of creation from nothing, and assume it to be a concept easily arrived at; but it is worth remembering that no philosopher of antiquity, without the aid of Revelation, ever distinctly taught it.

Plato's influence appears again in this definition, almost the same as one given in the Academy, of man as "a rational soul using a mortal and earthly body."[19] It is not surprising, in view of the Manichean influence of his early years and the later Platonic influence, that St Augustine should have leaned towards a psychological dualism all his life. This attitude had, and still has, profound repercussions among Christians in thinking about man: a tendency to imagine him as a soul imprisoned in a body.

3. Mediaeval philosophy

After the fifth century there followed, especially in the West, a period of several hundred years in which little original thought was produced, and scholars were mainly occupied with conserving the heritage of the past. With the breaking up of the Roman Empire and the chaos that followed, social conditions were such that little in the way of general intellectual advancement could be expected. From the death of Boethius about AD 525 until the coming of St Anselm in the eleventh century, the one outstanding figure is John Scotus Eriugena, who attempted a synthesis of philosophy and theology, gathering material from many sources, particularly from Neo-Platonism.

The great century of the Middle Ages was the thirteenth. But the achievements of that century would never have been possible without the rich and varied material of the past, not only of the ancient world, of the early Christian centuries and of the rapidly developing culture of the eleventh and twelfth centuries, but also of the Arab countries. In the Islamic world a rich civilization thrived, rich in its material accomplishments, in its science, its mathematics, its philosophy. The works of Aristotle, apart from his logic, were little known in Christendom until the twelfth and thirteenth centuries, when numerous translations were made, some from the original Greek, some from Arabic. Translations were also made of the works of the Arab philosophers, including their commentaries on

Aristotle.

Thus Western Christendom became familiar with the thought of such men as Alfarabi, Avicenna, Averroes and of the great Spanish Jews Avicebron and Moses Maimonides. A new and disturbing element was introduced into the intellectual life of the Middle Ages. The Aristotelian corpus and the Arabian commentaries confronted the mediaeval intellectual with a whole worldview other than the one he was used to, and in many ways alien, or seemingly alien, to it. It claimed to be a total view of reality: of the physical universe, of man – what he is and how he should act – of causality, of the ultimate principles of all things. It was a system constructed apart from Christianity: that is, apart from the religion which permeated Western mediaeval culture and gave it its spirit, its orientation, its guiding lights.

There was a shock in that encounter, in the novelty of the ancient philosophy suddenly returning to the world – not in the distant and academic and indirect way in which scholars had already been acquainted with it, but with the immediacy given by the original works of Aristotle and the interpretation (at times misinterpretation) of the mighty Avicenna and Averroes. Some vehemently opposed the new philosophy, others became intoxicated in their admiration of it. A middle position argued that it could not be rejected: there was too much truth in it for that; but it could not be wholeheartedly accepted: it contained serious errors and limitations, and Christianity was the true wisdom, not Aristotelianism *à la* Averroes.

The last attitude was that of St Albert the Great. This outstanding German theologian, philosopher and scientist, a member of the Dominican Order and the teacher of St Thomas Aquinas, was a man of encyclopaedic learning and an immensely penetrative intellect. He was very insistent on the need for observation and experiment in natural science,[20] a procedure he painstakingly practiced himself. His clear distinction between philosophy and theology marked him off from many of his contemporaries who confused the two.[21] Strongly defending philosophy, he helped promote its study in the Dominican Order. Always open to new ideas, always striving to be positive and constructive, he welcomed Aristotelianism, although he was by no means an uncritical acceptor of the Philosopher's teachings – nor of those of Averroes.

Albert's own teaching was somewhat eclectic, appropriating much from Aristotle, yet retaining and developing many Neo-Platonist and Augustinian themes. The result of his labours was an incomplete synthesis, an unfinished movement towards the integration of Aristotelianism into medieval culture.

St Thomas Aquinas. It was St Albert's greatest pupil, Thomas Aquinas (1225-1274), who gathered together the various materials of that age of rich culture and fused them into the most perfect synthesis of rational thought and Divine Revelation the world has ever seen.

The materials were certainly diverse. He extracted truths from the ancient philosophers (although Aristotelianism was the basis of his own philosophy, it was by no means the whole of it): he learned from Platonism, from Neo-Platonism, from Stoicism. He assimilated the best from the Arab and Jewish philosophers. He was vastly erudite in the mine of Patristic wisdom, Eastern and Western, but particularly St Augustine. The earlier Middle Ages provided further elements, e.g., in the debates, extending over several centuries, of the problem of universals. Finally, St Thomas' contemporaries were an indispensable help to him, both in the truths they taught and in the errors which provided him with the opportunity of probing more deeply and finding the truth.

The old caricature of the thirteenth century as a dull, ignorant, uniform period dominated by tyrannical ecclesiastical forces is a prejudice now generally abandoned. But something of that image tends to haunt the imagination of many; so it may be helpful to remind ourselves of the actual state of things in that century. It was a turbulent time when almost every shade of opinion sought a hearing: the dualism of the Albigensians and the pantheism of David of Dinant; the Augustinianism of St Bonaventure and the "radical" Aristotelianism of Siger of Brabant; physical science, mysticism, philosophy, theology, radicalism, conservatism.

St Thomas was a wonderfully prolific writer, composing commentaries, particularly on the Bible and on Aristotle; works on questions debated in philosophical and theological disputations; and many other writings, above all his great *Summa Theologiae*, which is a vast synthesis of theology, utilizing philosophy at every stage.

His erudition was great, and his intellectual penetration greater still. First and foremost a theologian, he was yet the prince of philosophers. His genius was at once deep, broad and balanced.

He wrote in a clear, simple Latin, with economy of words and a dispassionate objectivity. It is a style admirably suited to its purpose of explaining and defending the eternal truths of philosophy and theology, a mode of expression with a certain timeless universality; containing little trace of the historical period in which it was written, or of the personality of the author, or of the vehement debates that raged around him regarding some of his positions. The lucidity, tranquillity and universality of his intellect are mirrored in these same qualities in his writing.

No attempt will be made here to outline his philosophy: the following chapters will explain many of his teachings. Here a few distinctive features of his work will be noted.

Firstly, he achieved a synthesis. This was made possible by his understanding of the goodness and interconnection of all knowledge. Nothing was to be shunned or ignored: the physical sciences (still in their infancy, of course), philosophy, sacred theology – all have their place. But all are not side by side: some disciplines are more fundamental than others. Aquinas understood very clearly the relation between philosophy and theology, and therefore his work is free of the confusion between the two that spoilt the efforts of many earlier theologians. And from his insight into philosophy he gained an understanding of the nature of man superior to that of his contemporaries and of those who preceded him.

This appears clearly in his teaching about the relation between spirit and matter in man: the *naturalness* of man as a composite thing – not a "soul using a body". And the integration of spirit and matter was seen to be explained through the Aristotelian concepts of form and matter – the only way it can be explained. This throws light on the nature of human intellection, and St Thomas developed a doctrine that explained and harmonized sense knowledge and intellectual knowledge, and the process of intellectual abstraction. He was opposed to any theory that would make man less human by positing something extrinsic as an active principle of his understanding, e.g., Augustinian special divine illumination, or the separate agent intellect of the Arab philosophers. Each person is the integral principle of his own thinking. This position reinforces that of each one's personal responsibility, and of the dignity of the person.

The doctrine of act and potency is a key to an understanding of St Thomas' metaphysics. His distinction between essence and existence in all finite beings is an application of the more general concepts of act and potency. All his proofs for the existence of God depend on this doctrine, as do his explanations of creation, and of God's causality in relation to our activity.

Both during his life and after his death, St Thomas was ardently followed by some and vehemently opposed by others. Some saw in him a dangerous innovator promoting serious errors derived from Aristotle. Fifty years after his death Pope John XXII canonized him a saint and praised his teaching in glowing terms. That approval has been steadily continued by the Popes to our own day.

His teachings have been explored, penetrated, applied by such illustrious Thomists as Capreolus (1380-1444), Cajetan (1468-1534), Banez (1528-1604), John of St Thomas (1589-1644), down to Garrigou-Lagrange, Maritain and others in recent times. The labours of these men in developing and applying Thomism show clearly its living character: it is not a sealed system completely expounded in the thirteenth century and simply handed down from then on; it is a vital synthesis possessing immense potential.

However, in the decisive century following the death of St Thomas, it was not his ideas that had the greatest impact. In that time the ground was prepared for the modern systems of philosophy, in particular through growing scepticism regarding the power of human knowledge to attain super-sensible reality.

Transition to the Renaissance. With the English Franciscan William of Ockham (d. 1349), the history of philosophy enters a new phase.

Ockham emphasized the empirical and the singular in a way that weakened the reality of universal judgments, and led to the undermining of metaphysics. He tended to view reality as a collection of so many self-contained individual entities, and taught that no logical inference can be made from the existence of one thing to that of another. Knowledge of an effect gives us no insight into the nature of its cause. We can know it has a cause, but can identify the cause only by experience. And experience shows us the cause only by a process of elimination. We learn that fire causes heat by removing all other possible causes until fire remains the only one always present.[22]

Since effects are opaque, revealing nothing of their cause, and sensible experience alone shows which is the cause of any particular effect, it follows, he teaches, that the existence of God cannot be proved. So far as our natural reason can see, God may not be the cause of anything.[23] Neither can the existence of a spiritual and incorruptible human soul be proved.[24]

Thomas Aquinas had taught a real distinction between essence and existence in finite things. Ockham denied that distinction – for him, essence and existence name the same thing. Aquinas taught that the concept of being is analogous, having a flexibility in its meaning. Ockham taught that it always retains the same meaning. "From some accident which I have seen I abstract a concept of being which does not refer more to that accident than to substance, nor to the creature more than to God."[25]

As a theologian, Ockham was dominated by the thought of God's omnipotence and liberty. This comes out very clearly in his ethics. The source of the moral law is God's free will. In other words, if an act is evil this is because God willed it to be evil; if another act is good this is because he willed it so. But he is free and could have willed the opposite. Stealing and fornication are wrong because God forbids them. If he ordered them (and he would be quite entitled to), they would become good acts. God is free to order us to hate him; and if he should do so, hatred of God would be a meritorious act.[26] No act is intrinsically good or evil.

Inconsistently with this absolute voluntarism, Ockham insists on the need to follow right reason, and implies that reason can know, at least basically, the actual moral law. To be consistent he should have said that the moral law is knowable only through a revelation from God; for our reason cannot tell us what arbitrary choice God will make.

William of Ockham powerfully swayed Renaissance thought. He helped spread nominalism – the doctrine that a general term (horse, man, goodness) stands for a collection of individual things, not for a common nature possessed by many individuals. He drove a wedge between philosophy and theology by his scepticism regarding the power of human reason, and by his ascription of arbitrary freedom to God. The stress he laid on the need for observation and experience probably helped in the development of physical science, although it is becoming ever clearer to historians that observation and experiment were by no means ignored by earlier thinkers, e.g., Roger Bacon and Albert the Great in the thirteenth century.

Ockham's contemporary Nicholas of Autrecourt worked from similar premises, arguing that (a) one thing cannot be inferred with certainty from another: if we see a patch of white, for example, we cannot be sure that a substance exists in which the whiteness inheres (and so we cannot know that whiteness is an accident); (b) no causal argument is certain: if one event constantly follows another we become subjectively persuaded of a causal connection, but we cannot be objectively certain; (c) we cannot know there are substances, for we experience only sense data; (d) we cannot prove God's existence. We know with rational certainty only self-evident propositions – e.g., in mathematics – and data immediately perceived.

It is important to note that men such as Ockham and Nicholas, in spite of their drastic restriction of the power of human reason, insisted that the truths of faith are certain. Widespread crises of faith consequent on philosophic presuppositions belong to a later age.

The Renaissance is a bridge between the Middle Ages and modern times. There was, during this period, an intensification of interest in the beauty of sensible reality, and in the beauty of literature, especially that of Greece and Rome. A flowering of mysticism took place – some of it orthodox, some not. In science there was an insistence on observation and experiment.

Because of these elements and others, hostility was felt by many towards Scholastic philosophy. They rejected Scholasticism (whether represented by Thomists, Scotists or Ockhamists) as too dry and artificial, as consisting of abstruse subtleties and endless wrangling, as too remote from the method of observation and experiment.

[1]   Quoted by Diogenes Laertes, X, 139.
[2]   Ibid., X, 129.
[3]   Ibid., X, 118.
[4]   Ibid., VII, 86ff.
[5]   Ibid., 89.
[6]   *De Vita Beata*, XXIV, 3.
[7]   *Meditations*, IV, 23.
[8]   Cf. *Enneads*, V, tractate 5, n. 13; tractate 6, n. 2.
[9]   Ibid., III, 8, 10.
[10] Cf. V, 1, nn. 6 and 7.
[11] IV, 7, 8.
[12] VI, 9, 10.
[13] Cf. *Contra Academicos*.
[14] *De Libero Arbitrio*, II, 3, 7.
[15] *De Ideis*, 2.
[16] Cf. F. C. Copleston, *A History of Philosophy* (2003 printing), vol. 2, ch. 4, sec. 6.
[17] Ibid., sec. 7.
[18] *De Gen. ad Litt.*, IV, 22, 22.
[19] *De Moribus Eccles.*, I, 27, 52.
[20] St Albert, *Liber 6, De Veget. Et Plantis*, tract I, c. 1.
[21] Cf. his I *Summa Theol.*, I, 4, *ad* 2 and 3.
[22] *I Sent.* I, 3, n.
[23] *Quodlibet*, II, 1.
[24] *Quodlibet*, I, 12.
[25] *III Sent.*, 9, R.
[26] *II Sent.*, 19, O.

Chapter Three

FROM DESCARTES TO HEGEL

The modern period in philosophy got decisively under way with Descartes on the Continent and the empiricists in Britain. A characteristic of these thinkers was a suspicion of, at times a contempt for, the philosophic past. Part of the difficulty came from the unfavourable impression made on them by incompetent and hair-splitting Scholastics of their own time, an impression they wrongly transferred to Scholasticism as such. The fact that many Scholastics stubbornly clung to ancient scientific errors aggravated the situation. Hence we find a number of key thinkers at the dawn of the modern period with the ambition of reconstructing human knowledge from the foundations.

In England Francis Bacon (1561-1626) initiated such a plan in his uncompleted *Great Instauration*, taking a careful study of nature as his basis. Later David Hume attempted a similar reconstruction, building his system on an analysis of human understanding. On the Continent Descartes thought he was destined, by the use of the method he had worked out, to rebuild philosophy and the positive sciences on a firm foundation.

1. Descartes

René Descartes (1596-1650) was born in Touraine and educated at the Jesuit college of La Flèche. After extensive travelling and army service he lived in Paris for a few years, then spent most of the remainder of his life in Holland.

Doubt. In the *Discourse on Method* he speaks of the multitude of doubts and errors that afflicted him at the end of his schooling. He had attained little truth, except in mathematics. Philosophy has been cultivated for many centuries by the best minds that have ever lived, yet, "no single thing is to be found in it which is not subject of dispute, and in consequence is not dubious."[1]

Next he sought truth by travelling, but found the ways of men almost as diversified as the opinions of philosophers. One day in Germany he "remained the whole day shut up alone in a stove-heated room."[2] Here he began to plan his method. The next few years were spent perfecting its exercise. Negatively, he would reject "as absolutely false everything as to which I could imagine the least ground of doubt, in order to see if afterwards there remained anything in my belief that was entirely certain."[3] He had set aside from this methodical doubt "the truths of religion which have always taken first place in my creed."[4] Positively, he resolved to accept as true only that which he could clearly recognize to be so; and to build up a system in an orderly and logical manner.

Descartes puts forward the following three grounds for scepticism.[5] Firstly, my senses sometimes deceive me, so all sense experience is suspect. Secondly, in dreams I am often deceived into thinking I am awake, so there is the possibility that the whole of life is a dream. Thirdly, might not some great spirit, some "evil genius", deceive me into thinking the world is real, when it is all an illusion he causes in me? Reflecting on all he had learned and experienced, scrupulously applying his sceptical principles, he eliminated nearly all certitude from his mind.

The cogito. He declared that one certainty remained unshaken. "We must come to the definite conclusion that this proposition: I am, I exist, is necessarily true each time that I pronounce it, or that I mentally conceive it."[6] Even if an evil genius deceives me, "then without doubt I exist also if he deceives me." *Cogito, ergo sum* (I think, therefore I exist: this is the first principle of Descartes' philosophy. It is very similar to the "*si fallor, sum*" (if I am deceived, I exist) of St Augustine, but Augustine did not attempt to base a philosophy on it. By thought, Descartes means the content of consciousness, whether understanding, imagining, seeing, feelings of love or anger, etc. "By the word thought I understand all that of which we are conscious as operating in us."[7]

He had just found certainty; but in what did it consist? There was nothing in the cogito "which assures me of having made a true assertion, excepting that I see very clearly that to think it is necessary to be." Therefore, "I came to the conclusion that I might assume, as a general rule, that the things we conceive very clearly and distinctly are all true – remembering, however, that there is some difficulty in ascertaining which are those that we distinctly conceive."[8]

The knowledge attained immediately by reflection on his own consciousness did not establish very much. How often do I exist? "Just when I think; for it might possibly be the case if I ceased entirely to think, that I should cease altogether to exist."[9] Further, he only knows himself as a thinking thing, not as a bodily reality: his body may be an illusion. How can he get from certitude of his own mind and its contents to certitude of other things?

The existence of God. His first step was to establish God's existence. He gives three arguments.[10] One is from his awareness of his own dependence, the fact that his existence does not depend on himself. Things which are dependent suppose, as their ground, something independent and supreme – which is what we mean by God.

Another argument is from the presence he finds in himself of the idea of God. Arguing that the more perfect does not result from the less perfect, he claims he could never have formed such an idea for himself, but it must have been caused in him by God. The argument can be summarized: I could have derived ideas of corporeal things from myself, but not the idea of God. For I am finite, he is infinite. But I could never have known my finitude unless I had a standard to measure myself against. So the notion of the infinite is in me earlier than that of the finite. Comparing God with other things, "the idea which I have of him may become the most true, most clear, and most distinct of all the ideas that are in my mind."

Thirdly, Descartes gives his version of the famous ontological argument of St Anselm. He argues that whatever he knows clearly and distinctly to belong to something does really belong to it. "But it is not within my power to think of God without existence (that is, of a supremely perfect being devoid of a supreme perfection)." Therefore he really exists.

Descartes argued from the existence of God to the truth of other things. I understand that all things depend on God, and I know something of his nature, including the truth that he is not a deceiver (for deception is an imperfection; but God is perfect); "and from that have inferred that what I perceive clearly and distinctly cannot fail to be true."[11] In other words, God would be a deceiver if he constituted me in such a way that I would always be deceived. But he would have so constituted me if my intellectual knowledge, although clear and distinct, could still be false. As for the existence of the corporeal world, God has given me a strong inclination to believe in it. "Hence we must allow that corporeal things exist."[12] However, they may not be as they seem, for sense knowledge is obscure and confused; "but we must at least admit that all things which I conceive in them clearly and distinctly, that is to say, all things which, speaking generally, are comprehended in the object of pure mathematics, are truly to be recognized as external objects."

So Descartes' procedure is to start from self-consciousness, argue from that to an all-powerful Creator, and back from God's veracity to the truth of everything which is clear and distinct.

Mind and body. A very sharp dichotomy is made between soul (mind) and body. "Body is by nature always divisible, and the mind is entirely indivisible."[13] For by reflection I cannot distinguish parts in myself considered as a thinking thing, whereas I must distinguish parts in my body. Although I possess a body, "I have a clear and distinct idea of myself inasmuch as I am only a thinking and inextended thing", and "I possess a distinct idea of body, inasmuch as it is an extended and unthinking thing." So "it is certain that this [mind] is entirely and absolutely distinct from my body, and can exist without it." (Note he is not saying he is *only* a thinking thing; but that inasmuch as he knows himself clearly and distinctly he knows himself as a thinking thing – without deciding, at this stage of his investigation, whether he is also bodily.)

He concludes, from a scrutiny of his ideas, that man is formed of two substances, one thinking and inextended, the other unthinking and extended. He did not see that this destroys the unity of human nature, and makes a man into two beings. He inconsistently maintains that "I am not only lodged in my body as a pilot in a vessel, but I am very closely united to it, and so to speak so intermingled with it that I seem to compose with it one whole."[14]

For Descartes, all conscious acts belong to spirit: acts of imagination and sensible appetition as well as of understanding and willing. There is no real distinction between the sensible and intellectual orders; it is all a matter of degree, the latter being clearer and not so close to the body, the former more obscure and more intimately associated with the body. Consequently Descartes, not wishing to attribute spirituality to the lower animals, regarded these as devoid of consciousness: they are like ingeniously contrived machines.[15]

We do not directly know things, but ideas of things. That is why we cannot know immediately whether the world exists. We have ideas of colours, shapes and other sensible qualities, but we do not contact these qualities as really existing. Before engaging in critical reflection, "I believed myself to perceive objects quite different from my thought, to wit, bodies from which these ideas proceeded." "And having no knowledge of those objects excepting the knowledge which the ideas themselves gave me, nothing was more likely to occur to my mind than that the objects were similar to the ideas which were caused." Furthermore, a certain body appeared to be my own. "But afterwards many experiences little by little destroyed all the faith which I had rested in my senses."[16] Towers seemed round from afar, square from nearby. An amputee seems to feel pain in the missing member. I experience in dreams what I experience when awake; since the former feelings do not proceed from external objects, there seems no reason why the latter should.

Descartes' doctrine that we do not immediately know external realities, but only our own ideas, puts a chasm between the world and our consciousness. It is a doctrine that has had far-reaching consequences since his time. His solution, as we have seen, was to invoke the veracity of God as a guarantee of the world's reality. Most philosophers judge this to be a very inadequate answer.

Descartes' influence. Descartes appeared in a philosophic world which was in many ways unsure of itself, and his methodical scepticism dealt a shattering blow to the remaining confidence of that world. His aim was to ignore traditional philosophy (although he was far more affected by it than he admitted) and to reconstruct the philosophic edifice from the foundations. One historical result of his work was to turn men decisively away from the older ways, and set them building new systems of their own. Another result was the proliferation of extreme views on a number of questions, such as the relation of the psychic and the corporeal in man, and the correct method to be used in philosophy.

Regarding method, Descartes had a strong mathematical bias, and sought to explain things in an *a priori* way, deducing conclusions from what he regarded as intuitively seen first principles. As an appendix to his reply to the *Second Set of Objections* against his *Meditations on the First Philosophy*, he sets out in geometrical fashion his arguments for God's existence and the distinction between soul and body. A series of definitions is given, then postulates, then axioms, finally definitions.

This technique was employed by Baruch Spinoza (1632-1677) in his *Ethics*, and employed with ruthless logic. For example, Spinoza defined substance in a sense which led him to conclude that only one substance exists, namely God. All other things are modifications of God. He got rid of the matter-spirit problem by merging all reality into one. "Mind and body are one and the same thing, which, now under the attribute of thought, now under the attribute of extension, is conceived."[17] He also deduced a rigid determinism, saying that everything happens necessarily.

The Oratorian priest, Nicholas Malebranche 1638-1715), greatly admired Descartes, and was strongly swayed by him. Malebanche's view of the body-soul relationship was more extreme than that of Descartes. Arguing that "matter is nothing else but extension"[18] , he held that there can be no interaction between soul and body.[19] For Malebranche, this is an application of the more general doctrine called occasionalism; whereas others had taught that God is the supreme cause and created things are true secondary causes, he maintained that true causality can be exercised only by God. All other things are occasions of the divine activity.

"I say even that there is a contradiction in saying that you can move your armchair."[20] God moves the chair; I only seem to. Between created things there is parallelism, not causality; God produces effects in such an order that they parallel one another, and one thing *seems* to move another. My limbs undergo certain movements, and concurrently my chair is moved to another position in the room. But I moved neither my limbs nor the chair; God was the real cause. My movements were the *occasion*, not the cause, of the chair's change of position.

Since the world exercises no true causality, it does not bring about ideas in us. We cannot even be absolutely certain that the world exists except by turning to God's Revelation: the Bible assures us of the world's real existence. Malebranche explains our knowledge by saying that we see all things in God.[21] He is continually present to us, and we see his ideas of created things.

The doctrine of occasionalism was rejected by the great German philosopher Gottfried Wilhelm Leibniz (1646-1716), who taught a pre-established harmony between things. Leibniz was a man of many interests and unusual erudition. Central to his philosophy is his doctrine that all complex entities are composed of simple and indivisible monads. A monad is conceived by Leibniz as a sort of spiritual substance. Occasionalism taught that things are inactive; Leibniz endowed all things with activity. But he agreed with the occasionalists in saying that things do not act on each other. However, instead of explaining the world's orderly working by invoking the sole activity of God, Leibniz said that the harmony between diverse things is something pre-established from the beginning.[22]

The well known simile of the two clocks illustrates the difference between occasionalism and pre-established harmony. Suppose two clocks which don't work. They could be operated by an outside agency: by someone continually moving the hands and keeping the clocks synchronized. This represents the occasionalist position: God keeps the clocks going and keeps them adjusted. Now suppose two clocks which are mechanically sound and operate by their own mechanism. Further, they were originally synchronized and keep perfect time. So a harmony will be maintained between them, although they neither receive adjustments from without nor act on each other. This corresponds to Leibniz's position: each thing (each monad) acts independently of all others, and none has an influence on any other, but they have been so "set" by God that a harmonious universe results.

2. The British Empiricists

British philosophy in the early modern period, as most British philosophy since, laid stress on experience, and was wary of general systems elaborated deductively. It can usually be classified as empiricism, which holds that (a) all our knowledge arises from sense experience, and (b) we know everything *in terms of* sense experience, i.e., all knowledge is basically sense knowledge.

Thomas Hobbes. A crudely materialistic and mechanistic philosophy was proposed by Hobbes (1588-1679). "Life is but a motion of limbs", the heart is a spring, the nerves are strings, the joints are wheels.[23] External bodies press on our sense organs and cause knowledge. But the qualities sensed are not in the things causing them, except as movements. "Neither in us that are pressed are they anything else but diverse motions, for motion produces nothing but motion."[24]

Whatever we conceive has first been perceived by sense, either all at once or by parts: a man can have no thought representing anything, except subject to sense. "No man can therefore conceive anything but he must conceive it in some place, and endued with some determinate magnitude, and which may be divided into parts.[25] Reasoning is a process of addition and subtraction: e.g., two names are added together to make an affirmation, and two affirmations to make a syllogism. Hobbes declares that the expressions "immaterial substance" and "a free will" are as meaningless and absurd as "a round quadrangle".[26]

A copy of Descartes' *Meditations on the First Philosophy* was submitted to Hobbes for his comments, which were published with Descartes' replies. It is interesting to compare the outlook of the two men, one stressing intellectual concepts and the superiority of the spiritual over the material, the other emphasizing sensible images and the corporeal world.

In ethics Hobbes denied any highest good as the object of human life. "I put for a general inclination of all mankind, a perpetual and restless desire of power after power, that ceaseth only in death."[27] The fundamental law is that of self-preservation.[28] Men consent to live in a commonwealth rather than in a solitary condition because of their urge towards self-preservation. But in choosing life in society and submission to a Sovereign they renounce the right to do as they please and acknowledge the Sovereign's power, a power which is absolute except that the individual retains his right to self-preservation.[29] Hobbes' theory swings from the extreme of anarchy (when men live in isolation) to rigid totalitarianism (when they live in society).

He sees the reign of God over men as deriving from his irresistible power, and states that "the right of afflicting men at his pleasure belongeth naturally to God Almighty; not as Creator and gracious; but as omnipotent.[30]

John Locke. The outlook of Locke (1632-1704) was much more moderate. A student and fellow of Oxford, he travelled in France and Holland, and studied Descartes' philosophy. He was influenced by, and reacted against, many of the Frenchman's views. Locke's work, *An Essay Concerning Human Understanding*, is a foundation of later British empiricism.

By the term *idea* Locke means an object of internal perception, whether sensitive or intellective.[31] However, he makes no clear distinction between sense knowledge and intellective, implicitly merging the latter into the former. Rejecting all theories of innate ideas – in Platonism, Cartesianism, etc. – he insists that all ideas come ultimately from sensation. We are acted on by external bodies, which produce ideas in us.[32]

The primary qualities are really in bodies: they are solidity, extension, figure, number, motion and rest. We perceive these real qualities when we are acted upon by bodies possessing them. Secondary qualities (colour, sound, hardness, heat and cold, odour, flavour) are not really there, but in our senses alone: external bodies have only the power to produce these sensations. Heat is not really in the sun, nor is yellowness in gold, but in each case these is something which produces the respective idea – heat or yellowness – in us. Once we have been acted upon by things outside, and so given a supply of ideas, we proceed to form another set of ideas. We do this by reflecting on the operations of our minds, which reflection furnishes the understanding "with another set of ideas which could not be had from things without; and such are perception, thinking, doubting, believing, reasoning, knowing, willing, and all the different actings of our own minds."[33]

The material of all our elaborated knowledge is the simple ideas we get from these two sources. By a simple idea Locke means one that presents a "uniform appearance or conception in the mind, and is not distinguishable into different ideas."[34] A man may see motion and colour, or feel softness and warmth, in the same piece of wax, but these ideas are themselves simple. Simple ideas cannot be made or destroyed, but can only be found. When the understanding is once stored with them, "it has the power to repeat, compare, and unite them, even to an almost infinite variety, and so can make at pleasure new complex ideas."[35]

Essentially, Locke was a sensist, admitting knowledge only of the observable, and rejecting any intellectual penetration into the nature of things. He failed to see the full consequences of this position, however; and inconsistently taught the existence of substances and held that the existence of God can be proved. David Hume would be more logical.

Our idea of substance in general is of "the supposed, but unknown, support of those qualities we find existing, which we imagine cannot exist *sine re substante*, 'without something to support them'".[36] As regards particular substances, such as gold, man, horse, water, the only idea we have of them is of the combination of qualities or simple ideas we find in them, plus a confused idea of something to which they belong and in which they subsist, though we know not what it is.[37] "The idea of corporeal substance in matter is as remote from our conceptions and apprehensions as that of spiritual substance, or spirit."[38] The former is "supposed to be (without knowing what it is) the substratum to those simple ideas we have from without; and the other supposed (with a like ignorance of what it is) to be the substratum to those operations which we experiment to ourselves within."

Of body and spirit he says: "The simple ideas that make them up are no other than what we have received from sensation or reflection; and so it is of all our other ideas of substance, even of God himself."[39] We understand God by taking simple ideas of perfections – existence, duration, knowledge, power, wisdom, happiness – and enlarging them with our idea of infinity. The idea of infinity is itself acquired by taking some other idea and increasing it; we can take the idea of a foot and increase it to make two feet, then add a third to make three feet, and so on."[40]

What we really mean by man, whatever we say to the contrary, is an animal of a certain shape. "Whoever should see a creature of his own shape or make, though it had no more reason all its life than a cat or a parrot, would call him still a man; or whoever should hear a cat or parrot discourse, reason, and philosophise, would call or think it nothing but a cat or a parrot; and say, the one was a dull, irrational man, and the other a very intelligent, rational parrot."[41] Since we cannot have any positive idea of substance (it is but the unknown and unknowable substrate) we cannot know anything as necessarily flowing from substance. "It is impossible with any certainly to affirm that all men are rational, or that all gold is yellow."[42] (A Scholastic would agree regarding gold.)

Following Descartes, Locke maintains: "It is evident the mind knows not things immediately, but only by the intervention of the ideas it has of them."[43] He next puts the very pertinent question: "How shall the mind, when it perceives nothing but its own ideas, know that they agree with things themselves?" He answers that simple ideas must do so, because the mind cannot make them, so they must be the product of things acting on the mind in a natural way. These simple ideas, these products of things, represent things to us in the sense that they are appearances the things are fitted to produce in us. The idea of sweetness or bitterness in our minds answers the power of some body to produce it there. "And this conformity between simple ideas and the existence of things is sufficient for real knowledge." We shall critically examine this answer in chapter nine.

Locke is opposed to Descartes in a number of ways. Descartes posited innate ideas; Locke emphatically rejects them, and insists that the senses are the sole source of all our knowledge. Descartes held the existence of the world to be doubtful unless we see that God cannot deceive us; Locke is confident – although lacking absolute certitude – that the senses give us proof of the world's existence, and has no patience with sceptics who profess to doubt it.[44] Descartes emphasized abstract ideas and deductive reasoning; Locke concerns himself mainly with sensible images and has a strongly empirical approach.

But significant points of agreement exist, indicating Locke's dependence on the French philosopher. The "simple ideas" of Locke remind one of the "clear and distinct" ideas of Descartes. Both men start from what is given to consciousness, although they differ radically as to the source of the given. Both claim that we first know our own ideas, not reality. Both are dualists, viewing soul and body as two substances. Locke speaks of "the spirits that inhabit our bodies,"[45] and says that "sensation convinces us that there are solid, extended substances; and reflection, that there are thinking ones...and that the one hath a power to move bodies by impulse, the other by thought."[46]

George Berkeley. Born near Kilkenny, Ireland, of a family of English descent, Berkeley (1685-1753) studied and taught at Trinity College, Dublin, and later became Anglican Bishop of Cloyne.

He set out his philosophy in *A Treatise Concerning the Principles of Human Knowledge* (1710). Why, he asks, have philosophers fallen into so many errors, why have many ended in forlorn scepticism? The fault is mainly in false principles they have accepted, especially the view that the mind can form abstract ideas of things.[47]

In explaining what he takes to be the doctrine of abstract ideas, he reveals an utter confusion between ideas or concepts (in the Scholastic sense) and images. We have seen that Locke gave the term idea a wide meaning, and did not really differentiate between sense knowledge and intellectual knowledge. For Berkeley, all ideas are imagery. There is no difference between the concept of man and an image of a man. As a result he completely misunderstands the doctrine of abstract ideas. He thinks it means we have the power to *imagine* colour or motion, etc., without extension, although they do not exist without it. Also, that we can picture the common element in many instances of the same thing: such as *motion* which is not any particular motion, or colour which is not red, blue, white or any determinate colour. Similarly, the mind attains abstract ideas of compounded things like man by combining the qualities in which Peter, James, John, etc., agree and leaving out the differences.[48]

Berkeley states he lacks the power of abstracting ideas of this kind. He explains what he can do, and his identification of ideas with images appears clearly in the explanation. He can imagine a man with two heads; or he can consider the hand or eye in isolation from the rest of the body. "But then whatever hand or eye I *imagine*, it must have some particular shape or colour. Likewise the *idea* of man that I frame to myself must be either of a white, or a tawny, a straight, or a crooked, a tall, or a low, or a middle-sized man. I cannot by any effort of thought *conceive* the abstract idea above described."[49] The words I have put in italics – imagine, idea and conceive – are used without distinction by Berkeley; the distinction drawn by, for example, Aristotle or St Thomas between sensitive and intellective knowledge simply disappears, leaving only that of the external and internal senses. No wonder he is perplexed as to why the strange doctrine of abstract ideas should have become so widespread among men of speculation. It would indeed be a strange doctrine if it taught, as he thinks, that *images* can be had which possess no concrete, sensible characteristics. Berkeley does not criticize the traditional doctrine of abstract ideas, but the teaching of John Locke, or what he takes to be Locke's meaning.[50]

For Berkeley, things are constituted by collections of ideas, i.e., collections of sense-data: a stone, a tree, a book, etc., are a certain colour, shape and so on, found always together.[51] Because several of these sense-data "are observed to accompany each other, they come to be marked by one name, and so to be reputed as one thing. Thus, for example, a certain colour, taste, smell, figure and consistence, having been observed to go together, are accounted one distinct thing, signified by the name 'apple'." In other words, an apple is nothing but a collection of sense-data.

Material substance is a meaningless term. Philosophers call it a support, but it cannot be a support in the sense that pillars support a building; yet they do not explain what other meaning support has here.[52] "It neither acts, nor perceives, nor is perceived; for this is all that is meant by saying it is an inert, senseless, unknown substance: which is a definition entirely made up of negatives, excepting only the relative notion of its standing under or supporting.[53]

The secondary qualities of sound, colour and so on (proper sensibles in Scholastic terminology) are not really in things, but only in our perceptive powers. In holding this Berkeley was in agreement with most of the modern philosophers. And substance does not exist. What is left? Only primary qualities. So if there is a world outside us it consists of primary qualities alone: i.e., it has shape which is not the shape of anything, size which is not the size of anything, motion and rest without anything in motion or at rest! Such a weird theory should be repugnant to anyone; and it has a particular repugnance for Berkeley because such a world would be unimaginable, which for him meant inconceivable. "Extension, figure, and motion, abstracted from all other qualities, are inconceivable."[54] If the primary qualities cannot be separated even in thought from the secondary qualities, they too have only mental existence.

Berkeley draws the conclusion, which follows from his premises with rigorous logic, that bodies do not exist. Besides objects known, which exist only in the mind knowing them, there are only spirits or minds.[55]

Approaching the question from another standpoint, he argues that to be is to be perceived – "*Esse* is *percipi*".[56] Referring to the "opinion strangely prevailing amongst men" that sensible objects have a real existence, he insists that it involves a contradiction, because we perceive only our own ideas, and it is repugnant that any of these should exist unperceived. The tenet of the real existence of things depends on the doctrine of abstract ideas. For it is by abstraction that the existence of sensible objects is distinguished from their being perceived. He regards it as quite evident that all the things of heaven and earth, apart from spirits, have no existence outside a mind: "It being perfectly unintelligible, and involving all the absurdity of abstraction, to attribute to any single part of them an existence independent of a spirit. To be convinced of which, the reader need only reflect and try to separate in his own thoughts the *being* of a sensible thing from its *being perceived*."[57] To the objection that there may be real things *like* the ideas, he answers that only an idea can be like an idea. "A colour or figure can be like nothing but another colour or figure."[58]

The ideas of sense (the external senses) are imprinted by God, those of the imagination are excited by me. The former are more distinct and orderly, and are independent of my will, so they are called real things, whereas those of imagination, "being less regular, vivid, and constant, are more properly termed ideas, or images of things, which they copy and represent."[59] However, all alike exist in some mind. There are no extramental realities except spirits – the infinite God and finite spirits such as ourselves.

Descartes and Locke had thought that we directly perceive ideas, not real things; and Berkeley follows them in this. But ideas are necessarily in a mind. This is why he found it contradictory to assert the real existence of what we perceive.

Because of his ignorance of the philosophic past, he attacks Locke's notions of substance and of abstraction under the impression that he is attacking traditional philosophy.

He presents the paradox of remaining close to sensitive experience (he is rightly ranked as an empiricist), yet denying the real existence of sensible things. Empiricism and idealism have a closer affinity than is usually realized, as will become clearer in chapter nine, section two.

David Hume. History and literature were as prominent as philosophy in the interests of Hume (1711-1776). Born and educated in Edinburgh, he later travelled on the Continent and spent some years in France. His impact on the philosophic world during his lifetime left him disappointed, but his influence since his death has been enormous.

Hume is a convinced sensist, basing his philosophy entirely on sense experience. He distinguishes between sense impressions on the one hand, and thoughts or ideas on the other. By an impression he means a sensation or a present emotion; by a thought or idea a memory or image of the absent. An example of the first: a man feeling angry; of the second: a man thinking of anger.

Our impressions are the stuff from which all our ideas are composed. "All the materials of thinking are derived from our outward or inward sentiment: the mixture and composition of these alone belongs to the mind or will."[60] We can conceive a virtuous horse because we can combine the two impressions, virtue and horse. "All our ideas or more feeble perceptions are copies of our impressions or more lively ones."[61] He gives the following argument for this. Whenever we "analyse our thought or ideas, we always find that they resolve themselves into such and such simple ideas as were copied from a precedent feeling or sentiment." The idea of God as wise, etc., comes from a consideration of our own mind and an enlargement without limit of qualities we find there. When we suspect that a philosophical term is meaningless, we should ask: "From what impression is that supposed idea derived?" (Hume, like Berkeley, ignores ideas in the Scholastic sense and gives that name to images.)

Our factual knowledge is confined to what we experience. It admits of little dispute that "all our ideas are nothing but copies of our impressions, or, in other words, that it is impossible for us to *think* of anything, which we have not antecedently *felt*, either by our external or internal senses."[62]

This gives rise to considerable difficulties for Hume. For example, where does our idea of cause come from? When one billiard ball strikes another, all we experience is the two balls, and the movement of the second after having been struck by the first. We do not sense the power or energy, the causality, involved. Hume gives this explanation: when we experience constant uniformity, a new sentiment or impression arises within us, an expectation of the second event upon the occurrence of the first, and a transition from the imagination of the first to that of the second.[63] This sentiment is the original of the idea of cause. A cause is later defined as: "That after which anything constantly exists."[64] We know nothing of the intrinsic nature of causes or of anything else – apart from matters of fact which we sense, we know only the relations of ideas to each other, as in mathematics. "No object ever discovers [reveals] by the qualities which appear to the senses, either the causes which produced it, or the effects which will arise from it."[65] "The effect is totally different from the cause, and consequently can never be discovered in it."

Reason is powerless to explain the conjunction of events in an orderly sequence. Yet we always draw inferences based on the acceptance of order. So there must be some principle other than reason which determines these judgments. If we have a thousand uniform experiences (say of the coldness of snow) we draw an inference (that coldness is always to be found associated with snow). We did not know this on our first meeting with snow. But "reason is incapable of any such variation. The conclusions which it draws from considering one circle are the same which it would form upon surveying all the circles in the universe."[66]

If our general inferences are not to be explained by reason, how are they explained? By custom or habit. Custom seems to be the ultimate principle of all our conclusions from experience. The expectation of coldness in the presence of snow, or the feeling of love or hate when we are awarded benefits or injuries, and all similar operations, "Are a species of natural instincts, which no reasoning or process of the thought and understanding is able to either produce or prevent." We have no more insight into the relation between causes and effects than the lower animals have. "Though the instinct be different, yet still it is an instinct, which teaches a man to avoid the fire; as much as that, which teaches a bird, with such exactness, the art of incubation, and the whole economy and order of its nursery."

Morality is a matter of taste and sentiment rather than an object of the understanding.[67] Virtue is defined: "Whatever mental action or quality gives to a spectator the pleasing sentiment of approbation."[68] Vice is the contrary. Men are so constituted by nature that feelings of approbation or blame well up in them when they encounter certain kinds of behaviour. "Taste, as it gives pleasure or pain, and thereby constitutes happiness or misery, becomes a motive to action, and is the first spring or impulse to desire and volition."[69]

Hume held the Epicurean doctrine that pleasure is the highest good. Virtue does not willingly part with any pleasure except "in hopes of ample compensation" later in life. "The sole trouble which she demands is that of just calculation, and a steady preference of the greater happiness."[70] Reason is powerless; it is emotion that moves us. "Reason is, and ought only to be, the slave of the passions, and can never pretend to any other office than to serve and obey them."[71] This follows from Hume's subjectivism (the placing of morality in our sentiments, not in objective reality). The function of reason is to plan the means of satisfying sentiment.

Again in agreement with the Epicureans, he held that the "higher" sentiments are to be followed. He speaks of the pleasures of "conversation, society, study, even health and the common beauties of nature, but above all the peaceful reflection on one's own conduct..."[72] Further, he rejects the notion that all benevolence is basically self-love, and insists that man has within him a genuine disinterested benevolence.[73]

Alleged proofs of God's existence are invalid, because our knowledge, for Hume, is restricted to physical phenomena. For the same reason there is, strictly speaking, no idea of substance: since knowledge is of phenomena (either sensations, such as colour, or emotions, such as anger), and substance is asserted to be something deeper than these, it is a word without meaning – or at least without a meaning of the sort it is supposed to have. When we use the word substance, we are really talking about a collection of ideas; substance is "nothing but a collection of simple ideas that are united by the imagination and have a particular name assigned them..."[74]

Hume not only denies material substances, as Berkeley had done, but spiritual substances as well. For these would lack extension, and would therefore be unimaginable – which for a sensist means inconceivable. Furthermore, we have no idea of our self as a thing with a permanent identity. All we have is a series of perceptions, like the scenes in a theatre – but without any "theatre" where they would be enacted.[75]

Hume taught a pure phenomenalism: all we know is a stream of sensations and emotions and their further elaborations and combinations within us. Reason cannot tell us even whether an external world exists, for we know only our perceptions, not things themselves. Instinct, not reason, causes us to think the world is real.[76]

The philosophy of Hume owes elements to the ancient sceptics and to the Epicureans. It owes a great deal to Nicholas of Autrecourt in the fourteenth century.[77] Finally, it is a development of the less perfect empiricism of Locke and Berkeley.

3. Immanuel Kant

Immanuel Kant (1724-1804) was born in Konigsberg, East Prussia, and spent most of his life there. His family was of Scottish origin. After varied academic activities, he was appointed professor of logic and metaphysics at Konigsberg in 1770, but lectured also on many other subjects, including physics, geography and anthropology.

The philosophy he expounded in his later, or critical, period and found principally in the *Critique of Pure Reason* (1781) and the *Critique of Practical Reason* (1788) has exerted a tremendous influence on philosophic and religious thought from his own time to the present.

Kant sought a middle way between the intellectualism and universal principles of, e.g., Descartes and the radical empiricism of Hume. He agreed with Hume that all our experience is contingent and variable, and shows us only phenomena. But he was convinced there are necessary truths – mathematical propositions, for example. His solution was that since necessity is not found in the phenomena we experience, it must come from our own minds. This reminds one of Plato's teaching that true knowledge cannot be obtained from sensible things, but is brought forth from the soul, in which it dwells as a memory. Kant denied any innate knowledge, but held that the faculty of knowledge is so constituted that it confers meaning on the raw material of sensation.

All knowledge begins with experience. Here he agrees with Hume. But "it does not follow that it all arises out of experience."[78] "Our knowledge springs from two fundamental sources of the mind."[79] These are the powers of sensibility and of understanding – but Kant gives these powers a formative office: they *make* our knowledge.

"By means of outer sense, a property of our minds, we represent to ourselves objects as outside us, and all without exception in space."[80] Everything which belongs to inner sense is represented in relations of time. Space and time are not real: they are forms or characters of the mind. We did not learn of space through experience, because we cannot refer sensations to something outside us unless we already have the representation of space. "This outer experience is itself possible at all only through that representation."[81] Space is an intuition situated in us, not an aspect of outer things. When we ascribe space to things, or say things are side by side in space, we are speaking of them as they appear to us, not as they are in themselves.

We men are bound by the representation of space because we are so constituted, but there may be other thinking beings who are not.[82] Kant argues that we can never represent to ourselves the absence of space, although we can think of empty space. So it must be what makes appearances possible, and cannot be something that depends on them. Again, if space were a concept acquired from experience, geometrical principles would be contingent or non-essential, just as sensible perceptions are. So geometrical knowledge would be uncertain.

Time, too, is subjective. It is "a necessary representation that underlies all intuitions";[83] and "nothing but the subjective conditions under which alone intuition can take place in us."[84] It has no reality apart from our minds. He argues again that principles and knowledge having certainty can be derived only from what is fixed and necessary, not from the contingent and unnecessary. But such knowledge can be derived from the intuition of time (as in the general doctrine of motion). Therefore time is necessary: it is not an aspect of the contingent objects represented.

The things which affect our senses are totally unknown to us as they are in themselves. "What objects may be in themselves, and apart from all this receptivity of our sensibility, remains completely unknown to us."[85]

We could illustrate Kant's position regarding sensation by a mould into which molten metal would be poured to give it a certain shape. The metal would be determined to that shape by the configuration of the mould. Likewise, the raw materials of sensation, namely the things that affect our senses, are given a character in us – through the subjective forms of space and time – which they do not possess apart from us. But whereas the metal was given only a new shape by the mould, the transformation of things into objects of knowledge is utterly radical: we know *nothing* of them as they are in themselves. Drops of rain are mere appearances in us, and "even their round shape, nay even the space in which they fall, are nothing in themselves,"[86] but only modifications in us.

In addition to sensibility we have a power of understanding. This is fed by the senses, and forms concepts and makes judgments. The faculty of understanding, like the sensibility, is so constructed that it confers meaning on the things presented to it. When some object is given to the understanding, the latter applies to it certain inbuilt categories. We know the object according to, or in terms of, these categories – categories of unity, plurality, totality and other concepts of our minds.

"We cannot think an object save through categories."[87] They do not come from experience; on the contrary, they make experience possible.[88] The understanding is "the lawgiver of nature".[89] "However exaggerated and absurd it may sound, to say that the understanding is itself the source of the laws of nature, and so of its formal unity, such an assertion is none the less correct, and is in keeping with the object to which it refers, namely, experience."[90] The categories "are not in themselves knowledge, but are merely *forms of thought* for the making of knowledge from given intuitions."[91]

Kant teaches that all our (speculative) knowledge is confined to objects of experience. "The understanding can employ its various principles and its various concepts solely in an empirical and never in a transcendental manner."[92] When we strive to go beyond sense experience in our thinking, we lose ourselves in baseless opinions and empty abstractions.

I cannot know, for example, that I am a substance, because all that experience (introspection) gives me is my thoughts.[93] To say I am a substance which *has* these thoughts would be to transcend experience. Man lacks the insight to decide speculatively whether he has an indestructible soul or is merely transitory; whether he has free will or is determined in his actions; whether God exists or the things of nature are the ultimate. Such insight is lacking to man because he knows only his own representations, not things-in-themselves.[94]

In Kant's terminology, objects of knowledge are phenomena, things-in-themselves are noumena. We can have only a negative concept of a noumenon. It is "a thing so far as it is not the object of our sensible intuition."[95] This concept lacks positive content: it is simply of what something is not, so far as any determinate knowledge of ours is concerned. Positive knowledge of noumena would presuppose an intellectual mode of intuition. But we lack such a mode, so positive knowledge of things-in-themselves is impossible for us.[96]

Kant's doctrine cuts us off from the real world external to ourselves, leaving us in a world of our own construction. We can know that things-in-themselves exist, but we lack all knowledge of their nature.

Proceeding from Descartes' dichotomy between reality and our ideas, and Hume's phenomenalism, Kant thought the system he had worked out to be the truth. But it presented him with acute practical difficulties. Brought up in an intensely religious home (his parents were Pietists), he always retained a deep attachment to religious and moral values. What becomes of these values in the subjective world just depicted? The old arguments for God, the human soul's immortality, freedom of will are invalid, for they suppose knowledge of noumena or things-in-themselves. Kant wanted to retain these beliefs. "I inevitably believe in the existence of God and in a future life, and I am certain that nothing can shake this belief, since *my moral principles would themselves thereby be overthrown,* and I cannot disclaim them *without becoming abhorrent in my own eyes.*"[97]

He defended these beliefs by his distinction between the speculative employment of reason (with which we have so far been concerned) and its practical employment. Speculatively, truths about God's existence, etc. cannot be established – but neither can they be refuted: arguments against them are as invalid as those for them.[98]

Practical reason is concerned with the moral law and what can be known through that law. We have within us a consciousness of moral obligation, a sense of duty which admits no exceptions. If we act for pleasure or any other advantage, to that extent we are not acting from morality. Moral activity is that which proceeds from a pure and disinterested will, a will which acts from duty because it is duty, and admits no extraneous motives. If we picture a man standing by moral principles, refusing to compromise them, the admiration that arises for him, and the desire to have virtue like his, are increased as the purity of his moral motivation is more clearly manifested. If no other motive remains to him for acting as he does – his wealth, prestige, happiness, even his family are placed in jeopardy through his stand – our admiration increases accordingly.[99]

Each of us experiences within himself the grandeur of the moral law, and consequently his worth as a moral agent, as a being who must not be used as a means, but who is an end in himself. The unique dignity and the unconditional binding force of morality are unexplainable on empirical principles. The moral law opens to us the world of noumena, of things-in-themselves – but only practically: our speculative knowledge is not advanced.[100]

In his lofty conception of duty Kant agrees with the Stoics, and opposes the Epicureanism of Hume. If the will were determined by pleasure, there could be no room for higher and lower desires. "The man who cares only for the enjoyment of life does not ask whether the ideas are of the understanding or the senses, but only *how much* and *how great* pleasure they will give for the longest time."[101]

By morality man is connected with an intelligible order which only his understanding can conceive, a world which commands the sensible world.[102] Morality posits freedom, immortality, the existence of God.

Man is aware that he ought to obey the moral law, and thereby learns that he is free, for without freedom "no moral law and no moral imputation are possible."[103] But freedom can belong to man only as a member of the noumenal world, not insofar as he is a part of the phenomenal order, for phenomena are subject to necessity.[104]

Since morality demands perfect accordance of the mind with the moral law, and since this condition is never fulfilled by a man at any particular moment of his existence, the immortality of the human soul must be posited. "For a rational but finite being, the only thing possible is an endless progress from the lower to the higher degrees of moral perfection."[105] He can hope for adequacy "only in the endlessness of his duration."

The existence of God is a practical postulate. The reason is this. In the pursuit of the highest good (a pursuit the moral law imposes on us) a harmony between nature and the moral law is postulated as necessary. "Accordingly, a cause of all nature, distinct from nature itself, and containing the principle of this connection, namely, of the exact harmony of happiness with morality, is also postulated."[106]

Respect for the moral law makes necessary the above three suppositions – freedom, immortality and God. However, we still do not understand the nature of the three things posited.[107]

So Kant's argument is that the moral law demands the real existence of certain noumena or things-in-themselves. If they do not exist, morality lacks any foundation. But we experience the moral law within ourselves: we intuit its grandeur, its beauty, its unconditionally binding character. This firm experience is our guarantee of the noumena we have posited.

4. Idealism

Kant was accused of inconsistency in teaching the existence of unknown things-in-themselves. On his principles we are cut off from extra-mental reality. So how do we know it exists? Through practical reason? But surely that contention leads to impossibilities. For example, the same human action will be both determined and free at the same time – determined as it exists in the phenomenal world of our subjectivity, yet free as it exists in the noumenal world of things-in-themselves. Further, if we are really part of a noumenal world, and acting in that world, we should be conscious of the fact. But in Kant's system we are not conscious of this.

The idealist philosophers, who became extremely prominent in the nineteenth century, especially in Germany, took the logical step of dispensing with the mysterious thing-in-itself. Idealism is the doctrine that thought and its manifestations alone are real. What we call external reality is actually a projection or creation of thought, not something having a real and independent existence. The body-mind problem ceases; everything becomes an aspect of mind. To be is to be thought. The German idealists conceived reality as an absolute thought becoming conscious of itself.

Georg Wilhelm Friedrich Hegel (1770-1831) constructed the most complete expression of idealist philosophy. Absolute spirit, which he identified with reason or thought, is the only reality. "It is the substance, that through which and in which all actual reality has its being and existence."[108]

Through the vast stretches of time, this Absolute Thought gradually gains self-awareness. World history is "the description of the spirit as it works out the knowledge of that which it is in itself."[109] The primeval thought is like a seed, for it contains what it is to become. For Hegel, all reality is thought, and all history is thought becoming self-conscious.

Where does man fit in? His position, in a sense, is central for Hegel, since the Absolute is conscious only in man. However, when Hegel identifies reality with thought, he does not mean the personal thoughts of individuals. For metaphysical idealism, Thought is a totality which includes man, and the awareness each person possesses is an element in the life of the Universal Thought. Man's understanding is nothing less than the Absolute Thought becoming aware of itself.

While each individual has his place in this cosmic process, it is in society that thought achieves its fullest actualisation. And the whole of human history is a dialectic through which the Absolute progressively actualises itself. The Spirit labours slowly to comprehend itself, and the comprehension increases over the centuries. This comprehension appears in diverse forms in many fields, e.g., art and religion; but it finds its purest form in philosophy. The philosophy of each period contains that of the previous one, since it results from it. Achievements of the past are not dead, but are alive in the present, as in a higher synthesis. Philosophy and history resemble an individual, who is first child, then youth, then adult.

Hegel wrote and lectured on a wide range of subjects: metaphysics, aesthetics, politics, history, etc., interpreting all his data in the light of his dialectical idealism. His exalted confidence in reason and his vision of thought as something living and dynamic are in sharp contrast with the limited field and comparatively lifeless nature of thought in the conception of empiricism.

His influence is incalculable, not only in philosophy but in associated subjects. Phenomenalism and existentialism, Marxism and Fascism, evolutionism, the philosophy of history, cultural anthropology, modern liberal theology – all these owe much to Hegel, at least by way of inspiration.

Although he writes very clearly at times, for example in history, his expositions of his philosophy are usually extremely obscure, and one is often left with a *feeling* of the general trend of his thought rather than an understanding of what he is endeavouring to say. The mood is easier to grasp than the metaphysics. This partly explains how he has contributed to such diverse and mutually contradictory movements. His vision is poetical as well as philosophical.

Because idealism has fallen from favour, it is hard for us to grasp the influence it exerted in the nineteenth century. It flourished, in a bewildering variety of forms, on the Continent, in Great Britain (where its most brilliant exponent was F. H. Bradley) and in America. Certainly empiricism flourished too, but lacked the dominance it was to achieve in the twentieth century.

1   *Discourse on Method*, part 1. The quotes are from the translation by Haldane and
    Ross, *Philosophical Works of Descartes*, Dover Publications, 1955 edition.
2   Ibid., part 2.
3   Ibid., part 4.
4   Ibid., part 3.
5   *Meditations on the First Philosophy*, med. 1.
6   Ibid., med 2.
7   *Principles of Philosophy*, principle 9.
8   *Discourse on Method*, part 4.
9   *Meditations on the First Philosophy*, med. 2.
10 Ibid., med. 3 and 5.
11 Ibid., med. 5.
12 Ibid., med 6.
13 Ibid.
14 Ibid. *Cf. Reply to the Fourth Set of Objections*, first part.
15 Cf. *Reply to Fourth Set of Objections*, first part.
16 *Meditations on the First Philosophy*, med. 6.
17 *Ethics*, third part, prop. 2.
18 *De la Recherche de la Verité*, III, 2, 8, 2.
19 Ibid., VI, 2, 3.
20 *Entretiens sur la Metaphysique*, VII, 10.
21 *De la Recherche de la Verité*, III, *2, 6.*
22 Leibniz: article in *Journal des Savants*, Nov., 1696; translated by R. Latta, *The
    Monadology and Other Writings* (1965 printing), pp. 331ff.
23 *Leviathan*, introduction, p. 1.
24 Ibid., chapter 1.
25 Ibid., chapter 1, final paragraph.
26 Ibid., chapter 5.
27 Ibid., chapter11.
28 Ibid., chapter 14.
29 Ibid., chapter 21.
30 Ibid., chapter 31.
31 Introduction to *An Essay Concerning Human Understanding*, section 8.
32 Ibid., book II, chapter 1, section 3.
33 Ibid., book II, chapter 2, section 4.
34 Ibid., book II, chapter 2, section 1.
35 Ibid., section 2.
36 Ibid., book II, chapter 23, section 2.
37 Ibid., section 6.
38 Ibid., book II, chapter 23, section 5.
39 Ibid., section 23.
40 Ibid., chapter 17, section 3.
41 Ibid., section 8.

42 Ibid., book IV, chapter 6, section 4.
43 Ibid., chapter 4, section 3.
44 Ibid., book IV, chapter 11.
45 Ibid., chapter 3, section 17.
46 Ibid., book II, chapter 23, section 29.
47 *A Treatise Concerning the Principles of Human* Knowledge, Introduction, section 6.
48 Ibid., section 9.
49 Ibid., section 10.
50 Cf. Ibid., section 13.
51 Ibid., section 1.
52 Ibid., sections 16 and 17.
53 Ibid., section 68.
54 Ibid., section 10.
55 Ibid., section 26.
56 Ibid., section 3.
57 Ibid., section 6.
58 Ibid., section 8.
59 Ibid., section 33.
60 *An Enquiry Concerning Human Understanding*, section 2.
61 Ibid.
62 Section 7, part 1.
63 Ibid., part 2.
64 Section 8, part 1, second footnote.
65 Section 4, part 1.
66 Section 5, part 1.
67 Section 12, part 3.
68 *An Enquiry Concerning the Principles of Morals*, appendix I.
69 Ibid., final paragraph.
70 Ibid., section 9, part 2.
71 *A Treatise of Human Nature*, book II, part 3, section 3.
72 *An Enquiry Concerning the Principles of Morals*, section 9, part 2.
73 Ibid., appendix II.
74 *A Treatise of Human Nature*, book I, part 1, section 6.
75 Ibid., Book I, part 4, section 6.
76 *An Enquiry Concerning Human Understanding*, section 12, part 1.
77 Cf. supra, chapter II, near the end.
78 *Critique of Pure Reason*, B 1. In these references the pagination of the first edition is preceded by A, that of the second edition by B. The translation is that of Norman Kemp Smith.
79 B 74.
80 B 37.
81 B 38.
82 B 43.

83   B 46.
84   B 49.
85   B 59.
86   B 63.
87   B 165.
88   B 167.
89   A 126.
90   A 127.
91   B 288. Original italics.
92   B 297.
93   Cf. A 350.
94   Cf. B 509-512.
95   B 307.
96   Cf. Ibid.
97   B 856. Italics mine.
98   Cf. B 784.
99   Cf. *Critique of Practical Reason*, second part, pp. 249ff. Page numbers refer to the translation by T. K. Abbott in *Kant's Critique of Practical Reason and Other Works on the Theory of Ethics* (1963 printing). My quotes are from that translation.
100   Cf. Ibid., first part, book II, chapter 2, section 3; pp. 216-218.
101   Ibid., book I, chapter 1, theorem 2; p. 110.
102   Cf. book I, chapter 3; p. 180.
103   P. 190.
104   Cf. p. 188.
105   First part, book II, chapter 2, section 4, p. 219.
106   Ibid., section 5, p. 221.
107   Ibid., section 6, p. 231.
108   *The History of Philosophy*, introduction, I.
109   Ibid., 2.

Chapter Four

RECENT PHILOSOPHY

1. Empiricism

About the beginning of the twentieth century a powerful movement against the prevailing idealism asserted itself, particularly in Great Britain. Idealism, in its manifold forms, was felt to be totally unacceptable. Common sense rebelled against a theory that reality is but a projection of mind – whether of finite minds or of an absolute mind.

Idealists could not agree among themselves: for example, they accused one another of surreptitiously reintroducing realism. They could not defend the grand world-views they developed in their books. They proceeded in an excessively *a priori* manner, deducing their systems from so-called first principles, and ignoring empirical facts. Their method was alien to that of the rapidly developing physical sciences.

These and other complaints led to a resurgence of empiricism, and a distaste for idealism – in fact a distaste for any philosophy claiming to present ultimate truths or an overall explanation of things.

G. E. Moore and Bertrand Russell were among the first to assault the entrenched idealism of the British universities.

Moore (1873-1958) adopted a "common sense" approach. Many things are certain, whatever some philosophers have said to the contrary. We know bodies exist; we know the earth has existed for many years. We know a great many things, and we don't need philosophers to prove them to us. Moore's aim was to take his stand on common sense, then analyse concepts expressed by philosophers and others.

What is meant by moral obligation? What does "good" signify? Which classes of events do we name "sensory experiences"? What do I mean when I say: "There is in my mind a direct apprehension of this black mark"? He makes the most meticulous analyses of such concepts and statements, trying to see exactly what we mean when we use them.

Moore did not construct a philosophy, but put a lifetime of labor into clarifying concepts. Never satisfied with the results he achieved, he was ever striving for greater precision. Some say he did an excellent job of clarification and blew away much of the fog idealism had generated.

Others say he wasted his time on trivialities, and is intolerably boring.

If Moore emphasizes the clarification of concepts, Ludwig Wittgenstein (1889-1951) emphasizes the clarification of language. For Wittgenstein there are no philosophical propositions. Philosophy's task is to clarify our thoughts by probing the language in which they are expressed. Most of the questions philosophers have discussed are meaningless. We cannot answer them; we can only show their senselessness. And we can do this by coming to understand how our language works. When someone tries to say something metaphysical, we should "demonstrate to him that he has given no meaning to certain signs in his propositions."[1]

Wittgenstein's *Tractatus* was utilized by the group of logical positivists known as the Vienna Circle, under the leadership of Moritz Schlick. But the distinctive mark of logical positivism is its tenet that the meaning of a factual sentence is identical with its empirical verification – or, for A. J. Ayer, with its possibility of empirical verification.

A. J. Ayer. The school of logical positivism, already well known on the Continent, burst into prominence in Britain with the publication, in 1936, of *Language, Truth and Logic*, by A. J. Ayer (1910-1989). In this work, Professor Ayer maintains that philosophy is a logical examination of language. It studies whether beliefs are self-consistent, and shows "what are the criteria which are used to determine the truth or falsehood of any given proposition."[2]

"The propositions of philosophy are not factual, but linguistic in character – that is, they do not describe the behavior of physical, or even mental, objects; they express definitions, or the formal consequences of definitions."[3] "The possibility of philosophical analysis is independent of any empirical assumptions." Many questions look factual, but are really linguistic, such as the proposition that a material thing cannot be in two places at once. It is a matter of verbal conventions, and the use of relevant words in a particular way. The main philosophical part of the traditional problem of perception is "the problem of giving an actual rule for translating sentences about a material thing into sentences about sense-contents."[4]

Philosophers have wrongly thought they were discussing a factual question when it is "a linguistic question, being a demand for a definition." And the propositions given as answers are linguistic, although they may seem factual because of the way they are expressed. Again, the question: What is truth? is not a real problem. It concerns the meaning of the sentence, and "is reducible to the question 'what is the analysis of the sentence P is true?'"[5] The terms true and false connote nothing, but function in the sentence simply as marks of assertion and denial.

Charles Landesman points out, in criticism of Ayer's claim that an analytic proposition simply records our determination to use words in a certain meaning, that "...a semantic convention or linguistic rule is something optional and arbitrary..."[6] He rightly argues that such truths cannot be necessary: having four sides, in the understanding of square, would be the consequence of a decision made by English speakers, and might have been different.

Language, Truth and Logic leaves philosophy with no province of its own, and with no task except the critical examination of sentences – whether those of everyday life or those of the sciences. After having sufficiently clarified our everyday language, the philosopher can turn to science and clarify its language. This will involve a prior study of science; but it is necessary because "if science may be said to be blind without philosophy, it is true also that philosophy is virtually empty without science."[7]

Whatever logical positivists may have thought to the contrary, it is impossible to analyse language without manifesting one's standpoint concerning reality; and this is very clear in Ayer's case. An underlying philosophy about the world is constantly presupposed. He himself describes his views as deriving ultimately from Berkeley and Hume.[8] And he teaches very emphatically that our factual knowledge is confined to sense-data. Even the self is "a logical construction out of sense-experiences"; that is, "out of the sense-experiences which constitute the actual and possible sense-history of a self."[9] The self is not a substance: such a supposed substance is "an entirely unobservable entity"[10], which is not even revealed to self-consciousness, for "All that is involved in self-consciousness is the ability of a self to remember some of its earlier states." That is, "Some of the sense experiences which constitute A contain memory images which have previously occurred in the sense-history of A."

From their initial assumption that our knowledge of reality is confined to sense phenomena, the logical positivists concluded that any statement claiming to say more than the senses reveal is meaningless. Ayer asserts in his first chapter: "We shall maintain that no statement which refers to a 'reality' transcending the limits of all possible sense experience can possibly have any literal significance; from which it must follow that the labors of those who have striven to describe such a reality have all been devoted to the production of nonsense."[11]

Applying this to ethics, he argues that it is meaningless to ask whether an action is morally good or bad. (We cannot sense – see, hear, smell, etc., – qualities of moral goodness or badness.) If I say to someone, "You acted wrongly in stealing that money", this is the same as saying, "You stole that money", except that I am adding that I disapprove of the action.[12] (I do not sense *wrongness*.)

A man cannot contradict me; he can only express feelings contrary to mine. "So there is plainly no sense in asking which of us is in the right."[13] Ethical words have no truth-value; they are purely emotive, expressing and arousing feeling. Ethical judgments "have no objective validity whatsoever. If a sentence makes no statement at all, there is obviously no sense in asking whether what it says is true or false."

The same empirical criterion is applied to sentences about God. The word "God" is used of a being who is supposed to transcend the world of experience. So nothing meaningful can be said about either his existence or his nature. "God" is a meaningless word. Because the theist is saying nothing meaningful, he is saying nothing false. It is only when he claims to be "expressing a genuine proposition that we are entitled to disagree with him."[14] Ayer concludes that atheism, agnosticism and theism are all equally nonsensical, because all claim to be saying something about God; but nothing meaningful can be said about a senseless word.

To sum up: logical positivism teaches that philosophy should confine itself to clarifying the meaning of the sentences used in science and in everyday conversation. But meaning, when reality is under consideration, is found solely on the level of sense-experience – our minds are incapable of any higher knowledge of things. Therefore most of the traditional questions in philosophy – God, the nature of good and evil, the soul, the meaning of substance, etc., – are pseudo-questions; they utterly lack the kind of meaning philosophers have attributed to them.

Logical positivism underwent a quick series of modifications in trying to meet the objections hurled against it. In particular it was charged with inconsistency. The most basic inconsistency: logical positivism is based on the principle that empirical verifiability is required for meaning; but that principle cannot be verified empirically. Therefore it is a meaningless principle (from the standpoint of logical positivism itself). As a result of the criticisms, the logical positivism we find today is much less dogmatic and much more cautious than that of the 1930's.

Bertrand Russell. The best known British philosopher of the twentieth century is Bertrand Russell (1872-1970). His fame is due in large measure to his more popular books and essays, written in a way that appeals to many who would not touch his technical works. Also, his personal participation in controversial public issues helped make him known to people who otherwise would scarcely have heard of him. A sympathy with his outlook attracts many to him, and for this reason an examination of his views can give an insight into attitudes still widespread.

Russell became interested in philosophy partly because he hoped it would afford a defense of religious beliefs which he did not want to abandon. About his sixteenth birthday, before he had studied philosophy, he wrote down his beliefs concerning God, free will, immortality. He expressed his firm belief in God, a belief he was later to abandon, but resolved to take account only of scientific arguments for this position. "This is a vow I have made, which costs me much to keep, and to reject all sentiment."[15] He proceeds to argue to God from the likelihood of the creation of matter and force, and also from the regulation of the action of force on matter – the uniformity of nature.

He found himself unable to accept free will because "There is no clear dividing line between man and the protozoon. Therefore, if we give free will to man, we must give it also to the protozoon." He resists the rejection of free will, and states that it makes him miserable; but he cannot overcome it.

The immortality of the soul seems untenable in face of the theory of evolution. Man, it seems, is simply a perishable part of nature, his soul inseparably bound up with his body.

As his former beliefs slip from him, he even doubts the goodness of possessing truth, for "The search for truth has shattered most of my old beliefs"; it has "taken away cheerfulness and made it much harder to make bosom friends... One ought perhaps look upon all these things as a martyrdom," for the truth one attains may make others happier;

"though truth of the kind in this book (if that indeed be truth) I have no desire to spread, but rather to prevent from spreading." Gradually over a period of several years his religious interests waned, and "it was with a genuine sense of relief that I discarded the last vestiges of theological orthodoxy."

At Cambridge University he became a Hegelian, and was deeply influenced also by Kant. He aimed at "constructing a complete dialectic of the sciences, which should end up with the proof that all reality is mental."[16] But about 1898 he followed G. E. Moore in revolting against idealism. He became an ardent realist, and felt his new philosophy as a great liberation; he had hated "the stuffiness involved in supposing that space and time were only in my mind."[17] Although his realist views have since moderated, "I have never again shut myself up in a subjective prison."[18]

In *My Philosophical Development*, published in 1959, Russell states that his present understanding of the world is "a view which results from a synthesis of four different sciences – namely, physics, physiology, psychology and mathematical logic."[19] This really leaves no distinct field for philosophy as a study of reality, but replaces it with empirical science. And this scientistic outlook predominates in Russell's thought.

His explorations of the nature of knowledge, for example, are conducted from the standpoint of the scientist, not of the philosopher in the traditional sense. This gives rise to such conclusions as the following. Mental and physical occurrences may sometimes be identical, so that "the difference between mind and matter is merely one of arrangement."[20] Belief is a state of an organism. The belief *a car is coming* consists in "a certain state of the muscles, sense-organs, and emotions, together perhaps with certain visual images."[21] He adds that the belief, in theory, could be adequately described by a psychologist and a physiologist working together, and without mentioning the car.

Russell's approach is clearly shown in his statement that the philosopher's imagination "should be impregnated with the scientific outlook and that he should feel that science has presented us with a new world, new concepts and new methods, not known in earlier times, but proved by experience to be fruitful where the older concepts and methods proved barren."[22]

From one point of view Bertrand Russell's long intellectual journey is marked by a series of disillusionments. The religious beliefs of his boyhood were the first to go. Then he embraced idealism, only to reject and combat it. Mathematics not only became an absorbing interest, but was seen in an enchanted light as a thing of timeless truth and perfect beauty.[23] He retained mathematics, but abandoned his early ardor. "I have come to believe, though very reluctantly, that it [mathematics] consists of tautologies."[24] Its timelessness consists in "the fact that the pure mathematician is not talking about time."

2. Phenomenology and existentialism

In Europe, and to a lesser extent in America, phenomenology and existentialism have spread rapidly. In Great Britain, on the other hand, there is less enthusiasm for them. Many British philosophers think these Continental movements all but meaningless: their language is imprecise, their ideas vague and grandiose and suffused with emotion. The Continental philosophers have counter criticisms: empiricism as represented in the British universities is hardly worth bothering about because of its triviality, its subservience to physical science, its lack of concern with the anguish of man striving to know himself and his world. In short, it is too academic.

Phenomenology. The founder of phenomenology, Edmund Husserl, (1859-1938) was born in Prossnitz, Czechoslovakian Moravia. His early studies were in mathematics and science, but he found himself increasingly drawn to philosophy, finally settling into his life work of developing a new philosophy, phenomenology. He left a vast mass of writings, most of them still unpublished at his death. Interest in his writings increased after his death; and phenomenology, together with existentialism, is dominant in European philosophy.

It is not a homogeneous system, but a way of philosophising which varies greatly with its different exponents. Scheler, Heidegger, Merleau-Ponty all rank as leading phenomenologists, yet their doctrines differ substantially. Husserl is the movement's founder, but his followers criticize much that he taught, disagree among themselves as to which points are erroneous, and even on the interpretation of a great many matters.

Husserl craved certitude, and in phenomenology thought he had found it. He had much in common with Descartes: both were mathematicians as well as philosophers; both were distressed at the confusions and contradictions abounding among philosophers; both sought an absolutely sure basis for their thinking; finally, both thought they had found the right method and set themselves to develop and propagate it.

Their starting points are similar, too. Descartes started with the principle *cogito, ergo sum* (I think, therefore I exist). Husserl also starts with the data of consciousness. But for him the basis is constituted by everything immediately given to consciousness.[25] We *see* that some things are so, and these objects seen are the foundation of our thinking. If we are trying to verify a proposition, yet "we ascribe no value to the 'I see that it is so', we fall into absurdity."[26] We see what a house is, or a tree, or a color. Anything that appears in our consciousness can give a starting point for a phenomenological analysis.

Consciousness is not an undifferentiated unity, but every consciousness is consciousness *of something* – of a house, a color, etc. And this object – house, color – is given with the same immediacy as the ego itself. We simply find ourselves aware of objects, and it would be as impossible to deny them as to deny our own consciousness, for we cannot have consciousness which is not consciousness of something: consciousness is necessarily relative to an object.

This may seem a firm rejection of idealism in favor of realism. But it is not. Husserl spoke of a "bracketing" of existence, a leaving of existence out of account, to concentrate on the object that appears to consciousness without considering whether the object exists independently of consciousness or not. There is a big dispute among phenomenologists as to whether Husserl was an idealist or a realist.[27] Some passages in his writings seem to assert the real existence of the world, others seem to deny it. The solution may be that he would have liked to escape idealism, but was unable to do so. Having started with consciousness, as Descartes did, he was unable to get beyond it: he could explore the objects of consciousness but could not explain how they can exist independently of consciousness.

If existence is bracketed, that is, left out of account, then the phenomenologist cannot legitimately inquire into whether a real world exists. As W. Norris Clarke says: "There is no way in which phenomenology can even raise, let alone answer, such a question, since by its method it must restrict itself to the description of what actually presents itself in consciousness."[28] He notes that some forms of existential phenomenology seem willing to go further, but they thereby go beyond Husserl's bracketing of real existence.[29]

The phenomenological program has as its whole aim the clarification of the objects we directly experience. These objects are not ordinarily seen in their purity, but are seen through the mist and distortions of presuppositions, prejudices, unfounded assumptions. Phenomenology tries to remove the distorting factors so as to experience objects in their original givenness.

Consider the attitude of the average person to his life and experiences. He does not closely analyse or critically reflect; his usual attitude is one of acceptance at face value of what he experiences. By contrast, the empirical scientist stands back from the multitude of experiences that press upon us, for he uses a specific technique to enable him to capture things under a particular aspect.

The social scientist, for example, is not concerned with the individual circumstances and actions and emotions of your life or mine, except insofar as these provide him with useful data for his studies. The individual is for him just a statistic. Similarly, the physicist selects a slice of experience and understands it in isolation from all other aspects and in a highly mathematized fashion.

Phenomenology is dissatisfied with both the naïve worldview of the average man and the highly abstract and formalized concept of the scientist. The average man does not experience things in their pure givenness, but overlaid with social customs, distorted by presuppositions, deadened by routine. The scientist, *qua* scientist, knows an abstract model of a particular area of experience; he is in danger of accepting his model as the full truth, instead of seeing that life as it is directly lived is far richer and truer than any scientific formalization. Both the average man and the scientist fail to observe that every event has a significance, that each points to others, that the whole context must be sought if we wish to see the full meaning of any particular element.

Phenomenology attempts to ground the unreflecting everyday attitude and the abstract scientific one by analyzing concrete experience. This involves seeing each experience in its purity and grasping its significance by locating it in relation to all the other factors that contribute to its meaning. The world of lived experience is not justified by science; the reverse is the case: the abstract world of science is justified by the world of lived experience, which gives the first certitudes on which scientific constructions are based.[30]

Phenomenology, then, has many facets: it is an attempt to establish absolute certainty in philosophy by grounding it on the immediate data of consciousness; it is an attempt to overcome the idealist-realist problem; it is a method of investigating the phenomena we experience; it is a reaction against abstraction and against the view that the most reliable knowledge is that acquired by the positive sciences. It is more than a method, because it has specific teachings, for example on intentionality in knowledge, on phenomena as the deepest objects our minds can attain, on concrete as opposed to abstract knowledge. But many divergent views are found among phenomenologists, and many see it as a method of philosophising rather than a philosophy.

Existentialism. The meaning of existentialism is even more elastic than that of phenomenology. Some who are generally called existentialists disown the name. Some existentialists are Christians who attempt a vital penetration of their religion by way of their philosophy; others are atheists: John-Paul Sartre claims to disprove God's existence, and regards existentialism as an attempt to work out the consequences of atheism.

Modern existentialism owes much of its spirit to Soren Kierkegaard (1813-1855). He hated abstractions and universal systems: Hegel was for him a symbol of these despised modes of conceptualizing.

For Kierkegaard what matters is each individual person face to face with life in all its mystery and depth. Truth is intensely personal, and is reached by committing oneself, by becoming totally involved. Armchair philosophers cannot attain it. And the more one becomes involved in life, the more of a person one becomes. Existence does not mean something static, but a striving, a choosing, a process of becoming ever more fully oneself. Above all it has a religious meaning: the choosing of God in a leap of faith. It is in union with the transcendent God that human life finds its fulfillment.

In agreement with Kierkegaard, today's existentialists center their attention on man. They are not concerned with him in the detached manner of the anatomist or biologist, but proceed from the awareness each man has of himself, and try to elucidate the implications contained in this self-awareness. Their method is phenomenological. The philosopher should be a participant in the drama of existence, not a detached observer.

Man's freedom is stressed. He is able to surpass his present condition and find himself more fully. It is very easy to go with the crowd, conforming one's outlook and actions to those of the majority. But this is to live inauthentically. Authentic existence demands that a man make his own decisions, actively becoming what he feels he should be – even if this violates the conventions of society.

But what should a man be? The answer an existentialist gives will depend greatly on his attitude to theism. John-Paul Sartre proceeds in accordance with his atheism. Life and reality have no meaning; there are no objective standards to which our lives should conform, no God to whom we owe loyalty and from whom we can ask help. Basically, each person is alone; and in his loneliness he is faced with an awful responsibility: the task of living authentically – that is, of avoiding all hypocrisy and all mere convention and making choices that will be uniquely his own.

Yet, as Albert Camus forcefully stresses, the world in which he lives is an absurd world. The realistic person, according to Camus, will go through life knowing the absurdity of everything he does and everything that happens to him. He will know that his own choices have no more objective validity than those of anyone else. Despite this he will steadfastly commit himself to the way of life he has freely chosen.

Existentialism represents a spirited reaction to various trends: to systems that neglect the person in favor of the collectivity; to an exclusively technological approach to human problems; to unthinking conformity. Of course, one does not have to be an existentialist to object to these things; and more basic marks of existentialism are its hostility to abstract thought and universally valid principles, and its replacement of objectivity by subjectivity. Here the influence of empiricism can be easily seen, with its denial of universal ideas, and of Descartes with his concentration on his own thought.

It should not be supposed that the writers classed as existentialists make no attempt to develop an ontology, a science of being. On the contrary, Martin Heidegger devoted his principal work, *Being and Time*, to an extremely technical analysis of the nature of being. But he attacks the problem from the standpoint of man as he finds himself involved with being, and for this reason he makes intricate analyses of man, his consciousness and his involvement in the world. Sartre, too, explores the meaning of being in his major work, *Being and Nothingness*; but again from the standpoint of human consciousness and man's actualisation of his possibilities.

3. Postmodernism

"If you read a random dozen out of the thousands of books whose titles contain the word 'postmodern', you will encounter at least half a dozen widely differing definitions of that adjective."[31] This statement of Richard Rorty indicates the variety of viewpoints found under the umbrella of postmodernism. The reference to "thousands of books" indicates the interest this movement has generated in recent decades. As the name signifies, this movement goes beyond modernism; and by modernism is here meant the typical stances of philosophy from Descartes to recent years.

Especially in the earlier part of this period philosophers exhibited a confidence in their ability to find meaning, to construct solid systems, to advance the truth. But with the passage of time that confidence lessened. There has also been increasing disquiet concerning the kind of world that seems to be emerging, with worries about threats to human life arising from technology – through wars, damage to the environment, domination of our lives by an impersonal and ever more powerful technology.

Postmodernism exhibits scepticism about the capacity of reason to attain truth, and it opts for fragmentation instead of grand systems. It finds rationalism arid and inhuman. Postmodernist thinkers show impatience with an emphasis on scientific method, argumentation, attention to definitions. Kevin Hart sees the three marks of postmodernism as "anti-essentialism, anti-realism, and anti-foundationalism".[32]

Anti-essentialism denies that things have fixed natures which we can know. The mind cannot grasp *what* something is. Anti-realism denies that knowledge is of a real world independent of our thought. Anti-foundationalism is an extension of this, claiming that there are no firm grounds for any knowledge of the world.

Postmodernism therefore restricts itself to the particular, the fragmentary, eschewing systems and universal concepts. Bias, self-interest and the will to power are seen as distorting factors in any search for truth. The postmodernist viewpoint leads on to deconstructionism, which aims to break up "texts" into their components, to detect the motivations, influences and hidden agendas behind the surface meaning. The term texts refers not only to writing, but to any body of knowledge.

Michel Foucault and Jacques Derrida are eminent representatives of the outlook we are discussing. Foucault sees history in terms of the discontinuous, the chaotic, with a stress on the dominance of power as a shaper of belief. His prognosis is pessimistic, envisaging a technological takeover of human life, and viewing so-called scientific knowledge as shaped by political forces seeking control over people's lives.

Derrida is more optimistic, but no less dismissive of traditional positions. The tradition, he thinks, is bankrupt, manifesting a confidence it cannot justify. Yet he does not offer an alternative, for that would suppose a system, and he denies the possibly of a true system of thought. He "deconstructs" the views he encounters, but does not replace them with something allegedly better. In the words of Robert C. Solomon, for Derrida "...philosophy has no substance, and Derrida tries to make up for it by style".[33]

Derrida states: "Textuality being constituted by differences and by differences from differences, it is by nature absolutely heterogeneous and is constantly composing with the forces that tend to annihilate it."[34] Words and ideas have meaning through their relation to other words and ideas, and these through relation to yet others; and the meanings are constantly shifting. We cannot attain a stable underlying reality on which to ground our views. All predications depend on something outside themselves, something we cannot grasp, for it is absent from our thoughts.

A technical term, *differance*, is used by Derrida to signify something outside our thought but towards which thought tends and upon which are based the identities and presences in our minds. But *differance* cannot be clearly described – precisely because it is outside our thought. Comparing Kant and Derrida, Alex Callinicos says that Derrida "...sets *differance* in the place of the unknowable *Ding-an-sich* and, resolving the subject into the play of presence and absence, sets the categories themselves in motion."[35]

Postmodernism and deconstructionism are unable, from their very nature, to set out clear theses that can be examined and assessed – for they claim that all language is continually changing, with shifting layers of relations between words and concepts. So their views are not clearly stated. While they represent a reaction against characteristic themes from

Descartes onwards, they are at the same time a product of those themes. In particular, they are heirs of the theories of knowledge that cannot account for objective truth.

In the judgment of Alexander Solzhenitsyn: "For a postmodernist, the world does not possess values that have reality…a denial of any and all ideas is considered courageous. And in this voluntary self-delusion, 'postmodernism' sees itself as a crowning achievement of all previous culture, the final link in its chain. We can have sympathy for the constant searching, but only as we have sympathy for the suffering of a sick man."[36]

4. Pragmatism

According to pragmatism, the purpose of thought is not to attain objective reality, but to help us cope with problems. To accept a theory, for instance, is not to say that it is actually so, but that it is the best theory for dealing with our problems. In the words of a leading pragmatist, Richard Rorty: "…pragmatists do not think that truth is the aim of inquiry. The aim of inquiry is utility, and there are as many useful tools as there are purposes to be served."[37] We seek the best ways of satisfying our desires. Take the acceptance of the Copernican theory today, compared with its rejection centuries ago. We should not argue about whether we have got it right, or whether our ancestors were right. The concern should be about the achievement of ends. An end our ancestors had was to preserve the authority of the Bible, which might be weakened by non-literal interpretations. But we may argue today, says Rorty, that "… the benefits of modern astronomy and of space travel outweigh the advantages of Christian fundamentalism."[38]

Rorty sees pragmatism as proceeding from Darwinism; from human beings viewed as chance products of evolution.[39] It follows that there is no intelligibility to be found in things, and that they have no natures – there is not a way things really are, independently of their relations to other things and independently of our minds.

The questions philosophers have discussed, and which have been seen traditionally as having an intrinsic importance, are made, not found – and can therefore be unmade. Nor are there moral obligations rooted in an unchanging human nature.

Pragmatism and postmodernism are strongly influenced by Friedrich

Nietzsche (1844-1900), as indicated in these words from his fragment Truth and Lies in the Extra-moral Sense: "What then is truth? A mobile army of metaphors, metonymies, anthropomorphisms; a sum, in short, of human relationships, which, rhetorically and poetically intensified, ornamented and transformed, come to be thought of, after long usage by a people, as fixed, binding, and canonical. Truths are illusions, worn-out metaphors now impotent to stir the senses, coins which have lost their faces and are considered now as metal rather then currency."[40]

How should we live, according to pragmatism? No objective grounds exist for living in this way rather than that, for being kind to people rather than cruel. Still, the pragmatist opts for a way of life that recognizes the solidarity we experience between ourselves and others and the feeling that we should sympathize with the pain of others, seeing them as like ourselves in wanting pleasure and the avoidance of suffering. Not a rational case, but imaginative identification with other people is the driving force in treating them well.

5. Comparison of current trends

If empiricism and existentialism are dominant philosophies today, they are by no means the only ones. Thomism has a significant following, especially but not exclusively among Catholics. However, it has greatly declined from the prominent position it had in Catholic colleges and seminaries before the Second Vatican Council of 1962 to 1965. In the aftermath of the Council, Thomism and the whole Scholastic approach encountered much hostility. Phenomenology and existentialism were favored instead, leading often to views irreconcilable with orthodox Catholic beliefs. More recently this has moderated, and in these early years of the twenty-first century there are signs of a renewed interest in the thought of Aquinas, and its application to modern problems.

Marxism's large following has waned, but it still exercises an influence on many who would deny they are Marxists. A variety of trends are found in current philosophy: idealism (whether metaphysical or personal), realism (of many shades), evolutionism, pragmatism, positivism, postmodernism, etc. J. F. Mora gave a long list in 1960,[41] and declared that well over two hundred definitions of the concept "philosophy" could be found at the time.[42] There is no less variety now.

The United States accommodates all the above philosophies more representatively than Britain or most other countries. Influences flow into America from every part of the world and generally gain a hearing. Among typically American thinkers who have had a lasting effect on the climate of thought, the names of the idealist Josiah Royce and the pragmatists C. S. Peirce, William James and John Dewey are included.

There is not much communication between the major types of philosophy. Linguistic analysts use existentialism as a mine from which to draw examples of "meaningless" statements. Existentialists look on linguistic analysis as an ivory-tower discipline which ignores real human problems to concentrate on minute analyses of artificial sentences. They also charge empiricism with subservience to physical science and a consequent dehumanizing of man. They would emphatically disagree with A. J. Ayer's contention, quoted in section one of this chapter, that "philosophy is virtually empty without science", and with Russell's use of physics and physiology to solve philosophic problems.

They are not alone in their criticisms, especially about linguistic philosophy. Russell himself, despite his own activities in linguistic philosophy and his high regard for the *Tractatus*, saw Wittgenstein's later views as a disaster. Writing of his *Philosophical Investigations* (published in 1953) and the works that have arisen from it, he states that if their view is the right one, "Philosophy is, at best, a slight help to lexicographers, and at worst, an idle tea-time amusement."[43] He complains that this new philosophy, instead of concerning itself with the world and our relation to it, seems to be concerned only with "the different ways in which silly people can say silly things."[44]

A joke is told about an English philosopher who was asked: "Do you think life is worth while?" He replied: "That all depends on what you mean by 'while'".

Empiricists bring counter criticisms against phenomenology and existentialism. In particular they accuse them of obscurity. Take the following passage from *Being and Nothingness*, by Sartre. "Since human reality in its primitive relation to itself is not what it is, its relation to itself is not primitive and can derive its meaning only from an original relation which is the null relation or identity. It is the self which would be what it is which allows the for-itself to be apprehended as not being what it is; the relation denied in the definition of the for-itself – which as such should be first posited – is a relation (given as perpetually absent) between the for-itself and itself in the mode of identity."[45]

After wrestling with passages like this, it might be asserted, one should be more appreciative of the efforts on behalf of clarity made by the linguistic movement.

In the universities and in academic circles generally, little notice is taken of Scholasticism. This is an extraordinary situation, where the argument and reasoning of great thinkers – St Thomas, Maritain, and a galaxy of others in between – are casually ignored and problems such as free will, the nature of knowledge, the meaning of morality, are dealt with as though these men could have nothing relevant to say. It would be different if they had been found worthless after due study, and then dismissed. But it is assumed, without evidence, that they are not worth studying.

We have seen how the present situation in philosophy was reached. From Descartes onwards the problem of knowledge became more and more acute. One movement tended to assimilate matter to mind; the opposite one tended to assimilate mind to matter. There was a swing to intellectualism; and an opposite swing to sensism. Doubts spread. Can we have certitude or must we remain skeptics? Could the world be a projection of my mind? Or the thought of a universal mind? Can we know anything transcending sense phenomena? If not, how can we accept – how can we even think of – a purely spiritual God? And how can we perceive unchanging moral principles? Or man as a being having inalienable rights? Must free will be denied? If so, aren't the actions of a person just a product of heredity and environment, with one person no better or worse, morally, than another?

Linguistic analysis arose partly as a result of the spreading lack of confidence in the power of reason to understand reality. The first task, some of the linguistic philosophers argued, is to analyse our language and in that way to clarify our thoughts. We may then be able to see what is capable of fruitful investigation and what is not. Unfortunately, the area they found themselves left with hardly seems worth the mental energy expended in its investigation.

It should not be assumed that confusion in philosophy is an academic problem having no repercussions on the average person's outlook. On the contrary, philosophy is one of the principal influences on the modern mind. Our culture is shaped predominately by the leaders of thought, and filters down to the man in the street. That filtering process is much more rapid today than in the past; and the impact of ideas, especially on young people, is an increasingly obvious phenomenon. Of course a score of factors other than philosophy have contributed to the current climate of thought. Religion, art, politics, physics, experimental psychology – all these are formative influences. But they are not isolated from philosophy: they are affected by it, and it by them.

Even a cursory survey of the theological developments of the past three hundred years shows the great extent to which they have been shaped by philosophy.

Protestantism accords only a very limited place to philosophy in theological thinking, yet the views of Hume, Kant and others down to existentialism have caused profound modifications in Protestant thought. This has often happened through attacks on religion which have derived from Hume. Protestant theologians have tended to adopt Kant's answers to Hume. Kantianism in turn has led them into subjectivism.

Modern art is stamped with prevailing philosophic attitudes: this appears from its exploratory efforts, its groping for a significance, its rejection of the intelligible and objective. The pragmatic approach in today's economic and political theory is another effect of the lack of a stabilizing philosophy: if there is no underlying order in these spheres which the mind can grasp and be guided by, the alternative is a more or less arbitrary manipulation of society for the sake of selected purposes.

Only too often the physical sciences are elevated into a philosophy; and this is scientism. But it is logical if one adopts, for example, Bertrand Russell's view of knowledge; philosophy then becomes a handmaiden of these sciences. Since Freud, experimental scientists have tended to supply answers to questions previously considered philosophical – questions concerning, e.g., knowledge, free will, value judgments. Psychology is often forced to tackle questions that lie beyond its scope – because philosophy seems unable to settle them.

A host of practical factors have also made their contribution to current ways of thought, factors such as the rise of industrialism, the two World Wars, the weakening of class distinctions, the almost incredible improvements in transport and communications. Consequently we get such phenomena as a leveling of cultures and an information explosion.

No society can be understood without a knowledge of the forces molding it. And among the strongest forces is the society's philosophy – or philosophies. Certain factors are prominent today: in religion, a crisis of faith; in morals, a breakdown of traditional standards and no agreement as to what should replace them; in politics and civil life generally, protests, rebellion, violence. A person can find himself oppressed by a gnawing sadness as he searches his life and sees no meaning there. He doesn't want to remain on the surface of life, but is there anything beneath the surface? It is not a new feeling, but it now has a new prevalence.

Many feel alienated and lonely as they move about in a world where "God is dead" and life lacks meaning. Atheistic existentialism can have a powerful appeal for such people; and it certainly mirrors their mood. It accepts the view that reality is irrational and human life absurd. No meaning exists for man to uncover; and a man's dawning realization of this makes him see the absurdity of his life.

Albert Camus develops this thought at length. He rejects any leap of faith, in the manner of Kierkegaard, as a solution to the dilemma. What a person should do, if he has the courage, is to live in this absurd world, steeling himself against despair and also against the attempt to escape the meaninglessness of reality by wishful thinking. He must try to experience life to the full, instead of existing passively like a vegetable. What standards will he follow, what values will he reach for? Well, there are no objective standards or values, so he has to choose his own. Their meaning and worth will be purely subjective, purely arbitrary. The important thing, Camus thinks, is to make *some* choice, then commit oneself utterly to the consequences.

A man may choose to fight for his country, then commit himself with his whole soul to this purpose. Yet he should remain constantly aware of the meaninglessness of his cause; he should see that an enemy soldier could be equally justified in his allegiance to the opposite side, for all causes are objectively irrational. The authentic man sees the absurdity of life, yet freely commits himself to *something*, and lives his life in freedom and in protest against the irrationality of the world. At least his choices are his own – and so is the anguish in which he makes them.

Towards the end of the eighteenth century Kant surveyed the empiricism of Hume and saw that it led inexorably to extreme scepticism. Kant added: "Whether with such a terrible overthrow of the chief branches of knowledge, human reason will escape better, and will not rather become irrecoverably involved in this destruction of all knowledge, so that from the same principles a *universal_skepticism_should* follow (affecting, indeed, only the learned), this I will leave everyone to judge for himself."[46]

These are ominous words, and in our postmodernist days are closer to fulfillment than ever before; and with universal education it is not only "the learned" who are affected, but all classes.

1   *Tractatus Logico-Philosophicus*, 6. 53.
2   *Language, Truth and Logic*, Victor Gollancz, London, second edition (1946), p. 48.
3   P. 57.
4   P. 64.
5   P. 89.
6   Charles Landesman, *An Introduction to Epistemology* (1997), p. 165.
7   P. 152.
8   P. 31.
9   P. 125.
10 P. 126.
11 P. 34.
12 P. 107.
13 P. 108.
14 P. 116.
15 This and the following quotations from Russell's adolescent years are from the notes he reproduces in *My Philosophical Development* (1959), chapter 3.
16 *My Philosophical Development*, p. 42.
17 P. 61.
18 P. 62.
19 P. 16.
20 P. 139.
21 *Human Knowledge: Its Scope and Limits* (1948), p. 161.
22 *My Philosophical Development*, p. 254.
23 Cf. *The Study of Mathematics*; printed in *The New Quarterly* in 1907, reprinted in *Philosophical Essays* (1910).
24 *My Philosophical Development*, p. 211.
25 Husserl, *Die Idee der Phanomenologie* (1907), pp. 29ff.
26 *Ideen*, volume 1 (1913), p. 44.
27 Cf. Joseph J. Kockelmans, *Phenomenology* (1967), part 1, chapter 8.
28 Article "Thomism and Contemporary Philosophical Pluralism" in *The Future of Thomism*, p. 99, (1992), edited by Hudson and Moran.
29 Ibid., p. 100. (1992)
30 Cf. Kockelmans, p. 228.
31 Richard Rorty, *Philosophy and Social Hope* (1999), p. 263.
32 Kevin Hart, *Postmodernism: A Beginner's Guide* (2004), p. 99.
33 Robert C. Solomon, *Continental Philosophy Since 1750* (1988), p. 201.
34 Jacques Derrida, *A Derrida Reader*, edited by P. Kamuf (1991), p. 127.
35 Alex Callinicos, *Against Postmodernism: A Marxist Critique* (1989), p. 77.
36 Quoted in *Postmodernism and Christian Philosophy*, edited by R. T. Ciapalo (1997), p. 223.
37 Richard Rorty, *Philosophy and Social Hope*, p. 54.
38 Ibid., p. XXV.
39 Rorty in chapter two of *Deconstruction and Pragmatism*, edited by C. Mouffe

(1996), p. 15.

[40] Translation by Alasdair MacIntyre in his book *Three Rival Versions of Moral Enquiry* (1990), p. 35.

[41] In his book *Philosophy Today* (1960), p. 65.

[42] P. 66.

[43] *My Philosophical Development*, p. 217.

[44] Ibid., p. 230.

[45] Translation by H. E. Barnes, sixth paperbound edition (1969), pp. 64, 65.

[46] *Critique of Practical Reason*, first part, book 1, chapter 1, section 2; p. 142 of T. K. Abbott's translation (1963 printing).

Chapter Five

COMPARISON OF PHILOSOPHY WITH OTHER SUBJECTS

In this chapter we shall outline the position of Thomistic philosophy relatively to common sense, mathematics, physical science and sacred theology. The validity of that position will be more fully vindicated in the treatment of knowledge in the following chapters.

1. Philosophy and common sense

Suppose it were stated that we cannot be sure of anything until we have proved it from something else that we already know. At first glance this might seem reasonable; but a second look reveals that it is not. For it would make all certainty impossible. If one truth were founded on a previous one, and that on an earlier one, we would be involved in an infinite regression, and would never reach a foundation for our knowledge. Granted that we can have certainty, it is impossible that all our certainties be mediated by others; it is necessary that there be some we can know immediately.

Self-evident principles (also called analytic propositions) come into this category. A self-evident principle is a proposition or sentence which only needs to be stated, and its terms understood, for its truth to be seen. For example: The whole is greater than the part. Anyone who understands what "whole" and "part" mean immediately sees the truth of that sentence. Or again: Good is to be sought and evil avoided. The very notion of good is of something desirable, and therefore to be sought, while that of evil is of something repugnant, and therefore to be shunned.

No one who really understands such propositions can really dispute their truth; at most a person can tell himself he rejects or doubts them. These principles are not arbitrary creations of the mind, but arise from the intelligibility seen in things. We don't invent them; we find them.

There is another class of immediate certainties, namely judgments based directly on experience. The experience in question may be that of the external senses – sight, touch, etc. – or it may be introspection.

Take that of the external senses first. Sensation contacts things as physically present: it is an intuition. For this reason it cannot be erroneous, and neither can judgments deriving directly from it. Examples are the judgment that there is movement; or that bodies have dimensions. These judgments are not based on something reasoned to, but on something apprehended. This explains why, in everyday life, we have full confidence in the truth of what we sense.

If we merely think of, or form a mental picture of, say a building on fire, we don't conclude the building really is on fire; we are perfectly capable of conceiving or imagining such situations without there being any truth in them. Fiction writers do it professionally. But if we *see* the building burning down, and are sure we see it, we can have no doubt of the fact.

Now take introspection (reflection on our psychic processes – thoughts, emotions, etc.). This furnishes us with immediate certainties. When I judge, "I am now thinking of this table", I am sure the judgment is true because of the inner awareness I possess of my own thoughts. Introspection provides a lot of data for psychological judgments. We shall use it later in distinguishing between images and concepts.

Self-evident principles and judgments based immediately on sense experience are the source of all our reasoning, no matter how complicated or subtle that reasoning may be. They pertain to philosophy and to other sciences, as well as to common sense knowledge.

The term *common sense* is used with various meanings, so we must clarify our present use of it. It is a knowledge which dawns in man as soon as he begins to exercise his mind, and is common to the entire human race. No special education is required for it; on the contrary, its possession, in a rudimentary form, is an indispensable condition of later education. It contains three elements: the two we have just explained (self-evident principles and judgments about experience), and also the conclusions that can be easily drawn from these. Such easily drawn conclusions include, e.g., the conviction that the will is free, and many convictions about morality – that one has a right to defend oneself against an aggressor, that children should honour their parents, etc.

Common sense is infallible, because of its closeness to the truths it judges about. When a statement seems to be common sense but is erroneous, it will be found on examination to be outside the area just outlined as the province of common sense. If the statement that the earth is spherical had been offered to our remote ancestors, some would doubtless have rejected it as contrary to common sense. They might have argued that, if it were true, all the water would run down to the bottom of the sphere, or that any unattached objects in the lower part would fall off. But the statement that the earth is spherical is not really opposed to common sense: it does not contradict anything in the three categories we have explained. The suspicion that it does would be due to inadequate scientific knowledge.

It often happens that things are thought to be "just plain common sense" which in fact are errors; just as it happens that various truths of common sense are rejected by some people because of errors, prejudices and misunderstandings from which they themselves are suffering. Common sense is universal in that all have a share in it. It is a spontaneous knowledge: it arises naturally, as it were, without any special study or learning.

Some will object. If such marvellous knowledge exists – infallible, universal, spontaneous – how is it that we encounter so much error in the world? Among the educated we find many contradictions of common sense notions. Among uneducated peoples, instead of this common truth we find ignorance and gross superstition.

Firstly, although men's intellects arrive naturally at the primitive truths, they do not stop there. Pushing on to less evident things, error creeps in, especially under the influence of prejudice and passion. This is so at the individual level; it is often strikingly so if we consider the society into which the individual comes. The errors, the prejudices, the mental and moral darkness that can become established in a society will grow on the individuals who enter it. Then, like a cancer, the errors will eat into those first healthy truths, killing – or at least deadening – them.

Secondly, the common sense truths are possessed only obscurely, for the most part. Consider principles like these: Nothing is without a sufficient reason of being. Every agent acts for an end. The good is to be sought. Very few people think deliberately about such things, clarifying them in their minds. But they know them obscurely and act upon them; if they didn't, they would not act at all.

Philosophy arises from the self-evident truths and immediately experienced facts that common sense apprehends. However, it does not accept them because common sense affirms them, but because their truth is evident. And it reflects upon them, to understand them clearly and to vindicate them. Philosophy is more than a mature common sense. It is a knowledge of all things through their highest causes, proceeding under the light of reason. It is concerned with what things are (their formal and material causes), what makes them be (their efficient cause), and why they be (their final cause). The true philosopher sees the intelligible principles that explain things; all his thinking is done under the light of these principles.

The above considerations indicate the strength of philosophical argumentation, and the difficulty of it. Its strength is from its evidential basis: philosophical conclusions depend on no other science and on no authority. They rest solely on self-evident principles and on data directly experienced. Its difficulty springs from the fact that acute penetration into principles and reasonings is required before their truth can be clearly seen. And "acute penetration" is something that most people are not much good at.

The relevance, necessity and naturalness of philosophy appear from its relation to common sense. The latter is relevant, necessary and natural – we would see that very clearly if we tried to live without it. But true philosophy is a development of it. So a philosopher should be notable for common sense. And by paying heed to these first certitudes he will avoid many errors that he would otherwise slip into.

This indicates the way to approach the study of philosophy. Since its truths are radically contained in common sense, we should ascend from the common sense knowledge we possess to the philosophic knowledge we seek. It is a sort of organic development. Philosophy should then be communicated to others with the help of the common sense ideas at which our minds naturally arrive.

Common sense affirmations are rejected by philosophic sceptics. They would say that what I have called self-evident truths are in fact tautology. They would say our senses are unreliable; that we cannot be sure, for example, of the existence of bodies. I will not attempt to refute these criticisms here – they will be dealt with in due course; but I want to stress that philosophy has the task of vindicating common sense judgments, not naively accepting them on trust. G. E. Moore claimed, in a famous lecture, that he could prove two hands exist by letting everyone see them.[1] This is similar to Johnson's answer to Berkeley's doctrine of the non-existence of matter. Boswell tells us in his *Life of Samuel Johnson*: "I observed, that though we are satisfied his doctrine is not true, it is impossible to refute it. I shall never forget the alacrity with which Johnson answered, striking his foot with mighty force against a large stone, till he rebounded from it, – 'I refute it thus'."[2]

The man in the street will commend these experiments of Johnson and Moore as very good answers to the error in question. But they should not satisfy the philosopher: he should critically justify the stand taken by common sense, and show the source of the error. Otherwise he is not philosophising – is not striving to plumb reality to its depths.

2. The meaning of science

Very often the term science is reserved for the physical sciences. When told that a friend is studying science, we do not ask whether the science happens to be mathematics or philosophy or sacred theology; we know that our informant would not have used the word science had he intended any of these three disciplines. Nevertheless, these subjects deserve the name science according to its classic definition, which is: *certain knowledge through causes*. Let us examine that definition.

For knowledge to be truly scientific, it must be certain: if a scientist has only probability about something, he may be on the way to gaining scientific knowledge but the goal is yet to be reached, and he will continue his investigations in the hope of reaching certitude. The certitude intended, of course, is genuine objective certitude; if he subjectively convinces himself he is right, but genuine evidence is lacking, that state of mind is not true certitude. What is required is necessity of the thing known, and knowledge by the intellect of this necessity. There could be no science of winning lottery numbers, because no necessity exists for one number rather than another to be picked from the barrel: randomness, not necessity, prevails here.

Science cannot be concerned with necessary things without being concerned with causes, for it is causes that necessitate and explain things. When we merely know some effect, but are ignorant of its causes, our knowledge is superficial and incomplete. The term cause is applicable to the four causes enumerated by Aristotle.[3] If we were to fully understand all four causes of some thing – which in fact is never the case – our knowledge of it would be complete, for we would understand what produced it and why it was produced (the extrinsic causes), and also what it is in itself (the intrinsic causes).

Science tends to be thought of as something apart from the scientist – as a system found in books. But science is knowledge, and is therefore primarily a perfection of the intellect. What we find in books is a set of lifeless symbols, of which the living reality is in the mind of the person understanding the symbols.

3. Mathematics

Many philosophers have attached great importance to mathematics and the mathematical way of reasoning: Plato, Descartes, Spinoza are examples. But mathematics is not a part of philosophy, because the latter is concerned primarily with real being, whereas mathematics is concerned with quantity in abstraction from real being: discrete quantity in arithmetic and algebra, continuous quantity in geometry. It is the science that investigates the properties of quantity.

Take the notion of triangle studied by the geometrician. It has perfect triangularity, and it has nothing but triangularity. Any science abstracts from individuals and studies what is common to all the individuals, but when other sciences, natural philosophy included, study bodily things, they study them with their sensible qualities. Mathematics is different: it not only abstracts from the individual, but also from the sensible matter common to all the individuals. It is about quantity and its properties, but not the things that have quantity. So when the geometrician studies triangle, the individual triangle in white chalk is simply an aid to his thought, but the sensible matter of that drawing is of no interest to him whatever.

This explains the regularity of geometrical figures. If individuality alone were abstracted from, sensible qualities would remain for consideration, and these are not perfectly regular. Every actual triangle has minor irregularities, and falls short of what *triangle* means to the mathematician. But he abstracts from sensible matter, leaving only intelligible quantity and the qualities proper to it. Thus his concepts have a perfection and a simplicity that are never verified in actuality.

Because of the peculiar abstraction proper to mathematics there can be no induction in this subject; that is, no ascent from individual instances to universal laws. It is deductive, starting from essential definitions, analysing them and deducing their properties. The whole of mathematical science flows from the formal cause. Sense experience contributes only remotely; it has a preparatory role in providing the mathematician's intellect with the data for attaining notions such as number, triangle, straight line, etc., notions without which he could not begin his science.

And because of this abstraction, non-Euclidean geometries can be valid; they would not be if mathematics was concerned directly with realities, for they would then be contradicted by reality.

Mathematical modes of reasoning have a fatal fascination for some minds. Because of the purity, the simplicity, the orderly and necessary chains of deductive argumentation, this approach is thought to hold the key to understanding the universe. But that method, applied outside its field, quickly leads to disaster. I knew a student of mathematics who was awed by the wonderful mathematical ability needed to field a cricket ball! He explained that, to make an accurate catch, it would be necessary to calculate the speed of the ball when it met the bat, the force the batsman exerted, the angle of the bat, the direction and strength of the wind, and several other factors. The truth is that no mathematics at all would be needed. The explanation of the fielder's skill is physical, not mathematical. He would lack the data necessary for the calculations, apart from the arithmetical facility. What is true is that, given the data, the physical facts could be described in mathematical terms. But the facts, and their real explanation, would be physical, not mathematical. [4]

4. Empirical science

A great deal of confusion exists regarding the respective provinces of philosophy and the empirical sciences. It is often said that philosophy is broader and more comprehensive, or that it goes deeper than physics, chemistry, biology, astronomy, etc. This is true, but too vague. Actually, philosophy and the empirical sciences approach reality in diverse ways.

If a mineralogist is asked what silver is, he will enumerate its observable properties: sonorous, ductile, very malleable, with a certain melting point and boiling point, and so on. If asked to define these properties, he will be driven back to indefinable elements, which will be observed phenomena or sensations or operations of observation or of measurement.

Suppose a philosopher defines man as *rational animal*. He will define animal: *sensitive living body*. To clarify the notion of life he will say it is self-actuation. He will explain self-actuation in terms of identity and causality, and causality will be analysed into potency and act.

The two modes of understanding are quite diverse. The same diversity can be shown by contrasting the above definition of man with one given by a zoologist: *a mammal of the order of primates*. And if the zoologist clarifies the meaning of animal or of primate, he will do so in terms of the observable.

We noted in dealing with common sense that philosophy arises from experienced facts and evident principles. But, as the definition of man manifests, philosophy understands in terms of being; that is, in terms of the reality underlying what the senses attain. As the following chapters will show, sense knowledge attains only the most superficial aspect of things, their depths remaining unsensed. Now, the intellect takes either of two approaches, depending on whether it is studying empirical science or philosophy.

In the former case, the intellect strives to understand in terms of what is sensed; whether things are contacted by the unaided senses or with the help of instruments such as the microscope; or whether they are known through pointer readings and in similar ways; or whether through introspection, in the psychological sciences.

The philosophising intellect takes the opposite direction: from sensibles, and by the light of first principles, it investigates the very nature and intelligible properties of things. Unlike the positive sciences, it does not resolve or analyse its concepts into the observable, but into the intelligible. It attains the unsensed depths of things.

By means of observation and experiment the sciences collect material; and every single item of this material is reached through the external senses (unless, in psychology, through introspection). But a science is not just a collection of observations; it is a systematic account of some aspect of reality. However, the observational aspect proper to the empirical sciences precludes any penetration into the essences, the natures, of things.

This does not mean that the sciences know nothing of these natures: every science, from the fact that it is an account of what things are, is concerned in some way with natures. But the positive sciences attain directly only empirical signs of the nature of things: constant, observable, external phenomena which give rise to empirical laws established by induction. These laws are manifestations of the essences and causes which account for them, and in practice they take the place of the essences and causes. The order and constancy found among phenomena signify a necessity based in the nature of things: if no constant natures underlay the phenomena observed by the scientist, those phenomena could not be constant. The phenomena are pointers to something deeper, but it is with the pointers, not with the something deeper, that the scientist occupies himself. He investigates the facts, coordinates them into laws, and coordinates the laws into theories. But the whole process remains on the level of observed phenomena.

This coordinating and systematizing work, especially in physics, requires the extensive use of mathematics. The physicist uncovers harmony and intelligibility in the world, but as a physicist he cannot trace these to their ontological source, so he expresses them through mathematics. He finds order in the swing of a pendulum, and expresses it in this law: *The square of the period of oscillation of a pendulum is proportional to its length.* He studies gravitation and arrives at the result: *The force of attraction between two bodies is proportional to the product of their masses and inversely proportional to the square of the distance between them.*

A radical change has occurred in recent times regarding the degree of reality to be accorded to scientific theories. It used to be thought that they would show the very depths of physical reality. And the entities dealt with in physics, such as ether, electricity, atoms, were supposed to be like the things we see and feel. An atom would have a nucleus that resembled a tiny billiard ball, and other tiny billiard balls would be continually spinning around it.

This view has now been replaced by a conception of physics as dealing with the measurable in abstraction from that which is measured. Sir Arthur Eddington writes: "But now we realize that science has nothing to say as to the intrinsic nature of the atom. The physical atom is, like everything else in physics, a schedule of pointer readings."[5]

However, when Eddington goes on to discuss the substratum of the pointer readings, he proposes an idealistic explanation, reducing everything to "mind-stuff" or mental reality. He is not then thinking as a physicist, but as a philosopher – and the idealistic philosophy he expounds is untenable, as will appear later.

Thomism sees both physical science and philosophy as studying external reality, but in different ways. Ultimate questions are reserved for philosophy; it alone has the means of dealing with them. And because it handles ultimate questions it is superior to every other science except sacred theology. All the others give explanations which are relatively superficial, requiring to be grounded on the principles of philosophy. Even mathematical axioms presuppose philosophical principles. The axiom "two quantities which are equal to a third quantity are equal to one another" is resolved into the more universal metaphysical principle "two things identical with a third are identical with one another."[6]

This does not mean that the physicist or mathematician has to study philosophy before he can be certain of his own principles and conclusions; his science is intrinsically independent of philosophy, and common sense provides sufficient justification for the basis from which he works. But philosophy gives a more perfect justification.

Although the empirical sciences have no intrinsic need of philosophy, the scientist needs it – not as a scientist, but as a human being. Everyone needs a deeper knowledge than the study of phenomena is capable of providing; all need an insight into what lies beyond phenomena. The need is more pressing in the scientist than in most people, for science prompts questions it cannot solve, and a yearning to find the answers. What is life? Is everything designed for some end? How reliable is the picture of the world given by our senses?

In the absence of philosophy, the assumption is often made that empirical science is the most perfect expression of reality available to us. That assumption equates knowable reality with observable and measurable things – insofar as they are observable and measurable. Anything above that level is automatically ruled out. Man becomes a bundle of subatomic particles whirling in space; and even the nature of the particles remains unknown. That conception of reality, taken as the ultimate, is intrinsically repugnant; but it is unnecessary to take it as the ultimate if we admit a more basic philosophic grasp of being.[7]

5. Sacred theology

The word theology means "science of God". In chapters fourteen and fifteen the philosophic study of God will be treated; this is called natural theology, and is distinct from sacred theology. The latter, usually just called theology, is based on God's revealing of himself to the human race through the Bible and the Church. Teachings were given over many centuries: the first are in the Old Testament; then the coming of Christ and the teachings of the Apostles marked the climax of the Revelation. Christ made his Church the custodian and interpreter of that treasury of teachings – about God; about creation; about man: his nature and supernatural destiny, and the way of life that leads to that destiny. There can be no change in the content of the Revelation, but there can be a vast development in the understanding of it.

Take the teaching about Christ. It is revealed that he is God and man. But the meaning of this became clearer through the centuries, as the Church meditated on it and combated theories irreconcilable with it. The teaching of Arius (d. AD 336) was condemned: he held that the *Logos* or Word united himself with a soulless body, himself taking the place of the soul. Arius also denied the divinity of the Word, holding that he is the supreme creature and the first being to be created. On the other hand, Nestorius (d. AD 451) taught that the man, Christ, has a complete human nature, but is no more than a man; the divine Word dwells in him as in all the just; between the two natures, divine and human, there is only an accidental or moral union.

These doctrines and similar were condemned by the early Ecumenical Councils, and the revealed truths about Christ and the Trinity were gradually clarified. The key concepts through which the clarification was achieved were those of *person* and *nature*. If there were no real distinction between the human nature of Christ and the person possessing that nature – if these words were just different ways of saying the same thing – that person would be no more than a man, however closely he might be united to God in a moral sense. Numerous insights were developed concerning the perfection and power of Christ, his right to adoration, the value of his redemptive sacrifice, etc.

From this we can see how theology proceeds. Its principles are the truths revealed by God: truths about himself or other things as related to him. They are believed by the theologian on the authority of God, the Supreme Truth. In this they differ from the principles of philosophy, which are accepted by the philosopher because their truth is evident. The theologian's mind is illuminated by supernatural faith given by God, whereas the philosopher uses his unaided human reason. Theology is a true science: basing itself on revealed principles, it develops systematically by argumentation as rigorous and logical as that employed by other sciences.

A close relation exists between sacred theology and philosophy. Although superior to philosophy, theology cannot develop without it. The reason is that our knowledge starts from corporeal things and it is only by the aid of these that we can know God and divine things. The above example of the development of Christology shows how theology employs philosophy to gain an understanding of the mysteries of faith. Person and nature are philosophical concepts used here, and in the doctrine of the Trinity, to unfold the truth of these revealed mysteries.

Philosophy also has an apologetic function. Through it the existence of God is proved, as is the possibility of miracles and other truths necessary to defend the foundations of faith. Doctrines are also defended against adversaries by showing, philosophically, that they are not opposed to reason: as when it is shown, from the nature of intellect and will, and from the desire for perfect happiness, that the vision of God, to which man is supernaturally destined, is not repugnant to reason.

For the science of sacred theology to achieve maturity, a healthy philosophy is essential. The denial of this implies a chasm between natural knowledge and God's Revelation. In fact, all knowledge is harmoniously united, and man would remain in total darkness regarding the meaning of God's message unless he used concepts he already has to help penetrate the mysteries of faith. Nevertheless, theology, simply speaking, is far superior to philosophy or any natural knowledge, for as we have said, it comes from God's Revelation about himself, proceeds under the light of supernatural faith, and is concerned with an end for man which is above any natural destiny.

1   Proof of an External World, *Proceedings of the British Academy*, volume 25, 1939.
2   *The Modern Library* edition, p. 285.
3   Supra, chapter one, section four.
4   Cf. Aristotle's distinction between physics and mathematics: *Physics*, book II, chapter 2. See also J. Maritain: *The Degrees of Knowledge* (1959 edition), chapter 2, section 22.
5   *The Nature of the Physical World*, chapter 12; p. 259, Ann Arbor Paperbacks (1958).
6   Cf. J. Maritain, *An Introduction to Philosophy* (1962 edition), p. 73.
7   For an account of the relation phenomenology sees between philosophy and the sciences, an account which has a number of significant points of agreement with what has been said in this section, see the article by J. J. Kockelmans in *Phenomenology* (1967), edited by Kockelmans, pp. 540ff.

Chapter Six

KNOWLEDGE IN GENERAL

During the past three centuries theories about the nature of knowledge have multiplied, and philosophers have become more and more preoccupied with the question. And the diverse solutions attained have caused diverse positions to be held on other points, and have had repercussions in other fields, including empirical psychology and sacred theology. If modern philosophy is chaotic, this is largely because of errors about knowledge.

1. Knowledge: immanent and objective

When we reflect on knowledge, two characteristics occur to us: immanence and objectivity. Firstly, knowledge is immanent. That is, it is within the knower. If I see a tree or think of *man*, the apprehension is within me; it is not out in the tree or out in some universal man. Secondly, knowledge is objective. It extends to things outside us: the tree I see is not inside me, but out in the field; my concept of man is not a subjective construct of my mind, but fits every man. Knowledge is realistic.[1]

But these two seem to contradict each other. The first (the immanence) says: only that which is in the knower is known. The second (the objectivity or realism) says: that which is outside the knower is known. So it seems that if knowledge is immanent it is not realist; if realist it is not immanent. Idealists deny the realism to save the immanence. But it is unreasonable to deny the evident when it doesn't conform to a theory. A true account of knowledge must reconcile the immanence and the realism; it must reconcile both terms of the problem, and not suppress the problem by denying one term.

An objection may be raised here. It may be said that to set out the problem in the way I have is to *assume* that knowledge is objective. But all we are conscious of is its immanence, and we have to prove its objectivity – if we can.

I would disagree, and say that we are aware of things as outside us; we are just as much aware of this as we are of their cognitive presence within us. In section one of the previous chapter it was pointed out that some truths and facts are so evident that it is not necessary to reason to them, and that if this were not so every reasoning process would be lost in an infinite regression. Knowledge of things as outside us is among these immediate apprehensions.

Denial of this by some philosophers arises from difficulties they encounter in explaining knowledge, which leads them to reject something seen by other people as perfectly evident. We shall see presently whether the Thomistic theory of knowledge is able to avoid those difficulties and account for both immanence and objectivity.

But before doing so, a patent inconsistency should be pointed out in the procedure of one who criticizes a person for contending that knowledge attains external reality. The objector is saying: "You may be wrong in asserting the objectivity of knowledge." But his statement itself implies that objectivity, because it implies he knows the existence of the person whose proposition he is criticising, and knows that he puts forward the said proposition. It would be no defence for the objector to say he is only doubting, not denying, the truth of the other person's statement. Even to say, "The truth of your statement is doubtful", is to assert the existence of the other, and that he communicated his statement to the objector.

The immanent-objective dilemma can be solved if, and only if, there is a way of possessing a form which does not involve making it one's own, but allows it to remain other.

Consider what happens when something is physically appropriated; it is the opposite to the kind of possession that knowledge is. When some determination (some form, in Aristotelian and Thomistic terminology) is received in a determinable subject (in matter, that is), the reception can be called subjective, physical and compositive.

Suppose a piece of plasticine is moulded into a spherical shape. The plasticine is a determinable subject of shape: it can receive various shapes. It is now determined to spherical shape. The form received, i.e., the shape, is received by the plasticine as its own shape. This is called subjective reception. The determination or form is appropriated by the subject having it, so that it is the form of that subject and is divided away from other subjects. Similarly, heat received in water is the heat of that water, not of the fire that caused it, or of any other subject.

Secondly, and consequently, the reception is physical: that is, reception of the new form is by way of physical alteration in the receiving subject. The plasticine undergoes a physical reconstruction, which involved loss of its previous shape and acquisition of a new shape. The water gains heat through the physical alterations that take place in it.

Thirdly, the reception is compositive. This means that a third arises in the reception of the new form. When the plasticine becomes round, there are not just plasticine and roundness; there is round plasticine. When the water becomes hot, there are not just water and heat; there is hot water. The two are composed into a unity; and this is called compositive reception.

The reception just illustrated is that found in the order of physical (as opposed to psychic) being. The reception of knowledge is very different.

When a form is known it does not become the form of the knower, but remains that of the thing known.[2] The knower sees or imagines or understands the spherical plasticine or the hot water without appropriating them; he knows them as of other, not of himself. The reception is not subjective, but objective: the form remains the form of something other than the recipient.

Nor is the reception of knowledge physical. When the roundness of a ball of plasticine is observed, the observer's visual power does not become round. When he understands or senses that water is hot, his power of knowledge does not physically acquire heat. (This does not deny that physical modifications are had in the sense organs, but the modifications that take place there are preparatory to sense knowledge, not knowledge itself.) Therefore the reception involved in knowledge is not physical, but supra-physical: the act of knowledge does not consist in gaining a new physical constitution.

Finally, the union of knower with known is not a compositive union of the kind just illustrated. Such a union excludes objectivity, because from such a union a third arises, a compound of, for instance, plasticine and roundness which is round plasticine. If such a union occurred in knowledge, objectivity would be impossible; the knower would be apprehending the compound from knower and received form: and this would exclude all knowledge of outside reality.[3]

Kant taught a compositive union, holding that man confers meaning on the raw material presented to him; and he was completely logical in maintaining, as a consequence, that we cannot know things-in-themselves. The same subjective trap awaits every philosopher who posits a compositive union in knowledge, which includes all those who proceed in a way proper to physics and physiology, failing to see that a higher kind of union is required if knowledge is to be explained.

To sum up. Knowledge is a certain reception of form, but diverse from the material way of receiving form. Materially received forms are had subjectively, physically and compositively. Forms received in knowledge are had objectively, supra-physically and incompositively. Such a manner of reception, and it alone, explains the evident fact that things other than the knower are known. Also, as St Thomas says, if it sufficed for knowledge "that the known thing existed materially in the knower, there would be no reason why things which materially subsist outside the soul should lack knowledge."[4] Lifeless things and plants have forms materially, but they lack knowledge.

We must look more closely at this immateriality. In general, immateriality means an elevation above matter. But what is meant by matter? In one sense it denotes what Aristotle called primary matter, which is a pure potency or determinability in the order of substance, not anything actual. Now, mere elevation above primary matter is not sufficient to make something a knower: anything that exists is above primary matter, but not everything is a knower.

However, this elevation causes knowability. In other words, to be knowable requires some actuality or determinateness: the indeterminate as such is unknowable.[5] This is why primary matter is so obscure, and is not understandable alone, but only in relation to form. So to be knowable, determinateness or form is required – but nothing more; even the lowest substance, the most insignificant entity, is knowable.

Granted that something is knowable, what further degree of immateriality is needed for it to be also a knower? Four general levels of being are found in the world: inanimate things, vegetation, irrational animals, men. These levels show a progressive domination over matter. Inanimate things, like stones, are above primary matter. A plant is living, and exercises a certain domination over its environment, because it converts other things into its own substance through nutrition, it grows and it propagates its species. This activity is self-actualisation through which the plant increases its being and vitality – by its activity it becomes more than it was.

The activity of the inanimate thing is the opposite: the more it acts, the more it uses itself up and descends towards entropy. Physics shows the inanimate universe obeying the second law of thermodynamics – the law that entropy always increases. This process, if left to itself, would eventually bring the universe to a state of inert equilibrium, all its energy dissipated. This law does not apply to the activity characteristic of the living (although that characteristic activity is accompanied by entropic action). The living can be symbolized by a growing tree, the non-living by a burning candle.

The next stage, that of the irrational animal, reaches knowledge. The animal and the plant differ in this way: the plant converts other things into itself – it dominates matter to the degree of using others to perfect itself, but only by destroying them; the animal, through sense knowledge, acquires the very forms of other things, while they remain the forms of those others – it dominates matter sufficiently to receive other things without destroying them.

Man has a yet greater domination over matter, because by his intellect he can do more than sense: he can understand. The degree of immateriality relevant here will be dealt with later. For the present we are just clarifying the term immateriality and the basic level of immateriality needed for knowledge.

It might be noted that each of the levels, plant, brute animal, man, implies those below it. A plant also exercises the physio-chemical functions of non-living things; so does the brute and, in addition, the functions of vegetative life; man exercises physio-chemical functions, plus those of vegetative life, plus the activities of sense life, as well as rational activities proper to himself.

So the degree of immateriality found in a knower is such that the subjectivisation of matter is escaped: the determination coming from the thing known is neither destroyed nor appropriated, but retains its identity in the knower; it remains the form of another. To be a knower something must be free from the necessity of having forms only in a material manner – subjectively, physically and compositively. It must be able to have them objectively, supra-physically and incompositively.

Knowledge can be defined: *have form in oneself immaterially or objectively.*[6] This definition demands both the immanence of knowledge and its objectivity: it is in the knower and is his knowledge, yet is of another.

A couple of precisions should be added. When we speak of the knowing of another, we are not denying self-reflection. But firstly, the objectivity of knowledge can be more easily understood by seeing that things outside the knower are known; secondly, even in self-consciousness or self-reflection, two acts are needed: the act which is being reflected on and the act of reflecting on it. If we didn't have thought in our mind or perceptions in our imagination, if they were just blank, there would be nothing to reflect on. So even self-reflection is "of other".

It should also be noted that the terms material and immaterial are used in various senses other than those involved here. Immaterial sometimes means spiritual, that is, without a body or constituted without physical content. But the *relative* independence from matter, freedom from the possessiveness of matter, which is required for sense knowledge falls far short of spirituality.

2. The excellence of knowledge

Knowledge is an activity. But what kind of activity?

We spoke just now of the diversity between the acts of living and non-living things, and pointed out that a non-living entity dissipates its energy while a living one perfects itself. The reason for these opposed effects is that the activity of the non-living passes into something else, whereas that characteristic of the living remains in the operant. When a cup of hot water heats a spoon placed in it, the agent (the water) loses some of its own heat by acting on the recipient (the spoon). The activity is essentially towards another: the agent acts on another, not on itself; the activity is transitive. But when a plant nourishes itself from the soil, the agent (the plant) is not acting on a recipient and losing some of its own actuality. It is acting towards its own perfection, becoming more than it was previously. This activity is immanent, not transitive; it remains within the operant and perfects it.

Knowledge is clearly not transitive activity, but immanent: it perfects the operant, and doesn't pass into something else. But it is far more perfect than the immanent activity of the plant. In what does this greater perfection consist?

Looking again at the plant's act in nourishing itself, we see that it consists in the production of something other than the act itself. The act of nutrition changes food into plant, and the term of achievement of that action is other than the action. The act of nutrition ceases when its task is done, but the achievement remains; the plant, on the cessation of that act, does not lapse into a state of malnutrition.

Here is the difference between other living activities and that of knowledge (and of appetition). The act of knowledge is more immanent than those of nutrition, growth and generation; they are essentially towards a terminus distinct from themselves, but knowledge is itself an ultimate. This is true even when an expressed species is produced, because the species is *that wherein* the thing is known, and is for the sake of the knowledge.[7] Those other living activities are unto the perfection of the agent, but knowledge is itself such a perfection. They are merely actions, but knowledge is formally a quality, that is, a perfection of the knowing subject.

The cognitive union is so perfect that the knower becomes the known.[8] This is not intended metaphorically, but as a statement of fact. When two things, A and B, are united, how many possibilities are there? Well, firstly, A may become B; secondly, B may become A; thirdly, something new may arise. As we have seen, a third does not arise in knowledge. Nor, obviously, does the known thing become the knower: a landscape does not become the person who sees it. The only possibility left is that the knower becomes the object he knows.

In clarification of this apparent paradox, it must be stressed that we are speaking of a knower precisely as a knower; not, for example, as a man. We are not suggesting a man turns into a landscape when he sees one! But what happens to his visual power when he sees a landscape? Suppose he first closes his eyes. He is not seeing anything; he is in potency to vision, or more precisely, his power of sight is in potency to vision; that is, the power is able to be actualised, but is not yet actualised. Now he opens his eyes. What is his visual power now? It is no longer an unrealized potency for vision; it has been actualised by the landscape and, in act, *it is the landscape*. The capacity or potency to see has become actual seeing, the potency has been actualised as – a landscape. To the question, "What is your (actual) vision?", he can reply, "The landscape."

The same applies to any knowledge. If from not thinking, when asleep, he passes to thinking, his intellect passes from potency-to-thought into the object being thought about. Aristotle implies this in saying that in knowledge "The soul is in a certain manner all existing things."[9]

Raymond Dennehy points out that "…if knowledge is objective, this must mean that the intellect *becomes*, on the *intentional* level, the thing known. The alternative – that the intellect does not know the thing directly but instead knows the concept of the thing – is absolutely incompatible with epistemological realism insofar as it imposes a third thing between the knowing subject and the known."[10]

St Thomas notes that the perfection of each created thing is incomplete and that knowing beings have a remedy for the incompleteness because "There is found another mode of perfection in created things, according as the perfection which is proper to one thing is found in another thing; and this is the perfection of a knower inasmuch as it is a knower."[11]

This helps to explain man's deep urge to know, especially to know the noblest things. The person in whom this desire is mature does not seek knowledge merely for utilitarian motives, but for the very perfection, the fullness of being, that knowledge is. By nature he is one man, and is limited by space and time. Through knowledge he transcends the compass of his human nature and becomes many things. And he bursts the limits of space and time by knowing things that exist outside the small area in which his body subsists, and in times other than the present.

When it is said that the knower becomes the object known, this does not mean that he appropriates the natural existence of the object. A distinction has to be made between the form had by a knower and the existence exercised by that form.[12] The form is that of the known, but two existences need to be distinguished: the existence the form has in reality and the cognitive existence it has in the knower. The landscape has its own real existence independently of the person seeing it. But in his visual power the same landscape exists cognitively. So *what it is* is something of reality. *How it is* is from the knower. Because it is had immaterially, it remains what it is outside the knower, but within him it acquires a new existence, an immaterial existence.

The conclusion that two existences must be had is clear from the fact that many knowers can be having knowledge of the same thing: the one landscape, with its one real existence, is in many visual powers, with a distinct cognitive existence in each.

3. Intentional species

According to Descartes and many more recent philosophers, we directly know ideas, not things themselves. It is as though we knew the photograph of a certain man, but had never met the man. Our direct knowledge would be of the photograph, while the man would be inferred. Likewise, according to this position, we directly apprehend ideas (in the wide sense of cognitive representations, whether sensitive or intellectual), and then infer extra-mental beings which resemble these ideas.

Thomists utterly reject this notion of knowledge, insisting that it permanently cuts us off from reality. From a photograph we infer the reality of the subject pictured; but that is because our knowledge extends to things other than the photograph. If knowledge was essentially and primarily about ideas – if it was enclosed in a world of ideas – we would have no means of knowing whether any real world existed.[13]

Knowledge, according to St Thomas and his followers, bears directly on reality. Otherwise its objectivity would be impossible. Objectivity, however, is an evident fact, and its denial leads to inadmissible consequences.[14] It poses problems though, one of which is this: how can a thing be known when it is at a distance from the power? Another point is: how can a thing be known which, in its real existence, is not in the state in which it is actually known? For example, objects are had in an abstract manner in the intellect, but they do not really exist in that manner; the concept *man* is abstract, while all the real people of whom it is predicated are concrete individuals. This means that the intellect must make a contribution; it must supply the abstract state had by the knowledge.

So we are confronted with these facts: (1) things are known which, in their natural existence, are not within the faculty of knowledge, as a tree fifty metres away which I am seeing; (2) things are known in a state, e.g., universalised, which does not belong to them in their real existence. Yet knowledge is objective: it is not about our subjective states, but about real things.

This brings us to the notion of intentional species.[15] The word *species* as used here means a sign or similitude; it is a sign in the purest possible sense. Any sign manifests something other than itself, but other signs do so secondarily, whereas the intentional species does so primarily.

Take smoke as an instance of a secondary sign. It is first of all a reality in its own right, but functions in a secondary respect as a sign because it manifests fire – on seeing smoke we realize there is a fire. Similarly, a pallid complexion is primarily a reality (a quality), but secondarily a sign of illness. Again, a photograph is firstly a thing, but secondarily a sign of the man it represents: it is his likeness.

Now the sign we are discussing here, the intentional species, is primarily a sign and only secondarily a thing, a quality. What I know is the tree, but the physical tree with its natural existence stands in the garden; it does not dwell physically within my faculty of sight. Since it is not there physically, yet is known, its similitude must be there; and because it is the tree itself which is seen, the similitude must be a sign of a very perfect and special kind. It is certainly not equivalent to a photograph, for a photograph I look at is the thing my vision attains, and the man pictured there is only inferred, not seen. I think, "Here is a photo", not "Here is a man"; whereas in the other case I think, "Here is a tree", and only after reflection on the nature of knowledge do I reach the verdict that a species or sign must be present to make the knowledge possible.

A photograph presents itself and represents something else; an intentional species presents another without intruding itself. Its whole office is to show something other than itself; so it is not *that which* is known, but *that through which* something else is known. And this is achieved through the fact that the content presented in the species is that of the object, and not anything peculiar to the species.

The notion of intentionality – of the knower becoming what he knows without destroying either himself or the object – is one towards which phenomenology and existentialism are tending. Husserl worked out a theory of intentionality, but did not succeed in excluding idealism. He saw that the knowing subject is aware of an object, that his act can be characterized as consciousness of an object,[16] but failed to settle the status of the object and its relation to the knower. Sartre, too, insists that consciousness is always *consciousness of* something.

Species are of two kinds: impressed and expressed. Two reasons were given above for positing intentional species: externality of the object to the faculty of knowledge, and disproportion between the object and the state in which it is actually known.

The first of these (externality) makes necessary what is called an impressed species. A thing cannot be known unless it is present to the knowing faculty; so if it is not present in its own being it must be present vicariously, that is, through a species it causes in the power. When a person reflects on a thought in his intellect, he does not need an impressed species because the thought is already there – it does not need to be substituted for by a vicarious form. The same applies to the knowledge he has of his intellectual habits (such as the habit of mathematics), to the awareness of his own intellect and of his soul which he attains through introspection, and to the consciousness of his will and its habits and activity. That kind of union of the knower with the object is not the knowledge itself, for it is had even when he is not reflecting; but it constitutes the intellect ready for the act of reflection.

Apart from these exceptions, human knowledge is always of something external to the knowing power. When I remember a house I once saw, it is through an impression in my memory that I recall it; the house is not there physically – it may not even exist any longer. Even when I see a house, it is external to me, so a vicarious form must be impressed in my organ of sight before vision of the house can be had.

"That's all right as regards sight," it may be said, "but what about touch? If you touch the house, direct contact has been made, and surely no vicarious species is needed." But even the objects of touch are absent from the knowing power. The bricks whose hardness I feel are against my fingers, but do not enter my sense of touch; they remain outside, against the skin. So an impressed species is needed in this case too.

The second reason for positing intentional species is the disproportion usually found between the object and the state in which it is actually known. The only human knowledges where disproportion is not found are external sensation and sense consciousness.[17] Sensation is about a physical quality which is here and now acting on the sense, and which, through that action, is making itself known. Since it is sensed in and through its action, a strict proportion exists between the sense which is knowing and the object known.

Proportion is lacking in all other human knowledges. When I understand *man*, my act of understanding is identical with the object understood, for the knower becomes what he knows. But the concept *man* has an abstract character which individual men lack. Further, finite things, as they exist, are only understandable, not actually understood. But in my mind they are understood. It follows, then, that I must act to make these things proportionate to my intellect; I must make them become as they are actually understood; I must express them. The same applies to the internal senses of imagination, memory and the estimative sense: their objects are had in a state in which they do not actually exist. They can be known even when they no longer exist, as when we remember something we did in the past. We can imagine things that have never existed, such as a centaur. Moreover, the object of these senses, like those of the intellect, are from themselves only knowable, not actually known.

It must be concluded that the intellect and these three internal senses express their knowledge in an intentional species. Everyone is familiar with these expressions of knowledge, although most do not examine them philosophically. We speak of forming concepts and ideas. These are expressed species; in Thomistic philosophy those of the intellect are called concepts or ideas, while those of the internal senses are called images or phantasms.

They are not *that which* is known, but *that wherein* something else is known; they are formal signs. When I have a concept of *man* or an image of a house, I am knowing those objects (man or house); my knowledge is not confined to the concept or image, but is of that which the concept or image signifies. Generally I am not even explicitly aware of the intentional species – although I can make it the object of my knowledge by deliberately concentrating my attention on it.

To compare impressed and expressed species: when something is known which is external to the faculty of knowledge, as when a tree is seen, an impressed species (or impression of the object) is required. An expressed species (or expression of the object by the knower) is required whenever there is disproportion between the object and the state in which it is actually known – for example, because it is absent or because it is known abstractly but exists concretely. The external senses and the central sense have only impressed species, but every other human knowledge requires expressed species. An impressed species is needed in every human knowledge except intellectual reflection on objects naturally present to the intellect – namely, the intellect itself, its habits and thoughts, the will and its habits and acts, and the soul as manifested through thinking and willing.

We have been considering intentional species mainly in their cognitive aspect, that is, as signs of what they present. But they are also qualities: they are accidents inhering in the power that possesses them. From this point of view they are received appropriatively, being modifications of the subject having them.

The organ of sight, for example, is physically affected by light waves and that of hearing by sound waves. In the imagination, memory and estimative sense, physical modifications remain by means of which images can be recaptured; we could never remember anything unless traces remained within us of the knowledge we once exercised. But this kind of possession is utterly insufficient for knowledge: it has the subjective-physical-compositive character of the material possession of forms. A cognitive power is a vital principle of operation, not a passive receiver like a wax surface; and it reacts in its own immanent fashion to the impressions of things, uniting itself to the species to give rise to the objective-supraphysical-incompositive reception demanded by knowledge.

An objection. "You Thomists," a critic may object, "adopt a decidedly Procrustean procedure. You wish to uphold the view that knowledge is objective. Various weighty difficulties are urged against your view; and you reply by inventing a theory to counteract each difficulty. To meet the assertion that immanence excludes objectivity, you invent a new manner of possession – objective, supra-physical, incompositive – which allows you to eat your cake and have it: to accept both immanence and objectivity. Then another problem appears: it seems we directly know our own ideas, not real things. You meet this with a theory of intentional species. But another hitch occurs: science and common experience both show that knowers are physically changed when knowledge takes place. So you hold that these intentional species inhere in the manner of ordinary physical qualities as well as having an intentional mode of being."

In answer to this objection, I would point out firstly that the charge of Procrustean is as unjustified in this case as it would be in that of a scientist who put forward an explanation that fitted all the facts. The objectivity of knowledge is evident, not assumed; so is the statement that we directly know reality, not ideas. The existence of expressed species – images and concepts – is known to everyone by introspection. The intentional manner of informing is demanded by the fact of knowledge, while entitative or physical inherence is necessary because every quality needs a subject of inherence – it cannot just float around by itself.

Every study has its appropriate method; and it is a fatal error to attempt an analysis of knowledge by the methods of empirical science. A philosophical approach is essential.

[1] Cf. St Thomas Aquinas, *Summa Theologiae*, I, q. 85, a. 2.

[2] *Summa Theol.*, I, q. 80, a. 1.

[3] Cf. St Thomas, *Contra Gentes*, III, chapter 51.

[4] *Summa Theol.*, I, q. 84, a. 2.

[5] Ibid., I, q. 87, a. 1.

[6] Cf. St Thomas, *In Librum de Causis*, lecture 18.

[7] See the following section.

[8] Cajetan, *In I Summa Theol.*, q. 4, a. 1; John of St Thomas, *Curs. Phil.*, Vol III, ed. Reiser, p. 104a.

[9] *De Anima*, III, 8, 431b, 20.

[10] Dennehy, article "Maritain's Philosophia Perennis", in *The Future of Thomism* (1992), edited by Hudson and Moran, p. 73, original italics.

[11] *QQ. Disp. De Veritate.*, q. 2, a. 2.

[12] St Thomas, *In II De Anima*, lecture 24, ed. Pirotta, n. 553; Ferrariensis, *In I Con. Gent.*, chapter 44.

[13] This point is further developed in chapter nine, section two, under the subheading: The doctrine that we know directly only our own ideas.

[14] Cf. section one of the present chapter and also sections one and two of chapter nine.

[15] Cajetan, *In I Summa Theol.*, q. 55, a. 3; John of St Thomas, *Curs. Phil.*, Phil. Nat., q. 6, a. 3.

[16] Cf. *Ideen* I, section 84.

[17] The meaning of sense consciousness (or the central sense) will be explained in chapter seven.

Chapter Seven

SENSE KNOWLEDGE

1. The senses in general

A sense is a faculty of knowing which attains the singular, concrete qualities of bodily things. This is shown by experience. A sense never reaches the universal and abstract; only *this* individual is ever sensed, and not in its very essence, but only in the qualities it manifests in a corporeal power or faculty.

Denial of the corporeal character of sensation is inconsistent with the experienced nature of sensitive activities. It is also opposed to experimental evidence, which shows the constant correspondence between neural impressions and sensitive operations, whether of the external or internal senses. A dualist theory, such as that of Descartes, taking human nature as a conjunction of a body subject to local motion and a soul possessing life, finds it impossible to give any reasonable account of sensitive activities, or even of why a body is needed at all.

The senses are divided into external and internal. The external senses are the five to which the term sense is popularly restricted: sight, hearing, touch, taste and smell. Thomistic philosophy distinguishes four internal senses: sense consciousness (also called the common sense or the central sense), imagination, memory, estimative sense.

The distinction between external and internal is not from the location of the organ, as though those would be called external whose organ is in the exterior part of the body, and the others would be called internal senses. That classification would be accidental and not from the nature of the powers. The criterion is this: the external senses attain their objects without the mediation of another sense; the internal attain theirs only by the mediation of another sense. The external senses experience things as they physically affect the senses; this makes them the fundamental source of all our knowledge. The internal senses then know these things in their psychic existence, and further elaborate them.

2. The external senses

The ancient division into sight, hearing, touch, taste and smell is still accepted. But touch must be taken generically, and subdivided into at least two specifically diverse senses: the sense of hard and soft (pressure) and the sense of hot and cold (thermic). On reflection, we can see that these two kinds of sensation are irreducible to each other, and so must proceed from diverse powers. The distinction is also confirmed by experimental psychology.

The external senses are intuitive. Physiological changes always accompany sensation; but they are not the sensation itself, as is clear from the objectivity of knowledge. It is also clear from introspection, for what we are conscious of in reflecting on our sensations is of a different order from physical alterations. As shown in the preceding chapter, the impressed species whereby external things are known is itself of the intentional or immaterial order; it is not equivalent to a photograph or any other material representation.

Sensation is without an expressed species. For this reason it is strictly intuitive – that is, it attains things in their physical presence. This is extremely important for an appreciation of the fundamental character of sensation. Sensation is of a physical quality actually acting on the sense to produce the sensation. It is of the physical thing existing, singular and present.

Certainly the sense is not purely passive, for knowledge, as we have shown, is an *activity* of the knower: if it were a passive state it would be more imperfect than vegetative activity, for that is *exercised* by the plant. But the sense is at once passive and active; receiving the form of the sensible thing, it responds in its own vital fashion and the act of sensation is constituted.

Those who overemphasize the passivity of the sense destroy the objectivity of knowledge, making it a material reception of form. Those who overemphasize the activity of the sense equally destroy objectivity, for they leave unexplainable the attainment of the real, existing things of the world.

Consciousness reveals that sensation is strictly intuitive. Contrast sensation with other knowledge. When we imagine or remember or conceive something, we do not conclude from this apprehension that the thing actually exists. These powers are terminated at an expressed species and do not require the actual presence of their objects. It is different with sensation. We are not aware of any expressed species in the external senses. But we are aware of the object as physically existing and present. If we see something, and are sure we see it, we are certain it exists.

Certitude of the existence of corporeal things would be lacking if they were not immediately experienced, because knowledge merely of what something is does not show *that it is*. Experimental knowledge alone attains both the character and the existence of the known. And it necessarily attains both, so that sensation without its object present is impossible.

We saw in chapter three that many philosophers have expressed doubts about the world's existence, and have thought it needs to be proved. The trouble is, there is nothing more solid on which to base our proof: if the evidence of the senses is not sufficient, nothing is. But the perplexity of these philosophers is due to the fatal mistake of taking ideas as the primary object known, and failing to see that intentional species are pure signs which show something other than themselves (as was explained in chapter six). Granted that the species are pure signs, there is no difficulty in seeing that sensation gives us direct contact with existing reality.

As Raymond Dennehy says: "...contrary to the Kantian methodology, realism does not start philosophising with an examination of the intellect and its mechanism and then proceed to discover what and how this mechanism can know. Rather it starts out with knowledge of things and then proceeds to ask how this knowledge takes place." [1]

Proper and common objects. The proper object of a sense is that which is attained by this sense alone, and through which it attains other things. Colour, for example, is the proper object of sight. If colour were not known through sight, it would not be distinctly known at all. A person born blind has no distinctive knowledge of colour; the most he could attain would be a vague, analogous knowledge drawn from other qualities attained directly. But it would be extremely vague, for nothing else is much like colour. The same goes for the other proper sensibles: each is unique, irreducible to anything else.

The proper object of hearing is sound; of smell is odour; of taste is savour; of pressure-touch is resistance; of thermic-touch is temperature.

Not only is the proper sensible unique to the corresponding sense, but it is that through which the sense attains everything else that it reaches.

So when a sense knows movement, this is through the proper sensible. Sight detects movement of a thing through its colour: were it completely transparent it would be invisible, and its movement would consequently be unknown to sight. Touch attains the same movement, but not in the same way: here the resistance of the thing in motion conveys the movement to the sense.

The common sensibles are those objects known by several senses; known through the proper sensible in each case. They are five: movement, rest, number, shape and size.[2]

Most non-Scholastic philosophers call the proper sensibles *secondary qualities*, and the common sensibles *primary qualities*. However, this terminology suggests proper sensibles are not real, which makes it objectionable for those who accept their reality. For the modern terminology and the denial of the reality of proper sensibles, see Locke's teaching in chapter three above. A defence of the reality of proper sensibles is given in chapter nine, section three.

3. The internal senses

As was explained above, the internal senses are those powers of sensitive knowledge which attain their objects by way of the external senses; that is, in their psychic existence. The number of internal senses has been much disputed. St Thomas assigns four: common sense, imagination, memory, estimative sense.[3] These are arrived at by applying the principle, fundamental in St Thomas' philosophy, that powers are specified by their formal objects.[4] When objects are so diverse that the attainment of two of them by the same power would imply contradiction in that power, distinct powers must exist. So the number of powers will depend on the diversity of formal objects. Further, sufficient powers must be posited to account for all the facts, but no more than are necessary to do so.

The central sense. We are conscious of our own psychic acts: we are aware of ourselves seeing, imagining, desiring, etc. And we are aware of these acts as forming a unity. Now this would be impossible unless a special power existed to this end. Firstly, no sense can reflect on itself, because it is organic and cannot, as it were, stand back and watch what is happening within it. So a further power is needed in addition to the particular senses, a power whose object is the other sensitive acts.

Secondly, the unity of sensitive life would be impossible without a special unifying faculty. If sight, hearing and the other powers acted in isolation, sensitive life would be so many separate series of impressions, without order or use. In fact, sensitive life presents itself as a unity of external sensations, internal perceptions and appetitions. A person is aware of these as a unified whole. This work of unification is not performed by the intellect, for it has the concrete, singular character of sense knowledge; and it is present in irrational animals, as is clear from observation of them.

The faculty that performs this reflecting and unifying office is known as the central sense or sense consciousness or common sense. It is better to avoid the term common sense because it has a further, quite different meaning, as we have seen in chapter five.

St Thomas calls this faculty "the fontal root of all the senses."[5] In it the sensations of the external senses terminate; it feeds the other internal senses; it synthesizes all sensitive life. The alertness of our waking hours depends on it, and its inhibition causes sleep.

Like the external senses, it is an experimental or intuitive power. When dealing with the intuitive character of the external senses, we saw that they bring us their objects as acting on the senses. But we apprehend these physically present things as a unity: the colour, hardness, taste and odour of an apple are known, in a synthesis, as physically present – and it is the central sense which knows in this synthetic way; each of the external senses knows only its own object.

Bertrand Russell often pondered questions concerned with sensation and perception, but without reaching conclusions that satisfied him. He points out, for example, that in listening to music, one may deliberately notice only the part of the cello, and hear the rest, as it is said, "unconsciously".[6] How is this occurrence to be explained? How much of the music is one really knowing – only what one "notices"? Or the rest as well? What does knowing mean? Had Russell understood, and accepted, the distinction between external sensation and the central sense, he would have been in a better position to solve his difficulties.

Imagination. The central sense knows its objects as present. But we are able to know things in abstraction from their physical presence and absence. This happens when we imagine. The imagination is that power which receives the perceptions of the central sense and preserves them.

St Thomas says: " Imagination is, as it were, a certain treasury of the forms got through sense."[7] It reproduces them in their absence and associates them with one another. Regarding the reproductive and, especially, the associative functions, it must be remembered that imagination does not operate alone, but is influenced by other senses and by intellect and will.

The process is this. Sense consciousness (the central sense) apprehends the knowledge of the external senses, and from sense consciousness it passes to the imagination, which conserves it. But how can knowledge be conserved? When dealing with impressed species, we noted they have two aspects: they are primarily signs of things and secondarily modifications inhering in a power. In the imagination the impressed species of something remains as a quality in the organism. It is not there as actual knowledge – while it is being conserved it is not being known – but it can result in actual knowledge: it can be revived. So it is there all the time, but as a physical quality.

Because it is conserved in an organ, the perfection of its conservation depends on psychological and physiological factors, such as intensity of perception, emotion produced by perception, innate or acquired dispositions of the organism. As John of St Thomas says, a sensitive power "which retains and conserves species, does so by reason of the organ and according to the disposition thereof."[8]

When something conserved is known again, this is in an expressed species formed by the imagination, because the thing known becomes present to knowledge as actually known, whereas according to itself it is only actually knowable: so the "actual knownness" is through the vital activity of the imagination.

As indicated above, images are combined by association. This is due simply to the imagination if two images were originally received together; but for the elaborate imaginative constructions so necessary for practical purposes and in the sciences and arts, imagination needs other sensitive powers and the intellect. When a fiction writer constructs a plot, imagination is working creatively, but together with other powers and as an instrument of the intellect.

Memory. The memory is that sensitive power which knows things as past, or as previously known. It is awareness of the character of past that specifies memory, showing it to be distinct from imagination. I do not say I remember just because I have an image of something: this may simply pertain to imagination. When I have an image I may be sure I am not remembering, particularly if it is the result of creative imagination, as is the construction of a story. Or I may be uncertain whether I really remember or only imagine. Or I may be sure I remember, in which case there is something distinctive about this knowledge: an awareness of the past, of the previously known. It is one thing to imagine a house without associating it with anything in our past; it is another experience to remember a house we once lived in, to be aware of it as of the previously known.

This perception pertains to sense. It is found in irrational animals as well as in man: a dog obviously remembers its owner. St Thomas relates memory to awareness of magnitude and movement. "Time is known inasmuch as before and after in movement is known. Wherefore they too can be perceived by sense...To memory pertains apprehension of time according to a certain determination, namely, according to the distance in the past from this now in the present. Wherefore *per se* memory pertains to the apparatus of images, but *per accidens* to the judgment of the intellect."[9]

Estimative power. The necessity of a further sense is seen from the fact of instinct. The instinctive actions of animals have a number of characteristics: they are executed in the same way by all the individuals of the species; they need no individual experience; they are well done from the beginning; they are useful to the animal's nature – sometimes the individual, sometimes the species. An example is the nest-building of birds: although secondary variations occur, as in the kind of material used, the type of nest depends on the species of bird. Another instance is the rigidly organized behaviour of ants.

Instinctive behaviour cannot be explained without knowledge. Mere mechanical or reflex movements do not account for the harmony and proportion of instinctive actions, nor for the close correlation between these actions and other sensitive knowledge; as when an animal, stalking its prey, takes notice of wind direction, places of concealment, etc.

But what knowledge is specific to the estimative or instinctive sense?

It is not reducible to the senses already considered, as the various characteristics of instinctive behaviour prove: from its external or other internal senses an animal could not learn what befits or does not befit its nature, nor could it thus achieve the expertness shown in the intricacies of instinctive actions. Even man, with the aid of intellect, could not attain the perfection many animals show in their activities. Yet the actions are not from a power higher than human intellect; if they were, the power would show itself in other directions, for understanding produces versatility and adaptability, whereas instinct is rigid.

I saw a fanciful magazine article on ants, in which it was conjectured that they might some day replace man as the highest species! The prediction was based on the marvellous order and system of their lives. However, the logical conclusion from such orderly existence is the opposite to that reached by the article. It is the ants' lack of intelligence which accounts for the stability of the anthill; an approach to human intelligence would show itself in diversity and adaptability.

The power operating in instinctive actions is a kind of knowledge, but it is not any of the senses so far considered. What remains? That it is a sense other than those already dealt with. What is its object? Apprehension of what befits or is unbefitting to the animal's nature. An animal is so constituted that certain things are suitable to it, while others are harmful. It has a sensible power which apprehends the suitable and the unsuitable, as a lamb has an instinctive awareness that it should flee from a wolf – without comprehending why, of course. The power is called the estimative sense.

Man, too, has this, but does not require the complicated apparatus of instincts possessed by the lower animals, because he can guide himself by intelligence and will. In him the estimative sense is often called the cogitative power, because it operates in conjunction with intellect. It is very important in making practical judgments about concrete matters; in these judgments the cogitative power is used as an instrument by the intellect in synthesizing particular sensed facts with abstract, universal knowledge.

The estimative power presupposes a complex physiological structure, especially in the animals most guided by instinct. It belongs to empirical science to study the marvellous behaviour patterns of animals and unveil, as far as possible, the mystery of their operation.

Comparison. It was stated at the beginning of this section that the number of internal senses depends on the diversity of formal objects to be attained, and that sufficient, but only sufficient, to account for the facts must be posited. St Thomas says: "Since nature does not default in necessary things, there must be as many actions of the sensitive soul as suffice for the life of a perfect animal. And whichever of these actions cannot be reduced to one principle require diverse powers; for a power of soul is nothing else than a proximate principle of the soul's operation."[10]

The first thing needed after the external senses operate is a power of synthesizing the different impressions, so that a unity of consciousness is had. And this pertains to objects sensed as present. For this the central sense is required. A second necessity is the conservation and reproduction of the forms received; and imagination performs this work. A third necessity is the recall of the past *as past*; memory does this. A fourth requirement is the apprehension of the befitting and unbefitting; to which the estimative sense is ordered.

Although no knowledge can be explained on a physiological basis alone, all sense faculties are organic. But this means that each has a determinate structure, by which it achieves its object. So for diversity of objects, diverse organs, and therefore diverse powers, will be needed. The eye, for example, is structured for vision, not for hearing; and the organization required for hearing is so different that the two exclude each other. It would be impossible for one organ to perform both functions.

4. Emotional life

In philosophical psychology a long treatise on sensitivity follows the treatment of sense knowledge. That is beyond the scope of this work, but a few remarks will be made.

Beings with sense knowledge, whether man or irrational animals, have a sensitive inclination towards, or aversion from, things apprehended: they respond emotionally to what they know. The response is no more a bodily change than is knowledge but, like knowledge, it involves bodily change.

Appetition is contrasted with knowledge. Knowledge is a supra-physical possession of the known, in which the knower becomes what he knows. But appetition is an inclination towards real union with the thing known (or away from real union with something seen as menacing or in some way distasteful). Knowledge brings the thing into the knower; appetition urges the appetent out to the thing. It is not enough to know something desirable; we want real union with it. And because it is real, the union established by love is more perfect even than that of knowledge. In the words of St Thomas: "Knowledge is perfected by the thing known being united with the knower through its similitude. But love causes that the thing itself which is loved is in a certain manner united with the lover, as was said above. So the union of love is greater than that of knowledge."[11]

Affectivity is always dependent on knowledge. If no knowledge existed, neither would appetition. Appetition arises from knowledge, for if all knowledge were lacking of the goodness or badness of some object, no basis would exist on which to appetise it. This is not to say that motivations are always clear; they are sometimes very obscure.

But as Roland Dalbiez writes: "Psychoanalysis enables us to eliminate in a radical manner the pretended emotions lacking a cognitive motive. There is no emotion, normal or morbid, which is not motivated."[12] He goes on to say that the memory on which it is based may lie buried in the unconscious, but psychoanalysis will bring it to light and show it to be quite appropriate to the emotional state.

1   Article "Maritain's Philosophia Perennis", in *The Future of Thomism* (1992), edited by Hudson and Moran, p. 72.
2   Cf. St Thomas, *In II de Anima*, lecture 13.
3   *Summa Theol.*, I, q. 78, a. 4.
4   Ibid., q. 77, a. 3.
5   *In III de Anima*, lecture 3.
6   *My Philosophical Development* (1959), p. 142.
7   *Summa Theol.*, I, q. 78, a. 4.
8   *Curs. Phil.*, Nat Phil., q. 8, a. 1.
9   *In de Memoria et Reminiscentia*, lecture 2.
10 *Summa Theol.*, I, q. 78, a. 4.
11 *Summa Theol.*, I-II, q. 28, a. 1, *ad* 3.
12 *Vues sur la psychologie animale*, p. 107.

Chapter Eight

INTELLECTUAL KNOWLEDGE

Is there a difference in kind between intellective and sensitive knowledge, or is it just a matter of degree? The question is vital. On our answer depends our verdict on the nature of man, on morality, on the existence of God, on the meaning of science and philosophy.

Richard Rorty, denying a difference of kind between these ways of knowing, suggests "...that we think of pragmatism as an attempt to alter our self-image so as to make it consistent with the Darwinian claim that we differ from other animals simply in the complexity of our behaviour."[1]

We can begin by comparing images and concepts.

1. Images and concepts

An image is a sensible representation of a thing, as formed by the higher internal senses – imagination, memory and the estimative sense. This term, image, applies to the reproduction of any sense object: we imagine sounds and odours, etc., as well as things seen. A concept (or idea) expresses an understanding, and a comparison of the two reveals that they belong to diverse orders and that the concept proceeds from a far higher power than does the image. What are some characteristics of images and concepts, respectively?

1. An image is of the appearance of something: it is of a thing as manifested by colour, shape, odour, etc. But the concept of the same thing is of *what* the thing is, and is not in terms of sensible representations. If someone imagines an animal, all the marks contained in the image are external qualities apprehended by sense. The concept of animal is different: its content is the understood nature of animal. The same distinction is found between images and concepts of qualities, such as colour.

Can we form an image of colour? All we have is the image of a particular colour or colours: of red, blue, green, or some other colour, or of, say, a mosaic of many colours. But these are not images of *colour*, they are images of particular colours, whether one or many.

The concept brought to mind by the word colour is abstract and unimaginable, because it fits every colour – otherwise it wouldn't be the concept of colour. Now, because it fits every colour, its content cannot be limited to the manifestation of a certain colour or group. In other words, if the concept contained the picture of green, it would not fit red. Even if it pictured a mosaic, it would not signify *colour*, for that universal names the nature or essence, and not a group of particulars possessing that essence.

An attempt is sometimes made to equate images and concepts by claiming that we oscillate from one image to another, and that this gives rise to the illusion of a concept distinct from all images. For example, in thinking about *dog*, we may first have a picture of a fox-terrier, then of a bulldog, then of a spaniel. Instead of having a fixed image, a movement (generally unperceived) takes place from one representative of *dog* to another; and in this way we are aware of the numerous possibilities denoted by the word dog.

In reply, it can readily be agreed that fluctuating images of this kind are sometimes had, although most people would probably deny that this is what takes place when they think about *dog*. But the images only accompany the concept; they are not identical with it. This can be seen by comparing the various peculiarities of images with those of concepts. Besides, this theory implies that we never understand what is meant by *dog*, because the picture we have at any one moment is of a particular dog. Even the sum total of the pictures that occur to us on the subject represents only a tiny proportion of all the canine breeds, yet our understanding transcends all these representatives and is just as applicable to dogs we do not happen to imagine, and even to those we have never heard of.

2. The image is not only of the appearances of something, but of it as a singular. When we imagine a colour, we necessarily imagine it as *this* singular patch of colour; or if more than one colour is represented, as a group of singulars. Similarly, any image of an animal is necessarily of the singular. The concept is just the opposite; it is of the universal, as the same illustrations show. And that is why the concept fits all the individuals, as *colour* fits all colours. If it were limited to individuals, it would thereby be marked off from other individuals.

It might be objected that common images can be formed. When I hear the word man, an image may arise of a shadowy figure devoid of clear-cut characteristics, an image applicable to millions of men.

But in what way can this be called a common image? Certainly not in the sense that a concept is called universal. This image is as much an individual representation as a more vivid and detailed one would be, but the individual aspects of it – shape, colour, clothing, etc. – remain blurred, just as a photograph is individual whether clear or blurred. The common character, or the applicability to many men, is due to imperfection in the image. The more perfect an image, the more restricted is its applicability. So if I picture a man in a very vague fashion, the picture will be applicable to most men; but the more perfect my image, the more restricted will be its scope. If it is of a white man with dark hair, grey eyes, small ears and a square chin, its perfection will be much greater than in the previous case, but its applicability will be only to a small percentage of the human race. Any identification of concepts with common images would imply that intellectual knowledge is not merely a kind of sense knowledge, but that it is sense knowledge at a less perfect stage.

Another objection to the universal state of concepts is developed as follows. A computer can separate some particulars from others with a speed no human could match. Yet abstract intelligence is not attributed to the computer. Why, then, is it thought impossible that the human brain should be capable of making a selection of the particulars we wish to consider, to the exclusion of irrelevant ones? When thinking about animals, why should not the brain be able to select, say, bipeds for consideration, to the exclusion of snakes, horses, centipedes, etc.? Or white animals to the exclusion of other colours?

A first answer to this is that a universal is not a particular isolated from other particulars. Secondly, when we consider *biped* our thought is not limited to a singular instance, e.g., this man or this bird, of which we form an image. But the total inadequacy of the suggested explanation appears more forcefully if we try to see what image would be identical with the concept *animal*. What imaginable features have all animals got in common, so that by discarding everything irrelevant we would be left with those common features?

A determinate shape, say that of a monkey, must be excluded, because there are animals lacking that shape. Legs must be excluded, because some, including snakes, have no legs but are still animals. Feathers must be excluded, because most animals lack them. Even if we found something we could picture and which all animals possess, that organ or part is not what comes to mind when we think about *animal*.

3. An image may be reproduced externally, but a concept cannot. If

I picture a triangle I can draw it on a whiteboard. But the concept of triangle cannot be drawn. The reason for the difference is that images are individual, whereas concepts are universal. Any existing thing must be an individual: the abstract is not fitted for existence because it lacks the concrete determinations always found in existing things. An image of a triangle contains concrete determinations, and can be reproduced on a whiteboard. What does the concept of triangle contain? It expresses the very essence of this figure, but nothing else; it is equally applicable to a scalene, an isosceles or an equilateral triangle; it contains no material determinations, e.g., blue lines in ink, which an external reproduction must have.

Of any image we can say definitely that it is not the concept of triangle, because it necessarily represents sensible qualities, whereas the concept is necessarily of the very essence, and only the essence, of triangle, since it must befit every individual triangle.

4. A concept may be of something lacking sensible qualities, as when we think of truth, spirit or God. But it is impossible to form an image of anything that lacks sensible qualities, because images are about those qualities. Therefore concepts are not images.

5. Variation of images can occur without variation of concepts, which would be impossible if they were identical. This can be verified by thinking about some abstract subject, and varying the images. Understanding is always accompanied by imagery of some kind, but the precise kind of image does not matter. Some people tend more to word imagery when thinking of abstract things: when contemplating justice they will evoke a picture – or even an auditory image – of the word *justice*. Others generally have "thing" images: they will picture a courthouse, or scales. Any number of variations can be made without the concepts changing.

6. If concepts were images, communication by speech would be impossible. By words we could not signify our images with the exactness necessary to reproduce them in other people. To take some examples from the above, think what diverse images can be suggested by the words qualities, spirit, understand, identical, accompanied. There is agreement about which concepts are signified by these words, but not about which images shall be evoked by them. When I use the word identical, I may have an image of the written word, while you may imagine two sticks of equal length, and someone else may imagine identical twins. We agree,

however, about the conceptual meaning attached to the word, so the diversity of imagery does not matter.

But we can teach some birds to speak, it may be objected. And we can teach our dog his name, so that he comes when we call him. Are we to say, then, that "irrational" animals form concepts?

Reply. The abilities of birds, dogs, etc., in this matter can be fully explained without attributing the formation of concepts to them. So-called speech in a bird is developed through imitation of the words it hears, but does not presuppose concepts. And a dog becomes conditioned to the sound of his name; it is a case of association of images. The behaviour of brute animals is always explainable through sense knowledge. If they formed concepts the fact would be strikingly clear from their actions, as it is in even a very young child.

7. If concepts were images, judgment and reasoning would be impossible, because these involve the recognition of logical relations. But logical relations are not images. The connection between subject and predicate, or between the terms of an argumentation, is something that can be understood, but cannot be sensed.

2. The spirituality of the intellect

Argument from the immateriality of its object. We dealt, in chapter six, with the degree of immateriality required for knowledge in common. It appears from the comparison of images and concepts that some further immateriality must exist to account for understanding. The immateriality previously considered was sufficient to allow the having of forms in a way superior to the material way of having them. A materially had form is appropriated and becomes the recipient's form; but one had in knowledge remains that of the thing known.

However, there is a sharp difference between forms had by the senses and those understood by the intellect. Those had sensibly are of the external appearances of the thing known, retaining the various characteristics of matter: an apple known by the central sense is apprehended as *this* singular with *this* determinate colour, firmness, taste, odour. Only the qualities are apprehended, the qualities that inform the senses, the qualities conveyed by the action of the apple on the external senses. St Thomas writes: "Sense does not apprehend essences of things, but exterior accidents only."[2]

Intellect receives things in a higher manner; it receives the very natures or essences of things, not external accidents. "Thus differs the apprehension of sense and of intellect: sense apprehends *this coloured* (thing), but intellect apprehends the very nature of colour."[3]

This brings us to a higher degree of immateriality than sense knowledge requires. Forms had by the senses are held in a non-appropriative manner, but they retain their individual characteristics. In the intellect, on the other hand, forms are not only possessed in a non-appropriative manner, but the very forms are immaterial. That is, they are of essences (not of sensible appearances) and are universal (not singular). They cannot be contained in any image and cannot be externally reproduced. They are not sensible, but understandable.

The power that has forms in this high manner is beyond the senses and beyond the bodily order. We have seen that in knowledge the knower becomes the form of the known, so that "the knower in act is the very known in act."[4] But "the received is in the recipient according to the manner of the recipient."[5] By this principle St Thomas means that, for example, a quality received in an inanimate body, as heat in water, will exist there in the corporeal mode of the water; while a thing received in a sensible knower will exist in it in the supra-physical way proper to knowledge; and a thing received in an intellective knower will exist according to that knower's degree of being.

A concept, which is that wherein something is understood, is above the corporeal order: above every image, every external reproduction; it is something purely immaterial. But the intellect, in the act of understanding, becomes the known, becomes what it understands. Therefore the intellect itself is something above the corporeal order.

This means that understanding is not an act done by a bodily organ, such as the brain, but by a strictly spiritual faculty. By spiritual is meant something non-bodily, something having a higher being than a body, something not intrinsically dependent on a body in its being or its activity. A spiritual reality has no matter in its constitution. As we shall see, even the spiritual acts of man – acts of intellection and willing – are extrinsically dependent on matter, for man is a compound of matter and spirit. But what we need to investigate here is the conclusion that the intellect itself is not a part of the body.

The above argument can be formulated as follows:

1. That which, in its knowing, becomes something incorporeal, is of an

incorporeal or spiritual nature.

2. But the human intellect, in knowing, becomes something incorporeal.

3. Therefore the human intellect is of an incorporeal or spiritual nature.

We have already given the evidence for the premises of this syllogism, but it may help to repeat it in another way. Take the major premise (1). A thing acts according to what it is, not above what it is; otherwise there would be an effect (the activity) with no proportionate cause. Or to put it differently, insofar as the activity exceeded the operant, it would be activity without a cause. So a thing must act according to what it is, or proportionately to what it is. Therefore a knower which is incorporeal in its knowing is incorporeal in its being.

Now take the minor premise (2). The evidence for it is obtained by examining intellectual knowledge. Like all knowledge it consists in the knower becoming the known. But unlike sensible knowledge it means becoming an immaterialised form: a form which is abstract and universal, free from the concrete characteristics of the sensible – a form which is incorporeal. Therefore the human intellect becomes something incorporeal in the act of knowledge.

Finally, the conclusion (3). A power or faculty can be considered in two ways. It is an accident or attribute or property of the possessor, and it is a potency for activity. Sight is a faculty or attribute in the animal, a part of its equipment; and this is true whether sight is operating or not. But when it operates – when the animal sees – a potency is actualised: a potency to see becomes actual seeing. Intellect is a permanent piece of equipment, so to speak, of man. This is true whether it is operating or not. When it operates, the potency to understand becomes actual understanding. But the act of understanding, we have shown, is incorporeal. Therefore the faculty is an incorporeal attribute or property of man. Man has within him something transcending, and essentially independent of, the corporeal world – something spiritual.

Argument from reflection. A second proof of the human intellect's spirituality is from its capacity to reflect on its own acts. Abstract knowledge is intellective. But we are conscious that we can reflect on it; we can focus our minds on some abstract concept, or on a judgment. Take the sentence just above: "Abstract knowledge is intellective." That sentence is an intellectual judgment. And I can put it before me as an object of reflection, knowing the judgment and knowing my assent to it. The original judgment, the reflection on it and the judgment that it is true are all acts of the intellect: they are of the abstract, not of the concrete objects of sense perception.

If the intellect was not a spiritual faculty, reflection would be impossible, because it would then be organic, and reflection is impossible in an organic faculty. Why? Consider how an organic power operates. We have seen that it transcends the vegetative order, because it can have the forms of others, *as others*. But the operation does not transcend the corporeal order, because done through an organ. This involves changes within the organ: modification of the retina by light, modification of the brain in imagining, etc. Its operations are done through an empowered organ, and are restricted to the capacity of the organ. So if the organ is defective, the operation will be defective: a diseased retina results in bad eyesight. Similarly, the organic structure determines the kind of operation: we cannot see with our ears or hear with our eyes because diverse structures are required for each of these operations.

Now suppose an organic power reflected on itself, to have an explicit awareness of its own activity, an express knowledge of its own knowledge. It could not do this without its organ, for an organic power acts only through its organ: otherwise it would be supra-organic or incorporeal. But acting organically it could not achieve self-reflection without contradicting its own nature, for to know that it is knowing some object it would have to set itself up as the object of its knowledge. Now this is impossible to an organic power, because no body can act, simply speaking, on itself. One part of a body can act on another part, but the whole cannot act on the whole; if it did, it would be both active and receptive at the same time and in the same respect, which is self-contradictory. We cannot see that we are seeing, or hear that we are hearing. The closest the senses can get to self-reflection is when the central sense knows the activity of the other sensible powers;[6] but this is a reflection of one power on another, not of a power on itself.

Conjunction of intellective and sensitive knowledge. We have established that the human intellect is intrinsically independent of the body – it is not part of the brain or some other bodily part. As we shall see later in more detail, it is a property of the soul alone, and the human soul is spiritual.

But this raises problems. It seems to bring us to Descartes' position of the body and soul as two distinct substances. The unity of man would thus be lost; there would only be "the ghost in the machine". However, no dualism is implied in the Thomistic position. The relation of soul and body will be examined in chapter ten. But some light is thrown on it by the question that must occupy us now: How does the intellect get its knowledge?

St Thomas held that man's intellect is first in potency to thought, and that it derives all its knowledge from the senses.

The parallelism of sensitive and intellectual knowledge is evident.[7] As the body develops, so does intellectual functioning. It is very imperfect in a baby and improves as the child grows older. Secondly, as the body degenerates in old age, intellectual functioning is hindered. Thirdly, when sensitive operations are impeded by brain damage, drugs, illness or sleep, the intellect is unable to function efficiently.

Further, we can understand nothing except in conjunction with an image in the imagination. As noted in contrasting images and concepts, the former can be varied without variation of the latter. But they cannot be dispensed with; to do that would mean to stop thinking. When we wish to explain something, we resort to sensible illustrations, especially – and this is significant – when something abstract is being explained to someone unfamiliar with it.

Also, a person deprived from birth of one of the external senses is unable to form a concept of that proper sensible, except a vague analogical concept derived from the other senses. If he has never seen, he has no univocal concept of colour, for colour is contacted through sight alone. The paltry information he could be given about it would have to be in terms of hearing or other senses.

The above facts show a dependence of understanding on sensing, and a derivation of ideas from sensations. Another evidence of the same is from the soul's need of the body. If ideas were not obtained in some way from sense knowledge, why would a body be needed at all? The soul does not depend on the body for its existence, as will be shown. So it must need it for its operations. If it operated independently, the body would be superfluous; worse, it would be an evil to the soul, for it evidently hinders understanding at times, as just indicated. From the hypothesis that the intellect does not need the senses, it follows that the body is, simply speaking and not merely *per accidens*, a hindrance to understanding and a burden to the soul. And this helps explain the contempt some philosophers and others have felt for the human body.

3. The agent intellect

We now have to determine how the intellect gets its knowledge from the senses. Although empiricists rightly stress that all knowledge comes to us from sensation, they wrongly reduce the intellect to a sense and intellection to sensible knowledge. Ideas are spiritual, not sensitive.

When dealing with knowledge in common, in chapter six, we explained that an impressed species is a similitude of the thing to be known, and is required whenever the thing is external to the knowing power. But this is always so in regard to sensible things known by the intellect: they are outside the intellect. There are these two: an intellect apt to know sensible things once it attains them, and a world of sensible things separate from the intellect.

How is the gap to be closed? How is the intellect to be furnished with impressed species of the objects to be known? It is not enough to reply that the internal senses can produce the species in the intellect. They cannot do this alone because they are organic powers, whereas the intelligible species are supra-organic, that is, spiritual. Their incorporeal character can be inferred from the fact that they are of essences in abstraction from corporeal conditions. It follows that the activity of some intellectual power is necessary to account for the production of the impressed species.

There was a great deal of controversy about this in the Middle Ages, some, including Avicenna, Averroes and Roger Bacon, holding that a power outside man is responsible for this operation. The power was conceived as a substance separate from all bodies and giving the intelligible species of things to all men. St Thomas strongly opposed this. Its effect was to dehumanise man, to leave him passive before a supra-human power. He would be less perfect than plants or brutes in that they operate by their own powers, whereas he would be a passive recipient of intelligible species.

While agreeing that there is a certain passivity or receptivity about understanding, St Thomas adds that there is also action, "inasmuch as the intellect makes potentially intelligible things be actually intelligible. Accordingly it is necessary that in the nature of man there be the proper principle of each, namely, the agent intellect and the possible intellect..."[8]

We have these facts. Man's intellective knowledge is of a higher kind than his sensitive knowledge. But it is derived from that sensitive knowledge. And it requires impressed species, because of the absence of sensible things from the intellect. The impressed species must be produced by man, because he must be active in regard to his own thinking. Yet their production is not simply the work of a sensible power but demands an intellectual power, because of the abstract character of the species.

The name agent intellect, or active intellect, is given to this abstractive power. If we say, "a man thinks with his intellect", we are speaking of the faculty called by St Thomas, following Aristotle, the possible intellect. This is the power that does the thinking, and which we ordinarily refer to when mentioning the intellect. The agent intellect, on the other hand, is a power which prepares for thought; and it does so by illuminating the perceptions found in the imagination (taking imagination widely to include memory and the estimative sense) and abstracting from them the impressed species needed for the act of understanding.

We must not let the word intellect mislead us into assuming that the agent intellect thinks. St Thomas saw it as a distinct power from the understanding intellect, having an active preparatory role in regard to thought, a role necessitated by the fact that the concrete things of sense have to be immaterialised before they are fit to be understood.

How does the production of the impressed species take place? What are the respective offices of intellect and sense in this activity? The internal senses must have some role, since it is from their knowledge that the intelligible species are obtained.

Knowledge is realistic: it is not images or ideas that are first known, but things. An image in the imagination is a pure sign of a thing, according to its sensible qualities. What is known is *the thing itself*, but as it is sensible; and this is what makes it possible for the abstractive intellectual faculty, the agent intellect, to derive intelligible species from images, species of *the same thing* as is known by the imagination. But imagination knows the thing under its sensible aspect, while the agent intellect presents it as intelligible, or under the aspect of being.

St Thomas says of the abstraction that occurs: "The images are an instrumental and secondary agent, but the agent intellect is the principal and primary agent."[9] That the agent intellect is the principal and primary agent appears from the spirituality of intellectual species, whose production is beyond the ability proper to a corporeal faculty. But that the images are a secondary agent appears from the fact that what is known by the intellect depends on what the imagination attains. Understanding of a proper sensible, like colour or sound, requires that it should have been sensibly attained: a person born blind or deaf cannot understand it. And whenever an understandable object is abstracted from images, it owes its determinate character to the images. For example, from images of colours comes an understanding of colour; from images of a horse or horses an understanding arises of the nature of horse.

The relation between the agent intellect and the images can be illustrated by comparing the impressed species to a painting. There are the artist, the picture, the scene represented – say, a mountain. The picture is from the artist and from the mountain. It is from the artist as it is a picture, but from the mountain as it is *such* a picture: that is, representing a mountain and not a plain or a river or some other scene. Had the subject been a river, a different painting would have resulted. The artist corresponds to the agent intellect, the picture to the impressed species and the mountain to the thing present in the imagination.

The species is from the agent intellect as regards its intelligible character, and from images in the imagination as regards the thing presented. It does not derive one part of itself from the agent intellect and another part from images; the whole of it is from each: as actually intelligible, from the agent intellect; as a similitude or representation of a certain thing, from images. The same applies to the painting: it is wholly from the artist, as it is a painting; and wholly from the mountain, as it is a certain similitude.

The illustration is helpful, but must not be pressed too far. For one thing, the painting is copied from the mountain, not obtained by an intellectual abstraction from it. Also, knowledge is on a higher level than any material representation, and the conjunction of agent intellect and imagination is much more intimate than that of the artist and the exemplar. Both powers are rooted in the same person, and this causes a unification that would otherwise be impossible.

In the quotation above, St Thomas calls the images "an instrumental and secondary agent". We must examine the notion of instrument. For St Thomas, an instrument is something elevated above its proper level and applied by a higher agent. The proper action of a chisel is to cut, and it can perform this action without any higher influence being exercised on it. It can cut something simply by falling on it, for example. But is this proportionate and proper activity, the activity of cutting, sufficient for the carving of a statue? Clearly it is not, for that carving is artistic, and requires an artist as its principal cause. Yet it is true to say the statue was carved by a chisel; in fact, it is true that the whole statue was carved by a chisel, that there is nothing of it not due to the chisel. It is equally true that the whole statue was carved by an artist, that the work in its entirety is his effect.

What relation exists between the two causes? The artist is the principal cause, the chisel the instrumental cause. He uses it. It has its own proper power, namely, aptitude to cut. But from itself it lacks power to cut artistically. When used by the artist it is exercising its proper activity (cutting) but under a twofold influence from the artist: he is *elevating* and *applying* it to an artistic work beyond anything it could achieve on its own level.

Something is an instrument when a higher cause (a cause having a higher degree of being) makes use of its proper activity (such as cutting), but by elevating and applying it to a task above its natural ability.

In the formation of intelligible species, the agent intellect exercises an influence on the imagination. The proper work of imagination is to present things under their sensible aspects. And it continues to do this. But it does more, for it ministers to a spiritual power, the agent intellect. It specifies the latter to form intelligible species of those things which imagination knows in a sensible way. The specifying or determining activity is done by the imagination as elevated by the agent intellect. By an illumination of the intellectual order, the images are rendered apt for the abstraction from them of intelligible species. In this illuminating, the agent intellect abstracts the species.

The work of forming impressed species consists in making things which are only potentially understandable become actually understandable; that is, it consists in rendering them fully ready to be understood. Bodies are at first only potentially understandable to us, because our mind grasps them in an abstract and universal condition, whereas they exist as individuals with hundreds of concrete determinations. So they must be brought from that concrete way in which sense knows them to the universal way proper to intellect. The power that does this is the agent intellect, working in conjunction with images of the internal senses. Thus is actual understanding prepared for. What remains is for the possible intellect, informed by these intelligible species of things, to perform the act of understanding.

4. The possible intellect

As we have noted, by possible intellect is meant the power or faculty of understanding: the power which thinks. It is intellect in the strict sense; the agent intellect is called an intellect only presuppositively or as preparing for the act of understanding.

The charge is sometimes made against Thomists that they see the possible intellect as passive in knowing, as though it inertly received impressions from the agent intellect. In fact, it has its own highly active function. We have seen already that all knowledge is vital, immanent activity, transcending anything non-knowers are capable of. But this activity is much more perfect in the intellect than in the senses, because intellection is of the spiritual order, and reaches the very being of the things known.

Both passivity and activity are involved in the possible intellect. It is passive in the reception of impressed species. Before receiving them it is in potency to understanding: it can understand but is not doing so. Aristotle compares it to a writing-tablet on which nothing is yet written.[10] After it receives species, it remains capable of receiving further ones, through the continual action of the agent intellect bringing in the species of a multitude of sensed things. But on the reception of species it forms concepts through which it actively understands.

The concept. Whatever natural understanding we have, a concept is needed. We dealt earlier with the meaning of expressed species. Such a species is a special similitude which presents the known thing, and is needed when the thing is inadequate from itself for terminating knowledge, due to absence or improportion. In the internal senses of imagination, memory and the estimative sense, the expressed species is called an image or phantasm; in the possible intellect it is called a concept or idea.

What is required for an act of understanding is that the intellect should become the thing known, as it is actually known. Now, no finite thing is, according to itself, actually understood. Things are understandable, but an act of intellect is needed to make them understood. God alone is not only understandable, but actually understood – to himself. We shall see the reason for this in chapter fourteen. Sacred theology teaches that those in heaven see God without a concept because they share in his own understanding of himself. "To say that God is seen through a similitude is to say that the essence of God is not seen."[11] Apart from the Beatific Vision, no knowledge of God can be had without a concept, because of the chasm between the reality apprehended and the mode in which it is apprehended.

Even our thinking on our own thoughts requires a concept: they are not their act of understanding, but are acts that are understandable – by a reflection. Very obviously, the understanding of sensible things requires a concept. They are not physically present in the intellect; are singular – whereas they are understood universally; are not even actually understandable, but only potentially so, for their forms first need to be abstracted from matter.

The earliest thoughts. What is it that the human intellect first knows? What knowledge comes to the child to initiate his intellectual life?

Our intellect is first in potency to knowing, and intellectual knowledge has its origin from sense knowledge. But this involves a progress, in the intellect, from a most imperfect knowing to knowing in a more perfect way. The first knowledge of all will be the most imperfect because unelaborated, vague and closely wedded to sense perception. Cajetan says, in a famous sentence: "Being concrete in a sensible quiddity is what is first known, by actual confused knowledge."[12] This first knowledge is an awareness of being, but without any of the distinctions that will later be made. It is an abstraction from singulars – otherwise it would be sense knowledge – but is so weak that no distinction is made between modes of being, such as substance and accidents. It is an intellectual awareness of an indeterminate something.

The proper object of the human intellect. By the proper object of a power, it will be recalled, is meant that which is primarily attained by the power, and through which it attains other things. St Thomas says: "Of the human intellect, which is conjoined to a body, the proper object is the quiddity or nature existing in corporeal matter."[13] This follows from what we have seen. Firstly, the proper object must be of the nature or essence of something, because intellectual knowledge is distinguished from sensible knowledge by the fact that it seizes the natures of things, not sensible phenomena. This can be the nature of an accident, such as colour; or of a substance, such as horse. Secondly, the proper object is the nature of *corporeal* things. This appears from the earlier considerations of the relation of intellect to sense. In section two we saw the parallelism between sensitive and intellectual knowledge. When sensitive operations are imperfect – in a baby, in senility, through brain damage, drugs, illness, sleep – intellectual functioning is impeded. Also, nothing can be understood without some image in the imagination. From these evidences it follows that the proper object of the human intellect is not just any essences indiscriminately, but corporeal essences. They are the only ones within immediate reach of our intellect.

However, they are known as universal, not as singular. Corporeal things are not immediately understandable, but need to be abstracted from the concrete characteristics of matter.

The ultimate reason why the proper object of our intellect is corporeal essences, but as universal, is the truth that man is a union of spirit and matter. It is a substantial union; that is, the two form one nature. The meaning and implications of this will be seen more fully in chapter ten. The intellect is a power of the soul alone; and the soul is spiritual, but is so united with matter that one nature results. Since the intellect is not a part of the body, it understands without intrinsic dependence on the body. Further, it understands spiritually, for it is spiritual, and a thing acts according to its mode of being. But it is a power existing in a being compounded of spirit and matter. So it understands, initially, the corporeal things brought to it by the senses, but as rendered apt to be understood by abstraction from individualizing conditions.

Universals and singulars. Controversy about the meaning of universals goes back almost to the dawn of philosophy. And it continues today. The principles of the Aristotelian and Thomistic solutions have already been given, but we can now gather them together.

Words like man, equality, beauty, heat have a general signification, but what precisely is it they signify? Are they just words? According to nominalism they are. According to conceptualism they are ideas in the mind, and not mere words, but nothing in reality corresponds to them.

In opposition to these positions stands realism. But among realists – that is, those who hold that universals pertain to reality, and not merely to words or ideas – there is sharp disagreement about the nature of their reality. Plato taught extreme or ultra realism, saying that realities exist which, according to themselves, are universal. Equality, beauty, justice all name perfections never found in this world. Yet they are not empty words or mind-produced concepts, but the most real things of all, by comparison with which the corporeal world is a place of shadows. The things of this world are participations of these supreme realities, and our minds retain memories of the spiritual world of pure forms. To know is to remember.

According to moderate realism, held by Aristotle and St Thomas, it is true that universals are of realities. But it is necessary to distinguish between what is signified and the mode in which it exists. The only things capable of real existence are individuals. To this extent nominalism is right. But individuals can have a common nature: there can be many individuals of the same sort. All horses are of one nature.

The agent intellect abstracts from the individuals, and the possible intellect forms a concept of the nature common to many individuals. So the thing is universal in the understanding; the nature or essence or "whatness" is considered on its own, and is applicable to many individuals. But it cannot exist in reality in isolation. Every existing horse is an individual, distinct from all others, but is the same kind of thing as all the others. And this nature is considered abstractly in the intellect. The same applies to any other universal: man, justice, colour, etc. All existing men have something in common – their human nature. All acts of justice agree essentially; so do all colours – that is, precisely according to what is signified by *justice* or *colour*.

This nature, essence or "whatness", individualized wherever it really exists, is not according to itself individual – if it were it could not be multiplied in many different individuals. It is not according to itself universal either – if it were it could not be identified with individuals. But it can be considered universally in the mind. When we say, "Peter is a man", we are identifying the concept *man* with Peter. Yet we know man is not restricted to Peter; if it were, there could be only one man. But millions of other individuals exist who are as truly man as he is.

While the proper object of the human intellect is of things as universal, it would be a serious error to think the intellect has no knowledge of singulars. It would flatly contradict experience, and would make impossible any practical use of the intellect. We spend a good deal of our time judging and reasoning about singular objects: about work to be executed or actions to be performed. And some people with little speculative aptitude show themselves very capable in practical intellectual activity.

However, direct knowledge of corporeal singulars is had by the senses alone. The intellect cannot attain it because, in the words of St Thomas, "Our intellect understands by abstracting the intelligible species from individual matter. But what is abstracted from individual matter is universal. So our intellect directly knows only universals."[14]

The necessity of abstraction we have already seen: bodies in their natural state lack the immateriality required in intellectual objects. But we have also seen that intellectual abstraction is from sense knowledge and the *same thing* is known by the senses and by the intellect, although in diverse ways. Now, the intellect is able to know the singular by adverting to it in the imagination from which the universal is abstracted. By that reflection, says St Thomas, the intellect "has a certain knowledge about the particular according to a certain continuation of the intellect on the imagination."[15]

In this knowledge of singulars it is still the universal which is primarily and directly known, but by attending to the source of the universal the singular is known. The intellect really knows the singular, yet not in the way proper to sense – which is concerned only with the singular – but in the spiritual way proper to intellectual knowledge.

Because the singular is not self-understood, a concept is needed for the understanding of it, a concept distinct from that needed for knowing the universal.

We also have, in intellectual consciousness, a singular awareness of the acts of our mind and will, of the habits of these powers, and of the powers themselves, as well as a certain awareness of the soul's existence as shown through its acts.[16]

Criticisms of intellectual knowledge. Strange misunderstandings are voiced concerning the nature and value of intellectual knowledge. The concept is sometimes seen as a pale and static reflection of real things – a dim effigy of the flesh and blood world, an effigy without movement, without life, without appeal.

This criticism arises partly from the notion that the concept is an emaciated image.[17] It also fails to grasp the realist character of conceptual knowledge. To be correctly appreciated, understanding must be seen as a vital penetration of reality, revealing more than the senses can ever show us. The trouble is that we take the intellect for granted, and fail to see its magnificence.

Abstraction is severely criticized. By abstraction, it is said, we remove ourselves from the real world of concrete experience, and end in a conceptual world of our own making, a world of pseudo-realities like species and genera and specific differences. Or as Delbert puts it in criticizing metaphysics: "The botanist who wishes to describe the artichoke describes the stem, the root and the leaves. The metaphysician eliminates all that and studies the rest."[18]

There is a failure here to notice the difference between total and formal abstraction.[19] While total abstraction is very valuable – science, and even common sense, cannot dispense with it – formal abstraction is still more valuable, and is certainly not about the residue left after a process of elimination. But those who attack abstraction are often attacking the false notion of it as a mechanical sorting out of the common elements to be found in imagery.

Some complain that the intellect cuts the world into fragments, and claim that the senses alone give us a view of the whole.

But the view given by the senses is not nearly as comprehensive as sometimes thought. And it is always superficial. Certainly the intellect often selects a limited area for study, but this should be with the intention of making a synthesis later on. Our intelligence is the most synthetic power we have, far more so than the central sense; and the great network of the sciences – empirical, philosophical, theological – is a standing refutation of the charge that the mind splits the world into fragments. Of course, there is a big difference between what the mind is capable of and what each of us achieves; and when someone complains of faults of the mind he should ask whether they are proper to the mind or are faults due to misuse or disuse of the intelligence.

Another misunderstanding is that Thomists claim a comprehensive penetration of reality by the intellect; they are supposed to think it gazes into the depths of being as sight does into a sunlit pool of clear water.

This is far from the truth. The objections to intellect just dealt with all err by defect; but we must not exaggerate human intelligence and make it a faculty of pure intuition. It can indeed apprehend the natures of things – but only in an imperfect way. It is so far from having a clear vision of the objects it knows that it has to work laboriously on the data presented by the senses in order to obtain even a moderate insight. And of all the creatures in the world, man alone can be defined clearly enough to mark him off from the rest. He is defined *rational animal*; but we cannot see deeply enough to know, for instance, what essentially differentiates a cat from a dog: we have to be content with listing empirical signs in the manner of the zoologist. Even a genius, after heavy labours and with the aid of the accumulated knowledge of the centuries, can understand reality only very imperfectly.

One reason for the revolt against intelligence is the arduous discipline demanded by the search for truth. Some feel there must be an easier way, and allow themselves to be led by imagination and emotion; but that way ends in a foggy valley of illusion. The path of the intelligence is steep and difficult, but it ascends towards a clear summit of truth.

[1] Richard Rorty, *Philosophy and Social Hope* (1999), p. 72.

[2] *Summa Theol.*, I, q. 57, a. 1, *ad* 2.

[3] *QQ. Disp. De Veritate*, q. 25, a. 1.

[4] St Thomas, *In II de Anima*, lecture 12.

[5] *Summa Theol.*, I, q. 84, a. 1.

[6] Chapter seven, section three.

[7] Cf. *Summa Theol.*, I, q. 84, a. 7.

[8] *Contra Gentes*, II, chapter 76. Cf. *Summa Theol.*, I, q. 79. aa. 4, 5.

[9] *QQ. Disp. De Veritate*, q. 10, a. 6, *ad* 7.

[10] *De Anima*, book III, chapter 4, 430a 1.

[11] *Summa Theol.*, I, q. 12, a. 2.

[12] *In de Ente et Essentia, Prooemio*, ed. Laurent, n. 5.

[13] *Summa Theol.*, I, q. 84, a. 7.

[14] I, q. 86, a. 1.

[15] *QQ. Disp. De Veritate.*, q. 2, a. 6.

[16] Ibid., q. 1, a. 9; q. 10, a. 9.

[17] See the second difference between images and concepts, in section one above.

[18] *La Science et la Réalité*, p. 117.

[19] See chapter eleven, section one, infra.

Chapter Nine

A CRITIQUE OF IDEALISM, EMPIRICISM, POSTMODERNISM, PRAGMATISM

Let us first examine idealism and empiricism, especially in reference to the contention that they both lead to solipsism.

1. Idealism

Idealism – the doctrine that all is of and from mind – will not stand up to a critical examination. Take two objections made against it: that it cannot explain the physical sciences and that it cannot explain how we know there are other minds.

The sciences are based on the premise that there exist realities independent of thought. It is the scientist's task to obtain some understanding of these realities. Geology, for example, claims to investigate states of the earth which existed before conscious life appeared here. Astronomy claims to reveal facts which existed prior to their discovery: the earth did not begin to revolve around the sun when the Copernican system was accepted; on the contrary, the knowledge in question is true *because* it conforms to a reality independent of knowledge. In general, the advancement of science is a bringing into consciousness of a reality present independently of, and prior to, knowledge.

But if idealism were true, there would be only knowledge, without any independent reality. This would render it impossible for discoveries to be made by looking beyond the constructions of consciousness (for there would be no *beyond*), and equally impossible to say why one theory is true and another false. What would be meant by the statement, "The earth revolves around the sun," if *earth* and *sun* were mental furniture, not things independently of the mind? The same line of argument can of course be constructed from other knowledge, including common sense.

It places the idealist in an impossible predicament, because his philosophy compels him to accept both the testimony of consciousness and the claim that there is nothing beyond knowledge. So idealism contains an inherent contradiction.

Secondly, idealism cannot explain how we know there are other minds.

Idealists assert a universal consciousness of which each of us is a part. But how do they know this? I am conscious of myself as an incommunicable self, not as part of a larger mind. To say I am merely a part would be to ignore – and oppose – the evidence of my consciousness. If I am to posit thought as the sole reality, I must logically take it to be my thought, because I am immediately conscious of my thought but not that of others, and certainly not that of a universal mind.

Logically, idealism leads straight to solipsism; that is, the claim that I know only my own existence and that the world and other people are ideas in my mind. As G. K. Chesterton puts it, the idealist is a man whose friends are a mythology. Solipsism is so appalling that it cannot be seriously held. If I were a solipsist I could not even say that other people were mistaken in opposing solipsism – to say that would be to admit their existence! I would be a solitary self, imagining a universe of whose real existence I must remain agnostic.

2. Empiricism

It is not surprising that idealism should have lost its popularity, to be superseded by empiricism, which takes its stand on experience and admits no "metaphysical" realities. Whereas the basic principle of idealism is that the mind alone is active in knowledge, empiricism proceeds from the opposite pole, looking on the external objects of knowledge as actively impressing themselves on a passive subject. John Locke states: "The mind is wholly passive in the reception of all its simple ideas."[1] After receiving them its chief acts are to combine simple ideas into compound ones, to view ideas relatively to each other and thus acquire ideas of relations, and to separate ideas "from all other ideas that accompany them in their real existence; this is called 'abstraction'; and thus all its general ideas are made."[2]

So for empiricism the dominant factor in knowledge is the activity of external things impressing themselves on the knower. The latter's activity is one of combining, relating and separating; and even this is not seen as immanent activity intrinsically perfecting the operant, but rather as a mechanical and transitive production and juxtaposition of images. It therefore becomes impossible to admit any knowledge transcending that of the senses: so-called universals or general ideas are only images separated from the other images that normally accompany them.

In chapter eight, section one, we compare images and concepts, showing how they differ. Here we can simply note that empiricism proceeds logically in rejecting supra-sensible knowledge, once granted the fundamental empiricist principle of the knower's passivity, for this passivity precludes the abstractive activity needed for drawing concepts from sense-data. But that principle leads to disastrous consequences. One of these is solipsism. Solipsism is logically inevitable if we (1) hold that knowledge is through physical appropriation; (2) deny the reality of substance and of secondary qualities; (3) hold that we know directly only our own ideas. We will consider each of these positions.

The opinion that knowledge is through physical appropriation. In chapter seven we saw that non-knowers receive forms in an appropriative manner: the form received becomes that of the recipient: heat received in water or shape in plasticine is the heat of *that water* or the shape of *that plasticine*. Now if this occurred in knowledge (assuming knowledge were even possible on such a supposition), the knower would be attaining his own modifications. Precisely because the form (heat or shape) was *his form*, that is, something of himself, in knowing that form he would be knowing only himself. Physical appropriation would make knowledge of anything external absolutely impossible.

This means the knower would be condemned to solipsism. The people, trees, houses of his perception – what would they be? Not real entities subsisting independently, but only interior images consisting in the knower's modifications. Therefore to avoid solipsism it is absolutely necessary to hold that the possession in which knowledge consists is non-appropriative: that is, it is of a mode transcending the physical manner of receiving forms.

But empiricism rules out any supra-physical or non-appropriative having of forms. For empiricism asserts the passivity of the knowing subject. But a subject which passively receives determinations impressed on it by an external agent is not exercising that dominance, that vital activity, essential to the transcending of physical appropriation. Briefly, empiricism allows no manner of receiving forms other than the appropriative manner; therefore it becomes impossible for the knower to apprehend anything other than himself. And this is solipsism.

Denial of the reality of substance and of secondary qualities. Common sense judges that there exist secondary qualities, such as colour (or proper sensibles in Scholastic terminology), primary qualities, such as shape (common sensibles), and an underlying substance which supports these qualities. Now what happens if we reject the first and third of these – secondary qualities and substance?

We have already seen how Berkeley worked out the consequences.[3] He realized the impossibility of shape, size, motion, rest and number existing without a subject: shape that is not the shape of anything, size that is not the size of anything, and so on. So he gave them a subject, namely the mind: there is no external physical world; the world exists only in the minds of spirits.

He rightly saw the absurdity of primary qualities existing on their own. But he went too far in asserting the existence of spirits, for these would be unknown if knowledge originated from impressions passively received: I would know only the impressions – to get beyond them to the cognition of spirits would require an intellectual activity and insight contrary to empiricist principles. Proceeding consistently with empiricism, I would be left enclosed in a world of images – and with no grounds for asserting that anything else, or anyone else, exists.

The argument can be formulated in this way. Things are either corporeal or incorporeal. But on empiricist principles the incorporeal (if it exists) is unknowable. Therefore corporeal things are left. However, if I go on to deny substance and secondary qualities to bodies, I have reduced them so far that it becomes impossible to attribute independent existence to them. Therefore they exist dependently on the percipient. But the only percipient I am aware of is myself. So solipsism follows.

Substances cannot be admitted by empiricism because a knowledge of substance supposes an active penetration by our minds into a reality underlying the phenomena revealed by the senses. Nor can the objectivity of secondary qualities be explained unless knowledge is, contrary to the empiricist view, a non-appropriative having of forms.

The doctrine that we know directly only our own ideas. According to Thomists, our knowledge is immediately of realities, not of ideas or images. They hold this because they see the intentional species as a pure sign wherein reality is known. If this is denied and it is held instead that the idea or image is *that which* is immediately known, it becomes logically necessary to say that I never know anything except my ideas or images. If the idea is *that which* is known (not that wherein reality is known), I will attain only an idea of reality, not reality itself. So I will never know whether anything real corresponds to the idea.

We can illustrate this by supposing a prisoner in solitary confinement whose total information about current events in the outside world was limited to what he saw on a television screen. He could not be sure that anything factual corresponded to the scenes he witnessed and the statements he heard. It could all be fiction invented by his jailers. To judge whether the stories he witnessed were of real events he would need to assess them in the light of factors other than the stories themselves – particularly his memories of reality prior to his imprisonment.

Now to apply the illustration. What the prisoner saw on his television screen corresponds to what is known according to the theory we are discussing. He saw images, but could not know, except by inference, whether they were of real events in the city outside or only acts performed on a film set. Similarly, in this theory it must be said that we cannot know, apart from inference, whether the cognitive images and ideas which we experience are of real things, or are simply mental constructs with no extra-mental reality corresponding to them.

At this point it may be objected: but we can verify them in the same way as the prisoner verified his television stories. He could use his experience to decide whether what he saw was reliable. And even though we do not know reality immediately, we can reason to reality from the ideas we immediately experience.

The answer must be that we could not do so because of this radical difference between the two cases: the prisoner possessed knowledge other than that which he acquired from television; but according to this theory the totality of our knowledge is removed from reality. In other words, everything in the mind is an idea (using that word widely to include imagery) and ideas immediately manifest themselves, not real things. It follows, then, that the thinker is trapped inescapably in the net of his ideas. He cannot know whether a real world corresponds to them, or whether other people exist, or even whether his own body exists. Here again solipsism is inevitable.

This theory of knowledge was taught explicitly by Descartes, Locke,

Hume and Kant. It was this which made it necessary for Descartes to try to prove the existence of a material world – proof is superfluous for one who claims to attain the world directly through his senses. Descartes appealed to God's truthfulness: he would not deceive us into thinking a real world existed. Locke attempted to solve the problem by maintaining that data of the external senses must be produced by things outside operating on us.[4]

Neither position will stand examination. Regarding Descartes' explanation: if we knew only ideas, we could not even know God existed, for God is something other than our ideas. The foundation of any argument for the existence of some reality must be a reality already known. But this theory denies that we know any reality whatever. Therefore it leaves no foundation from which to argue to a reality. As for Locke's explanation, why could not the perceptions arise from the mind itself? Hume points out that experience cannot help us here because "The mind never has anything present to it but the perceptions, and cannot possibly reach any experience of their connection with objects. The supposition of such a connection is, therefore, without any foundation in reasoning."[5]

Hume admits he has no answer, but says nature is too strong for principle where extreme scepticism is concerned, and will impel us to put aside our philosophical doubts and act like other men.[6] He should have seen that a theory which leads to such bizarre conclusions must be fallacious, and that we should look elsewhere for the truth.

As we have seen, the theory is by no means confined to empiricism; it is also a cardinal tenet of idealism. It is inevitable on empiricist as well as idealist principles. The reason empiricism cannot escape it is, once again, the doctrine of the knower's passivity. Granted his passivity, the possession of forms in knowledge must be appropriative. Just as heat received in water is the heat of that water, not of the fire that produced it, so the passive reception of forms in knowledge would make them forms of the knower, at most resembling exterior things. But the knower could not get outside himself to see whether any external reality corresponded to the forms which he found in himself.

In conclusion. It follows that the avoidance of solipsism requires that knowers have forms in a supra-physical and non-appropriative way, that substances are real and that things – not ideas – are directly known. These conclusions in turn rest on the premise that knowledge is an immanent and vital activity (not a transitive one), an activity unique to knowers. Yet we must not swing to the other extreme and deny all activity to external things – this is the typical error of idealism, Things really act on the knower, who responds in his own vital fashion.

The problem of the nature of knowledge is a specifically philosophical one, not a scientific one. Modern empiricists often fail to realize this, and treat the question rather from the standpoint of physical science. Bertrand Russell is an excellent example. He writes of perception: "My own belief is that the problem is scientific, not philosophical, or, rather, no longer philosophical."[7] The theory of perception is greatly simplified "if we learn to imagine what is called 'perceiving an object' as a remote effect of the object, which resembles it only approximately and only in certain respects."[8] He goes on to deny intrinsic distinction between the mental and the physical. Elsewhere he states that we know the external world as "the unexperienced cause of experienced effects."[9] Again: "The starry heaven that we know in visual sensation is inside us. The external starry heaven we believe in is inferred."[10]

Russell fails to see that such an inference would be unjustified, because there would be no foundation on which to base it. It is perfectly true, as he points out, that we can often infer an unexperienced thing from one that is experienced. However, the peculiar position here is that, on his assumption that all knowledge of external reality is inference, there would remain no basis from which to infer. It would be like a man trying to raise himself by his shoelaces. I do not deny that a man can raise himself from the ground by grasping something external and tensioning his muscles; but I deny that he can do so if the something is his shoelaces.

3. The reality of proper sensibles

Many would assert that at least in one area it can be shown by experience and by physical science that knowledge is subjective, not objective: namely, regarding the nature of proper sensibles. Most scientists and non-Scholastic philosophers, as well as some Scholastics, hold that colour, sound, hardness and softness, heat and cold, flavour, odour exist only in the sense, not in the things that are sensed.

This theory, called interpretationism, holds that only the causes of proper sensibles exist in things; for example, there are no colours or sounds in nature, but only vibrations which are apt to produce sensations of colour or sound in us. The opposite explanation, called perceptionism, holds that proper sensibles are real. A defence of that position will be given here.

Interpretationism is incompatible with the concepts explained in the previous chapters, and according to which the knower becomes the known. Interpretationism, on the contrary, maintains that proper sensibles are manufactured by the knower upon a stimulus from the object, and that therefore they do not present the object, but are only its effect. The object is present causally, not formally. Knowledge not only produces something which lacks non-cognitive reality, but the quality it produces – colour, sound, etc. – is that which is basic in sensation, that through which all the common sensibles – shape, etc. – are given. So interpretationism removes us from direct contact with the people, houses, trees, and so forth which our senses seem to be intuiting; positing instead qualities lacking extrasensory existence as the medium whereby we come to a knowledge of reality.

Before considering difficulties proposed against perceptionism we must see more precisely what it involves. Firstly, it does not require that an object should be known as it is at a distance from the sense. Things are sensed in their very action on the sense; and by that action they are within the sense. So if a distant star is seen, the object acting on the sense – the object which is *per se* seen – is the light from the star *in its condition as it affects the sense*. The star may have ceased to exist during the years the light took to reach the earth. Also, the light would have been greatly modified in its long journey. Again, take the vision of a faraway mountain range. It is seen according to the light acting upon the organ of sight. But this is light that has been modified by other objects between the mountain range and the eyes – by mist in the atmosphere, by light from cities, etc. If the range appears blue instead of green, can we blame our sight for inaccuracy? No; sight is seeing its object as it impinges on the sense-organ. It could rightly be accused of error if it saw what an observer close to the range would see, for it would not then be sensing its object in the way it is present. Briefly, what is sensed is the object in its action on the sense, and therefore in the condition in which it then exists.[11]

The colour we see is that which acts on the sense of sight; the sound we hear is that which acts on the sense of hearing. Similarly, when we chew an apple, we taste the mixture which affects the taste buds, a mixture which may contain elements other than the apple: remains of food previously eaten, secretions in the mouth, etc. We say that when we are sick food sometimes loses its customary taste; but to speak more accurately, we are then tasting a mixture containing elements not normally present in the mouth.

The sense of touch – whether the sense of resistance (pressure-touch) or of temperature (thermal-touch) – also needs analysis. The resistance we sense when we grasp a brick is together that of the brick and that of our hand. When we dip a finger into warm water two heats are present to the sense of touch: the heat of the water and that of the finger. So we cannot experience *merely* the heat of the water. For this reason the water will seem hotter if the finger is cold than if it is warm.

Perceptionism, while avoiding subjectivism, is emphatically not naïve realism. It recognizes a subjective element in the senses of touch, taste and smell; it insists on the incompleteness of all sense knowledge; it takes account of the hindrances often encountered, not only from external factors but also from defects in the sense organs.

Now we come to some specific objections to the objectivity of proper sensibles.

Objection. A person who has had a leg amputated seems to feel pain in the missing foot. How is this error reconcilable with the objectivity of the senses?

Reply. The error concerns localization of an object, not the reality. The pain is in the nerves in the trunk of the body, nerves which were extended to the foot, and the pain is imagined to be in the foot.

Objection. Some people find a food pleasant tasting, others find it unpleasant. The same occurs in the case of smell and touch. Now the real thing cannot be pleasant and unpleasant together. So either the quality perceived is not objectively there, or else some people – those who perceive it wrongly – suffer an illusion.

Reply. The senses of touch, taste and smell report more than the objective character of the thing sensed; they also report the reaction of the sensing subject. There is an "interested" or subjective element in these three senses. They report the subjective reaction of pleasantness or unpleasantness in their possessor, a reaction that varies from one person to another. Two people may experience an equivalent sweetness in their coffee, but one also experiences the pleasantness this sweetness has for him, the other its unpleasantness for him.

Also, as said above, there may be a real modification of the taste due to other elements with which the coffee is mixed in the mouth. Or possibly it happens, analogously to colour-blindness, that one person is incapable of perceiving some qualities that others perceive. Some certainly perceive more acutely than others.

Objection. Physics shows that colour, sound, heat and other proper sensibles have nothing corresponding to them in external reality except vibrations. And variations in a proper sensible, in a sound for example, are in accordance with variations in the vibrations.

Reply. Physics shows that determinate sensible qualities have determinate vibrations corresponding to them, but does not show that the vibrations alone are real. All qualitative changes, chemical changes for example, have local movement associated with them; but this does not justify us in identifying the quality with the movement. Perceptionism maintains that the qualities of sound, colour and so on are real independently of perception, but that they arise (in reality, not in the sense organ) from determinate vibrations. The conclusion that the proper sensibles are real qualities of things is a philosophical one, not a conclusion from physics. And so is the opposite thesis. Physics is concerned with observable and measurable phenomena – and nothing beyond. But to conclude there is nothing beyond would not only be a violation of reason and common sense; it would also be an assumption going beyond physics. Physics rightly occupies itself exclusively with the observation and measurement of the vibratory aspect of sensible qualities; which does not mean those qualities are vibrations.

Objection. Sensation can be produced by artificial stimulation. Pressure on the eyes can produce a flash of light. Electrical stimulus to the appropriate sense organ or to the nerves of, for example, sight or hearing, will provoke sensation; and the response depends on the nature of the organ or nerves, not on that of the stimulus. In other words, the same stimulus will produce either colour or sound, depending on which organ is stimulated. This shows that the proper object of the senses must be subjective, their character depending on the nature of the sense organ, and their existence being caused by an external stimulus.

Reply. The above phenomena can be explained consistently with perceptionism. One theory attributes the light and sound in these cases to the internal sense of imagination, not to the senses of sight and hearing. This explanation claims that a disposition towards the experiencing of colour and sound has become fixed in the nerves and cerebrum by a lifetime of exercising the powers in question. When the artificial stimulus is applied, colour or sound is *imagined*, not truly seen or heard. The faculty involved is the imagination, whose object does not need to be physically present, not the intuitive external sense of sight or hearing.

A second theory grants that the phenomena are in the external senses, but explains them without denying their objectivity. This theory claims that real colour or sound is produced *within the organ itself* by the mechanical or electric stimulus. It is argued that these organs have the specific end of recording colour or sound – their intrinsic constitution is wholly towards this. If pressure on the eyes or electricity stimulating the nerves produces even the faintest of light waves, it is not surprising that sight should register them. Similarly, if electric stimulus of the nerves of hearing gives rise to sound waves, it is only to be expected that they will be registered by the hearing. Precisely because of the constitution of these organs, light waves and sound waves can be very readily produced within them, and therefore the qualities of colour and sound.

Objection. If a number of people view a soap bubble, each looking at it from a different angle, each will see the same part of it in different colours. But the same part cannot really be differently coloured at the same time. Therefore the colours seen are not really in the soap bubble.

Reply. We have explained above that perceptionism accepts the modification of light between the external object and the visual power. That provides the solution to this difficulty. The really existing colour is changed before reaching the viewers. For one, rays of a certain length are eliminated by interference, for another those of a different length. The fact that different colours are seen from different positions is a problem for interpretationists too, and they solve it by appealing to the same scientific fact: elimination of rays of a certain length. That fact solves the dilemma of the soap bubbles for either perceptionism or interpretationism, while leaving open the philosophic question of whether colour is an objective quality of things or a subjective quality of sight.

Objection. If colours are objective, would we not be compelled to say that a thing is coloured even in the dark? An apple really has a round shape whether we see it or not; has it also a red colour when no light exists by which to see it?

Reply. No. When not illuminated it has a permanent disposition to absorb certain light rays and reflect others – that is, a disposition to give rise to colour. But colour comes into being only upon illumination.

Objection. A person suffering from colour-blindness sees colours that are not really there. Some colour-blind people see as blue what those with normal vision see as green. But the real thing cannot be together blue and green. Interpretationism alone is able to explain the apparent contradiction: colour is subjective, and dependent on the constitution of the visual organ; if this is defective in someone a colour will exist for him different from that which normal people see.

Reply. Even if, through a defect of the organ, a colour arose within the eye, this would not rule out its objectivity. It would be subjective if it *existed only in sensation*; but not if it were present *as a real colour* which *became an object of vision*. The colour-blind person would be in error when he located the colour in an external thing, for instance a signal light, but this would be an error of imagination and judgment, not an illusion concerning the existence of a proper sensible. But the usual explanation of colour-blindness would be that the person sees some colours and fails to perceive others. For the colour we see is usually a mixture of several colours. The colour-blind person fails to perceive one or more real colours; but those he does perceive are real. Because his sight registers certain colours to the exclusion of others, the result is a colour that normal people do not see in that thing.

Objection. If we look straight at a bright object, then close our eyes, we seem to still see it. How is the seeing of an after-image compatible with the objectivity of sight?

Reply. While knowledge is not a physical modification, an act of sensation presupposes such a modification; sense knows corporeal things and knows them in their action on the sense organ. In the case of sight, the thing seen causes photochemical qualities in the retina, qualities which remain for a short time after we look away from the thing. It is through those still present qualities that we retain an image of the bright object we were looking at.

Objection. An experiment with Newton's disc demonstrates that colours are not objective. The disc shows all the colours of the spectrum while it is stationary, but when rotated rapidly it shows white. Real colours in the disc could not be changed to white through rotation and back to the colours of the spectrum by halting the rotation. So the colours are not really there.

Reply. This can be explained through the photo-chemical qualities mentioned in answer to the previous difficulty. The qualities caused by the colours of the disc remain briefly in the retina. With the rapid turning of the disc the qualities merge in the retina, producing white, which is a composite of all the colours together. The error that arises in this phenomenon does not consist in taking as objective what is merely subjective, but in imagining the whiteness to be located in the disc.

Objection. In half-tone printing, colours appear which are not objective. If a red block is printed over a yellow one, the result appears as orange; if blue is printed over yellow, green appears. But the yellow and green are not really there. This can be verified by examining the page with a magnifying glass. In the first case, one sees yellow and red dots; in the second, yellow and blue dots.

Reply. The position here is similar to that in the previous difficulty, and is also related to the imperfection of our vision. The individual dots are too minute to be distinguished except with a magnifying glass – or sometimes with the naked eye close to the paper. As a result, a confusion or blending of colours takes place in the eye.

4. Postmodernism and pragmatism

We noted in chapter four that while postmodernism and deconstructionism are a reaction against characteristic themes in modern philosophy, they are also a product of those themes. They deny that things have intelligible natures which we can know and they deny ordered structures in the world. We are immersed, they claim, in an ever-changing flow of fragments, with no objective intelligibility that the mind can grasp.

Pragmatism, like postmodernism, denies that things have objective natures. The aim of thought is not to see things as they are, but to help us cope with our experiences. No objective grounds exist for doing this rather than that, but we should view others as we view ourselves, namely as seeking pleasure and avoiding suffering, and we should further this aim.

The presuppositions of postmodernism and pragmatism concerning knowledge have already been examined in our discussion of the nature of knowledge, and their weaknesses shown. Here we can note that these positions are self-contradictory.

Foucault claims, for instance, that bio-power is a menace, and that we should help the oppressed. He is implicitly presenting these claims as objectively true – otherwise his statements would be meaningless. Likewise, the general statement of postmodernism and pragmatism that there is no objective truth is itself a statement that claims to be objectively true. It amounts to saying: It is objectively true that there is no objective truth.

Richard Rorty poses the dilemma himself.[12] Suppose, he says, that pragmatists are asked whether they have *discovered* that what was thought to be objectively true is actually subjective, or have they *invented* it. If they say they have discovered it, "we are in danger of contradicting ourselves". (He doesn't go far enough: if they say that, they *have* contradicted themselves!) Alternatively, if they say they invented it, "we seem to be being merely whimsical...If truths are merely convenient fiction, what about the truth of the claim that that is what they are? Is that too a convenient fiction?"

The objection he poses is unanswerable; he has destroyed his own philosophy. He proceeds to dodge the question by saying it is framed in terms the pragmatist rejects. "The distinction between the found and the made is a version of that between the absolute and the relative..." But pragmatists, he says, reject that distinction. In fact, the objection is clear and straightforward, and does not depend on any particular philosophical presuppositions. Rorty does not answer it because it is unanswerable.

1 *An Essay Concerning Human Understanding*, book II, chapter 12, section 1.
2 Ibid.
3 Chapter three, section two.
4 *An Essay Concerning Human Understanding*, book IV, chapter 4, section 1.
5 *An Enquiry Concerning Human Understanding*, section XII, part 1.
6 Ibid., part 2.
7 *My Philosophical Development*, p. 250.
8 Ibid., p. 252.
9 Ibid., p. 228.
10 Ibid., p. 10.
11 Cf. J. Maritain, *The Degrees of Knowledge* (1959 edition), chapter 3, n. 23, footnote.
12 See *Philosophy and Social Hope* (1999), introduction, p. XVIII.

Chapter Ten

CONCERNING HUMAN NATURE

An understanding of human knowledge allows us to reach conclusions about man – his nature and activities – which would otherwise elude us. Some of these conclusions will be examined in this chapter. They harmonize with the theory of knowledge we have been explaining, but if that were false a quite different philosophy of man would be demanded.

1. Spirituality of the human soul

In chapter eight we proved intellectual knowledge to be of a superior order to sense knowledge, and from this difference saw that the intellect belongs to a higher order of being than the senses or other corporeal things. We must now examine the soul in which the power of intellect resides.

The intellect was shown to be spiritual, and consequently not a part of the body. No power subsists out on its own, but is based in some substantial principle which has and exercises the power.[1] By studying a power we can reach conclusions about the thing that possesses it. We found, on studying the intellect, that it is spiritual. And from this it follows that it is the property of a spiritual soul. The reason is that a thing can act only according to its capacity; a living body, for example, can operate in an organic manner, but not supra-organically or spiritually. If it did, there would be action without an adequate cause. Since the acts of the intellect are above the bodily order, and therefore the intellect is a spiritual power, the substantial principle which possesses this power must be a spirit.

We need to look carefully at the notion of spirit, for it is difficult to understand, yet an understanding of it is vital. One difficulty is intrinsic: as we have seen the proper formal object of our intellect is the essences of bodily things; and this means that when we wish to understand something transcending bodies, we can do so only through bodily things.

There is also an extrinsic difficulty, due to social conditioning. Most people just don't think about spirits, and such studies form no part of their general education. A person subject to this environment for most of his life will find it a great effort to break his acquired accustomisations of thought.

Because the being of a thing determines what it can do, the higher the being the more powerful is its activity. There is a progression in being, and consequently in operation, from inanimate things to vegetation, to brute animals, to man. Each of these levels above the first shows a further domination and a more perfect activity.

Man, through his intellect, becomes the things he knows, making the perfections of other things in a way his own. And by his will, as is shortly to be shown, he can unite with the good that he knows. Vast, transcendent realities become his own through knowledge and love, the truth and goodness and beauty of which Plato and others have spoken. Such a world is the place of spirit, a world surpassing the fleeting phenomena of sense. For a spirit, in its own entity, surpasses the sensible world, and its proper powers and activities are proportionate to its being.

A spirit can be defined operationally as a being that understands and loves (by a love of the will, not sensible love). And it operates in that way because it is intrinsically free of matter – there is nothing corporeal in its constitution.

This might sound negative, saying what something is not. But that suspicion is caused by the fact that bodies are first in our knowledge and are alone attained directly by us, which leads to the illusion that the more bodily and tangible something is, the more real it is. Reason shows the opposite to be true: matter is a principle of limitation, and the higher something is in the scale of being, the freer it is from matter. Spirit transcends matter entirely. So in saying a spirit has nothing corporeal in its constitution, we are implying something very positive. A spirit lacks matter because it doesn't need it, because it is too real to need it. It is more real – that is, it has more being or entity – than any corporeal thing. And from the greatness of its being follows the greatness of its activities, although in this study we have proceeded from an examination of the intellectual activity of the human spirit to conclusions about its entity.

Bodily things are extended and occupy space. This is a severe limitation. They are restricted to a particular place at any one time. And their activities are restricted – for one thing, they are incapable of self-reflection in the strict sense. A sensitive power cannot reflect on itself because self-reflection involves a complete return of a power on itself, in order to know that it is knowing. But an extended thing cannot exercise a complete return on itself. A spirit is free of this limitation, and therefore is capable of self-reflection.[2]

The extension of bodies brings us to another point: they are composed of parts. A spirit, on the contrary, is simple or lacking essential composition. This too appears from the power of intellectual self-reflection. Now, what has parts can be disintegrated. For this reason bodies are constantly in danger of destruction. They are vulnerable to attack from any agent capable of disrupting the equilibrium of parts their being depends on – whether the attacker be wind or acid, a steamroller or a germ, or any of a million things. This is danger to which a spirit is not subject, for its essence is uncomposed, and therefore indestructible.

The conclusion is awe-inspiring when realized. A spirit is immortal: it is something which can never cease to exist, for it contains no potentiality to dissolution. The condition needed for a thing to be dissolved is composition of parts. A spirit, as its spiritual operations show, lacks parts. Therefore it cannot be dissolved.

The only possible way it could cease to be is by annihilation, not by dissolution. But annihilation, or the reduction of a thing to pure nothingness, could be caused only by God, because the existence and conservation of finite things depends on his causality, so its cessation likewise could be accomplished only by him. But his activity is towards being, not nothingness; nor is it in accordance with infinite wisdom to create something which is naturally fitted to last forever, and then annihilate it.

Kant objects that the soul might possibly be changed into nothing, not by dissolution, but by a gradual diminution of reality until nothing remained.[3] This objection takes a truth applicable to accidents, and wrongly applies it to the underlying subject which possesses accidents. A colour, for example, can fade away until nothing of it remains; but this does not remove the substance that had the colour. The heat of water can diminish, but the water itself remains. The reason for the difference is that the quality – colour or heat – has no independent existence, but inheres in something else, whereas a substance exists in its own right, not as a participant in the being of something else. Kant, of course, thought speculative knowledge is confined to phenomena, while things-in-themselves remain unknown; and the Aristotelian distinction between substance and accidents could have no place in his philosophy.

2. The will

As explained in the previous chapter, intellect is a power belonging to the spiritual soul alone. There is one other power to which the same applies, namely will. Like sensitive knowledge, intellectual knowledge is followed by an inclination towards, or aversion from, the things known. In the case of sensitive knowledge, the appetitive power is called sensitive appetite;[4] while the appetitive power following intellect is called will.

The existence of some appetitive faculty is obvious. We are familiar with the loves and hates, the hopes and fears, etc., that exist within us, and which must be referred to some power. They are not knowledge, which is supra-physical union with the known; whereas these appetitions and affections are about *real* union with, or aversion from, things known. They are consequent on knowledge (consequent causally, not temporally), for we cannot appetise something we know nothing whatever about. They are about things whose real possession is apprehended under the aspect of good or evil.

But how do we know there is a real distinction between sensitive appetite and will? We have seen that intellectual knowledge transcends anything a brute animal is capable of; must the same be said of the will? It must, as we shall see. Man has sensitive knowledge and affectivity in common with the lower animals. But just as he has a power of knowing transcending anything they are capable of, he has a corresponding power of loving transcending sensitive appetite. This conclusion is logically denied by empiricists, for they admit only sensitive knowledge, but it logically follows from the acceptance of two specifically distinct orders of knowledge.

Granted that the intellect is spiritual, an intellective appetite must exist. For knowledge is followed by inclination, and is not static and self-enclosed. But sensitive inclination is not proportionate to intellectual knowledge, which reveals a marvellous world unknown to the senses and a whole range of lovable and hateful objects of which sense apprehension cannot be had. So an appetite must exist corresponding to intellectual knowledge; which means an appetite as spiritual as the intellect itself, since it is specified by the intellect – intellectual knowledge gives the appetite the object under the aspect of good or evil understood.

This does not mean that will is only concerned with things sense cannot reach, but that the aspect under which will is attracted to things is diverse from the aspect known by sense. Will can be attracted to the physical qualities of a person – but as apprehended intellectually. Will can be attracted to the pleasant taste of a cake – but, again, as apprehended by intellect.

Distinction between will and sensitive appetite is not separation. There is a close conjunction between the operations of the two powers, just as there is between intellectual and sensitive knowledge. It is impossible to will anything without some movement of our sensitive appetite accompanying the act of will, just as it is impossible to understand anything without an accompanying image. This is one reason people easily confuse the two sorts of appetition, and think of will as identical with sensitive appetite; in the same way, they identity intellect with sense.

We have said that the will is attracted to sensible pleasures, but as known by the intellect. Similarly, when some spiritual good attracts the will, the sensible appetite responds too; which happens because the images accompanying the spiritual good represent it, in their own sensible manner, to the lower appetite. The appetitive life forms one whole, not two isolated series.

3. Freedom of will

Have we freedom of will, or are our actions determined? This is another of the many problems with a history stretching back to antiquity, and still being debated today. We saw in chapter one that Plato attributed all human decisions to education and physical constitution. Some today do the same. The reasons given sometimes pertain to the general philosophy of the opponent of free will. But there is a dilemma pertaining to the very nature of will which can be expressed like this: If the will is subordinate to the intellect, it is not free; if free, it is not subordinate to the intellect.

We have just considered the subordination of the will to the intellect, saying that it is specified by intellectual knowledge, that it is attracted or repelled by what the intellect sees as good or evil. If something is seen as in no way good, the will cannot want it, for no motive exists to draw the will. It is impossible for the will to be attracted without any attractiveness being understood; just as impossible as the eyes seeing in total darkness.

Further, if the intellect judges two things to be good, it seems that the will must choose the one judged to be the greater good, otherwise it is acting against its intellectual specification. It is unnecessary, of course, that what appears good to the intellect should really be so; one can ardently desire what one erroneously judges to be good. The point being made here is that if something is judged, in a particular situation, to be the only good or the greater good, it must be chosen. Some philosophers have emphasized the principle of subordination, and consequently denied freedom of will.

But others have accepted freedom by denying this principle. They have argued: If free, the will is not subordinated to the intellect; but it is free; therefore it is not subordinated to the intellect. The denial of subordination means that the will acts in an arbitrary and blind manner, unguided by the intelligence. It is action without a motive, for only knowledge provides motives.

It seems at first glance that acceptance of the first position is irreconcilable with free will. But the second position equates free will with a blind indeterminism which would degrade man, instead of ennobling him. If that was free will, it wouldn't be worth having.

The common sense person, uninterested in philosophy, will brush the problem aside, and say he is sure of freedom because he experiences it. This is insufficient for the philosopher, whose task is to assign reasons and solve difficulties. But the testimony of consciousness should be rationally assessed, and not ignored. Each of the extreme positions of determinism and pure indeterminism emphasizes one term of the problem and denies the other. A true solution must reconcile both.

Three arguments for freedom of will are given below: the first two are from the testimony of consciousness; the third is based on the nature of will and intellect, and provides the means of solving the determinism versus indeterminism dilemma.

Argument from experience of moral responsibility. We are aware of certain factors relating to moral integrity or responsibility, factors without which such integrity would be an empty term. Personal responsibility involves doing good actions and avoiding evil, even though we could have done the opposite. Consider the difference between a driver who deliberately runs down a pedestrian, and one who does so accidentally. The result is the same in each case, but the moral character of each incident is quite different. But if freedom of will were lacking, the cases would be morally identical: neither driver would have been responsible for what he did.

This brings us to a second point: some actions are praiseworthy, others blameworthy. Freedom of will alone accounts for this. A person acting in a certain way because forces outside his control determine him to do so merits neither praise nor blame; and he receives neither if we know his condition – if he is insane, for example.

A third point is experience of remorse following a bad action, together with the resolve to act differently next time. The remorse felt by the first driver in the above illustration, if he repents of his action, is different from the sorrow (but not repentance) felt by the second driver after his accident.

The argument can be formulated in this way. These three things relate to the experience of personal responsibility: some actions should be done and others avoided, though the opposite course is possible; some actions merit praise, others blame; repentance occurs, and is different from mere sorrow about an unfortunate happening. But every experience demands an explanation; and the only explanation here is free will, for moral responsibility is impossible otherwise. Therefore free will exists. There is no question-begging here, for these factors are experienced, not assumed.

Denial of free will implies denial of some of human nature's noblest qualities, reducing them to illusions. It is a denial that can only be posed speculatively, not practiced. A serious attempt to practice it, in education, law, general social life, would mean chaos.

Argument from the experience of freedom. In the doing of a free act, we experience our freedom. This is not the experience of something that guarantees freedom, as in the argument just expounded, but is direct consciousness of the freedom itself. First, while deliberating about which choice to make, I am conscious that none of the possibilities draws me invincibly. Any may be chosen and any rejected; I am the arbiter and the decision is mine. Then in the very choice itself, as one alternative is willed and the others rejected, I experience that I am doing this because I want to, and could have chosen otherwise.

So the very dominion of the will over its act is experienced by intellective consciousness. This experience, of course, is had only while the act is being exercised: while the deliberation and choice are being done. But it is remembered afterwards. Experience is concrete, not abstract. An act of will is dynamic – a doing; it is not a static product like something made. So it is experienced as it occurs, and is experienced as it is – as a free activity.

An objection is sometimes put that the so-called consciousness of freedom is really unconsciousness of necessity.[5] Man fails to see the true cause of his behaviour, the chains that bind him to this action rather than that. Ignorant of the hidden causes, he supposes himself free: he thinks himself the determinant, when in reality he is determined.

One answer to this objection is that we can distinguish our free actions from our necessary ones. Many things force themselves on us, and we are not free to reject them: things we see and hear, for example; we cannot choose whether to see or hear them. There are other things we seem free about: whether to go out or stay at home, whether to travel by bus or train. If necessity reigns in all these cases, why are we aware of it in some and completely unaware of it in others?

This leads to a second answer to the objection. If our supposed consciousness of freedom were really unconsciousness of necessity, the greater our ignorance of the causes of our actions, the greater should be our illusion of freedom. The opposite is the case: the more aware we are of our motives, the more conscious we are of freedom. Suppose I can travel into the city either by bus or train. I have the half-formed intention of going by train, and then, passing the bus stop, I see a city-bound bus about to move out, and impulsively jump on. On another occasion, having plenty of time, I deliberate as to which would be the better choice; I consider fares, time of arrival, proximity to my destination. Then I choose the bus. In which case was I more certain of freedom? Obviously, in the second. Why? Because I was more aware of the causes motivating me. In the first case it might be argued that my action in leaping on the bus was forced upon me by causes beyond my control, that I lacked freedom. But in the second case the causes were clear: the two possibilities and the reasons in favour of each; my domination of the deliberation and of the choice exercised.

Many psychologists would remain unconvinced. They would insist that their study of the unconscious mind and their experience with their patients leaves them with little sympathy for the arguments of philosophers in favour of free will. By the time a child is old enough to engage in so-called free acts, his character has already undergone a constant moulding process for several years; and his apparently free acts are determined by his character. His very "wanting" to do something is fixed. The real master, as psychoanalysis shows, is the unconscious mind.

It is not unfair to answer that much of the difficulty comes from the fact that psychologists often have their views in this matter "determined" by the psychological theory they have been taught. The situation is further aggravated for them by the circumstance that many of the people they study are mentally ill, which can easily lead them to overstate the morbid elements in human personality. I have no wish to deny that freedom is weakened – can even be destroyed at times – by psychiatric disabilities. But we should not imagine everyone has his freedom crippled. The contrast between the average person and one afflicted by a severe psychiatric condition is very marked – at least to one well acquainted with the second person.

The contention that the unconscious mind is the real master of our desires, and therefore of our actions, would equate the behaviour of an obsessive or compulsive with that of a person without these problems. Both would be driven by unconscious urges of whose nature they were ignorant. All reasons would be rationalizations. But as S. I. Benn and R. S. Peters point out,[6] the term "rationalization" is a verbal parasite which flourishes because of the presence of genuine reasons with which it can be compared.

An inherent contradiction is involved in rejecting consciousness of freedom as an illusion, and holding instead that the unconscious mind is our master. My reason for saying so is this. The question of free will versus determinism is not one that leaves people indifferent, but one capable of provoking powerful emotions, whether towards the acceptance of freedom or its rejection. When a controversial issue like this is at stake, we need to be able to think it through with a reasonable degree of impartiality – otherwise our decision will be unreliable because of the motives that influenced it. But the required impartiality presupposes freedom – otherwise the causes controlling our willing would make us judge in accordance with our personal preferences. In other words, the (unfree) will – dominated by unconscious drives – would coerce the intellect into assenting to the position the person wants to hold. Jones may be certain of freedom, and Smith equally certain of determinism.

Each thinks he is judging rationally, unaware of the dictatorship his unconscious is exercising over him. If Smith gives the right answer, this is not because he is reasonable but because that answer happens to be the one prompted by his unconscious.

So when a psychologist claims that determinism due to unconscious drives is the reasonable position to hold, his statement contains the implication that *he is not determined by unconscious drives* in the assertion of that position. If he insists that, in this particular case, the evidence is clear to him, how can he reject the even clearer and more widespread experience called "consciousness of freedom"?

Argument from the nature of intellect and will. Freedom of choice means that an agent can decide its own actions. It is not constrained from without, by cosmic forces or any other external cause. And it is not impelled from within by some necessity arising from its own nature. It is free from both these restraints, the external and the internal. So the free agent is one that decides whether to act or not, and when various actions are possible, decides which to execute. It is as though a tree were indifferent as to whether it should produce apples or oranges, and could decide this for itself. This doesn't happen with trees, and the reason is that their nature determines them to certain actions. In other words, the determination or actuality or form according to which they act is one they have no control over; so the acts proceeding from it are necessary, not free.

Suppose a dog chases a rabbit. This activity is not so intimately bound up with his nature as that of a tree in producing a specific fruit. There is this difference: the dog has powers of sensible knowledge and appetition, which open to him a greater range of activities than those of non-knowers. He comes to know other things, appetise them, and act accordingly – for example, by chasing a rabbit. That type of action can be called spontaneous, to distinguish it from the rigid operations of non-knowers. However, the dog's actions are not free, between he is not able to choose between possibilities, but his nature constrains him to follow the strongest urge.

The free agent has a further eminence over forms. This eminence consists in the freedom to choose between forms. Its action will still be according to some form, for every action is determinate (it is *this* rather than something else), so it must proceed from some determination or form within the agent, just as do the operations of fire or a tree or an irrational animal. But the higher some being is, the more perfect are its powers of operation. The brute animal acts with the spontaneity deriving from sensible knowledge. The free agent acts with the liberty deriving from intellectual knowledge. Freedom of choice is domination of the form according to which action proceeds; that is, the free agent chooses the form according to which it will act – chooses how it shall be specified or determined. And that means it has domination over the resulting action.

That is the action of a free agent. It remains to be shown that the human will has this domination and so is free. We have seen that the will is specified by good understood. But when something is understood as good, is it seen as completely good, with no shadow of the undesirable about it? If it were, the will would have to choose it, because the will goes after good, and if a thing were seen as purely good no reason could exist to shun it, or even to remain indifferent to it.

While no freedom of choice would exist there, the position is otherwise concerning the particular good things of everyday life. All these have this characteristic: they are attractive in some respects, unattractive in others; that is, somewhat good and somewhat bad. Buying a car has attractive aspects, but a brief consideration shows disadvantages – the expense, the danger of accidents, and so on. Whatever instance comes to mind, disadvantages can be quickly detected: the good thing will cost too much money or too much effort, it would mean going without some other good thing, it would prove a disappointment in the end, there would be sorrows associated with it, and so on.

So this conclusion is reached: the particular goods the human intellect is confronted with are not seen as purely good, and therefore do not compel intellectual assent.[7] Although will, from its nature, is specified or determined by good understood, none of these goods is understood as compelling acceptance. They are seen as possible motives for action, not as necessary motives. Something can be said in their favour, but something can be said against them. This applies even to our consideration of God; choosing him involves difficulties and the renunciation of things opposed to his will, so from the practical standpoint adherence to him is not viewed as an unmixed good.

While the intellect is in this uncertain state, no choice can be made, for the intellect is deliberating, and is not yet able to bid the will: "Do this, not that." Everyone has often had the experience called "being in two minds" about something, or "having half a mind" to do a certain thing. These expressions indicate the indecisiveness of mind where no motive appears sufficient for a definite judgment that a particular action is to be done. And viewed abstractly, no motive is sufficient; all that can be said, abstractly, is that this or that action is choosable, not that it must be chosen.

How is the impasse broken? It cannot be broken by the intellect or by the choosable things. The things remain the same – they remain only "choosable", not "compelling choice". And the intellect judges accordingly, which means it is in a state of indeterminacy about making a decision. But the will itself may take away the indeterminacy by adhering to one of the possibilities and rejecting the others. Thus a new situation arises: a determinacy now exists, a befittingness of this form rather than another. And in a strictly practical judgment about the situation, the intellect bids: "Do this action, not that." This practical judgment of the intellect is the form according to which the will acts in actually willing a particular thing. But it is a judgment *caused by the will*, for it is a judgment of a determinate befittingness that arose on the part of the will; and it arose freely, for the will is not determined from its nature to this imperfect good rather than that.

The argument can be summarized as follows. The form according to which the will acts is the strictly practical (practico-practical) judgment that a certain action is to be done (or omitted). The human will is free about particular things if it can choose this form, that is, if it can cause this judgment. But it can do so, because (a) particular things are from themselves only choosable, not things that must be chosen; and (b) the intellect understands them as only choosable. So the will alone establishes that befittingness which causes the intellect to bid: "Do this here and now." But the will freely establishes this befittingness, for from its nature it is not determined to this rather than that.

To return to the dilemma with which we opened this section, it can now be seen how the will is free and yet subordinate to the intellect. First, the intellect sees the imperfect goodness that attracts the will; then the will takes away the indeterminacy; then the intellect, faced with a new situation – the new bent of the will towards the good object – bids:

"Choose this." The will does not break free of the intellect, but operates in its light at every stage of the deliberation and final choice. The will neither coerces the intellect nor is necessitated by it. It does not coerce it into judging that something is fully befitting which really isn't – on the contrary, a real befittingness now exists, established by the will itself. But the intellect does not necessitate the will, because it is the latter which establishes the befittingness according to which the intellect judges.

What is to be said of the objection that the will must follow the good which is judged to be greater (or greatest)? In a sense this statement is true, but must be rightly understood. We all experience cases where we abstractly believe one choice to be better than another, yet we go ahead and choose the lesser good. Abstract knowledge is insufficient; any knowledge is insufficient except that most practical of all judgments which is specified by the option of the will for one object rather than the other. The greater good in favour of which the intellect irresistibly judges has that character because of a befittingness freely established by the will.

Some philosophers reject free will because they think it involves action without a cause. If so-call free actions result from a cause, how can they be free? An effect depends on its cause, and therefore is not free. On the other hand, causeless action is absurd; and even if it were possible it would not be a perfection, but would make its possessor a creature of unaccountable, irresponsible whims.

The analysis of freedom we have just given is manifestly not of causeless activity. Causality is exerted by the will itself, and the intellect also causes – by proposing ends for attainment (final causality) and by specifying the will's actions. The notion that free activity would be causeless comes partly from taking causality exclusively in terms of the physical causality at work among bodies. But there are grades of reality, with an increasing domination over matter; and when the level is reached on which intellect and will are situated, causality there is not identical with that proper to bodies. The will is a real cause, but different from others in that it can choose which effect to execute, whereas a physical cause has no choice. Fire, for example, is the cause of the heat in a kettle of water, but the effect is necessary – the fire cannot choose to cool instead of heating.

Free will is sometimes rejected on the grounds that it is incompatible with the confident (and generally correct) predictions we all make about the behaviour of people we know. It is argued: We can predict a person's behaviour fairly accurately if we know him well. It is to be expected that we could predict it even more accurately if we knew him better. As in the case of scientific phenomena, the more data we have the better our predictions. Now, this shows determinism to be true. If people acted freely, we would not be able to say in advance which alternative they would select.

This argument disposes of the spurious notion of free will as causeless activity, but does not refute the genuine concept of freedom.

First of all, while our predictions are usually correct if we know the person well, they are sometimes wrong; and it would be begging the question to assume that they would always be right *if* we knew him thoroughly.

Secondly, in many everyday happenings one obvious course of action presents itself, and we have no particular reason to seek an alternative. If we wish to make a three-kilometre journey and the only transport is a bus, we will ordinarily catch the bus instead of walking. The prominence, or the easiness, or the conventionality of a particular choice leads us to select it. Because that choice is the obvious one, and nothing significant militates against it, we have no good reason to trouble about other possibilities; but that does not show that we are unfree to do so.

Thirdly, each new choice a person makes does not appear without antecedents, but is related to his character and his habits. He will sometimes act in an unexpected way (out of character, as we say), but acceptance of free will does not imply that he must be forever acting in unaccustomed ways. When he finds himself in a situation where a decision is called for, he will assess the position in the light of his accumulated knowledge, and will be inclined to follow the volitional habits he has developed through free acts over the years. But he *can*, and sometimes will, do otherwise.

4. Union of soul and body

All who admit a spiritual soul in man are faced with the question: Is man really one thing, or is he two in some kind of collaboration? Plato thought man is a soul using a body, the soul being the true man. Before living on earth in a body, each person had dwelt in another world as a pure spirit, and will return there after death. His aim should be to avoid future incarnations by detaching his desires from earthly things. Descartes, too, maintained that soul and body are two distinct substances, and although he insisted they are intimately united, he was unable to give any reasonable explanation of their union. Today those who accept a spiritual human soul generally reject Cartesian dualism; but while they explicitly reject it, most remain deeply influenced by it.

If man were two substances in some very close union, there would necessarily be two series of actions. When two men row a boat, each is a distinct operant, and his activity remains distinct from that of his companion, even though only one result occurs – the boat's movement. It would be the same if man were two entities, a body and a soul. Even though they acted harmoniously, two would be acting, not one; and there would be two activities, not one.

That concept of man contradicts his consciousness of himself. When someone says: "I drove the car", or "I thought about you", he experiences the unity of his ego, and knows himself as the source of his acts. He is aware of his body as part of himself, not as something alien in which he is dwelling. And bodily acts, such as seeing, hearing, remembering, are as much his own as are those of intellection and willing.

Man's unity cannot be explained by Cartesian dualism; and the realization of this has caused some to deny a spiritual human soul. They then assume, very often, that anyone who accepts a spiritual soul is a dualist. However, the Thomistic position is very far from dualism. We cannot explore it in detail here, but we can outline it.

St Thomas, following Aristotle, explains the union of body and soul through matter and form.[8] A physical entity is not indeterminate matter (substantial potency) but something specific, for example, a horse. That constituent which determines it to be a horse is called the substantial form. As regards man, the form that makes him human is his spiritual soul. The soul is at the same time a form and a soul: it is that which constitutes him as the specific thing he is, and which constitutes him living. And being a spirit, it places him in the highest grade of life – intellectual life.

The soul is not an efficient cause, or agent, united with a body which it moves. It is the formal cause of the body; which means that it constitutes, with primary matter, a determinate body. In other words, the soul does not merely make the body alive: it makes it a body, and it does this by being the formal or determining part of it. So when we speak of the human body, meaning that complete thing we can see and feel, we are not speaking of something that *has* a soul, but of something that *is* partly soul: the soul is the form, and the form is part of the complete thing.

The sentence "Man is composed of body and soul" is inaccurate if *body* is used in the everyday sense. In that sense *body* means a reality which is actual – a going concern, so to speak. But when a Thomist says, "Man is composed of body and soul", *body* does not signify anything actual. It means a material principle which cannot exist in isolation because of its indeterminacy. What exists is an entity resulting from the actualisation of a potency; or to put it in another way, from the determination of an indeterminacy; or again, from the informing of matter. But the potency, or indeterminacy, or matter, does not exist as such – to exist a thing must be actual, not potential.

After death the corpse is not, strictly speaking, a human body; it is a different thing from the body that previously existed. Just as in any other substantial change, the matter is no longer informed by the same form, and therefore the substance that previously existed no longer exists. The form still exists, for it is unique among substantial forms, being a spirit as well as the informing principle of a body. But the man does not exist: a disembodied soul is not a man.

When the soul is spoken of as a spirit, this does not mean a pure spirit, namely a being which is complete without a body. A separated soul continues to exist because it is intrinsically independent of matter, but it is incomplete in that separated state, requiring matter in order that a human being be constituted.

The hylomorphic union of human nature rules out the possibility of reincarnation of the soul in a succession of bodies. While the soul specifies the matter that it informs, making it human, the matter individualizes the soul, so that the person is *this* particular individual, e.g., Tom – not Dick, Harry, Anne, Mary or anyone else. The soul is not an isolated thing ready for union with any body that happens to be available, like a spoon of sugar that can be stirred into any cup of coffee. It is more like a key that will fit only one lock.

Another consequence is that each person had only one chance of existence. Unless a particular sperm fecundated a particular ovum, that individual would not have come into being. Another sperm and ovum would have resulted in another individual. Even the same sperm and another ovum, or vice versa, would have produced a different individual. This is obvious enough from the biological standpoint and in regard to the body. But the hylomorphic union of soul and body means that *different matter necessitates a different soul*. Souls are not like a row of motors, any one of which can be placed in any chassis.

A human being is a contingent reality – that is, he need not have existed: his existence lacks necessity. But we rarely realize how almost unbelievingly contingent he is. Tom could not have existed unless a certain sperm had united with a certain ovum, which implies he could not have been conceived a week earlier or a week later. Moreover, he could not have had other parents. So his existence demanded a convergence of millions of events from the beginning of the human race to the time of his conception: all the events needed to ensure that his ancestry be exactly as it was. If his grandparents had not lived, or had not married, or had not conceived when they did, he would never have existed. The same applies to his great-grandparents, and his great-great-grandparents, etc. Think of the fortuitous factors on which even one marriage depends, or even the factors leading to the couple meeting in the first place – the chance that they lived in adjacent suburbs, or had a common interest in sport, or were introduced by a mutual friend. The existence of each of us is very contingent indeed.

5. Integration versus schizophrenia

Is the bodily side of human nature a help or a hindrance to the spiritual? From what we have seen of the nature of man, in this and earlier chapters, it is clear that, simply speaking, it is a help, although per accidens it can be a hindrance.

It is simply speaking a help. Although the human soul can exist apart from the body, that state is not natural to it. It would be strange if the state of the separated soul were better than that of the complete human being, in spite of being unnatural.

The perfectioning of the higher powers of intellect and will depends dispositively on the perfection of sensitive powers. Imagine a person deprived from birth of the five external senses. He would never know anything, because all human knowledge begins from the senses. He would remain unconscious all his life. Sensation is necessary for the very existence of higher knowledge. And in general, the perfection of intellectual knowledge and of acts of will depends greatly on the perfection of sensitive life, especially on that of the internal senses and the emotional powers. This is strikingly clear from cases of brain damage or senility. The intellect and will of these people have not been damaged, for they are spiritual faculties. But their impaired sensitive powers are unable to serve the intellect adequately, with the result that it is unable to function as it should. And this affects the will: feeble understanding and judging result in feeble willing, and a diminution of freedom. Psychiatric disorders, too, exhibit the tie-up between sensible and intellective life. Disturbed imagination and emotions affect thinking and willing; while conversely, these influence the imagination and emotions.

Keen senses and ardent sensibility are more apt instruments of a high intellectual and volitional life. But due order must be maintained, these lower powers not being allowed to impede the higher, while the higher powers themselves must be rightly used. Otherwise chaos can result, whether initiated by the sensitive level storming the intellectual, or by errors of intellect and badness of will. The second possibility should not be forgotten, for there are sins of the spirit as well as of the flesh.

Disordered sensitive life can be a great hindrance to truth by causing a mental lopsidedness. Man strives for intuitive knowledge, that is, immediate apprehension of physically present things. He achieves this in external sensation. And this intuitive quality gives to sensation a vividness and concreteness not found in other knowledge. For this reason things sensed seem more real than those understood, and they draw us more easily. We have the feeling that because one thing is known more concretely than another, it is a more real thing. But the only realities man can contact directly are bodily things, which are on the lowest level of being. And the senses contact bodies only in their most superficial aspects – through colour, shape, and so on. In fact, they do not know the nature of these superficial aspects; as St Thomas says: "Sense apprehends *this coloured* [thing], but intellect apprehends the very nature of colour."[9] So there is the ever present danger of the understanding becoming warped by the vividness of sense experience.

Imagination, too, can play havoc with the intellect. Sensible qualities reproduced in the imagination contain much of the vividness and concreteness found in external sensation. By contrast, the apprehensions of the intellect seem, to some people, pale and unreal. So the illusion can arise that the objects of the imagination are more real than those of the intellect. This can go so far as to deny the reality of anything unimaginable. It may be a symptom of the extent to which this fallacy has spread that the words *unimaginable* and *inconceivable* are popularly used as synonymous. But to be conceivable is to be understandable, and the more elevated something is in the order of being, the more understandable it is – although not necessarily to us.[10] Imaginable things, on the contrary, are always corporeal.

Because of the sensible origin of its knowledge, the intellect must contend with a bias towards sensism, which in some respects is easier to grasp and accept than is an intellectual philosophy. Deeper penetration, however, shows the inadequacy of any form of sensism. A vague and restless awareness of this inadequacy, without knowing how to diagnose or overcome it, is part of the explanation of the confusion in modern philosophy.

Preponderance towards the sensible explains the difficulty of seeking a higher good when sensible goods solicit us. They seem so warm and inviting, while the goods understood by the intellect seem so cold and unappetizing. Our emotional powers are drawn to the palpable things of sense, and the will can easily follow. Swinburne speaks of:

"the lilies and languors of virtue
and the roses and raptures of vice."

The preponderance towards hedonism must be guarded against in searching out the true good for man.

Man tends to an ontological schizophrenia. On the one hand, sensible realities draw him vehemently, distorting his intellect and warping his will. This is a pull towards the surface of reality. On the other hand, unseen things attract him with their dimly perceived truth, goodness and beauty, their promise of a nobler and larger world than that accessible to the senses. This is a pull towards the depths of reality.

Some people with an awareness of vast realities beyond their grasp, realities they are struggling towards, feel that the body is a barrier in reaching them, and consequently that the body is an evil; while those who move in the opposite direction become immersed in sensible things, their outlook and lives become superficial, and fundamental things seem so many ghostly reflections of the sensible world.

We have seen the reason for this schizophrenia. Man does belong in two worlds. A compound of matter and spirit, he is attracted to each. In himself he sums up the whole of creation: the mineral, vegetative, sensitive and spiritual kingdoms all meet in him. This is what it means to be a rational animal. Because he is corporeal, he is vulnerable from matter – subject to illness and death for example, as well as to the lopsidedness we are discussing. Because he is rational and therefore has free will, he can disrupt himself as no irrational animal can: he is in danger of this terrible ontological schizophrenia, which is more fundamental than the psychological variety.

But he is a person, not a chaos of conflicting elements. And the remedy is integration. The lower powers are for the sake of the higher, so the sensible level must not be allowed to dominate. But this does not mean to become unfeeling: that would starve the intelligence and will. The ideal position would be to have keen senses, particularly the internal senses, and a strong emotional life; but guided and elevated by a powerful intellect and a healthy will. A knowledge of truth, at least a practical knowledge, is essential; otherwise a realistic coordination of actions is impossible, for light is lacking by which to coordinate them.

The achievement of integration of powers is something that must be worked at. So must intellectual penetration into the meaning of things: facility in this comes only slowly, and obstacles from a distracting imagination and from lazy habits of mind are difficult to eradicate. It is like any arduous undertaking for which we find ourselves unprepared. But it is worth the effort.

The philosopher is sometimes caricatured as an oddity remote from normal life and living in his own abstract world. This is very far from being a picture of the true philosopher. Jacques Maritain insists that the metaphysician should be keenly and profoundly aware of sensible objects, and steeped in existence by acute sensitive perception and by experiencing the sufferings and struggles of real life. He continues: "The Thomist philosopher is dubbed scholastic, a name derived from his most painful affliction. Scholastic pedantry is his peculiar foe. He must constantly triumph over his domestic adversary, the Professor."[11]

Instincts of man regarding his nature. A true philosophy of man should harmonize with the deepest longings and instincts of man regarding his life and destiny. Nature does not act pointlessly, so these instincts must have some basis. I am referring to such things as the longing for happiness and for immortality, the striving after justice and beauty, the inherent sense of the dignity and value of each human person, the desire for immutable truth. Such aspirations are explainable in the concept of man sketched in this and the previous chapters, but are unexplainable in an empiricist framework. Empiricism reduces all knowledge to sense knowledge, leaves no room for any destiny after death, reduces all good to what can be appetised sensibly. Man differs in degree, but not in kind, from the other animals.

It is not wishful thinking to want a fulfilment of these desires; it is as much a realistic goal of human endeavour as any of the things people desire – an urge to eat suggests that food is a requirement of human nature; an urge towards friendship suggests the same about that. If we find, as we do, that man also yearns for perfect happiness, for life after death, for absolute truth, justice and beauty, why assume these are idle dreams, impossible of fulfilment?

1 For the necessity of substance, see chapter twelve, section two.
2 Cf. chapter eight, section two.
3 *Critique of Pure Reason*, B 414, 415.
4 Chapter seven, section four.
5 Spinoza urges this argument; see *Ethics*, first part, appendix.
6 *Social Principles and the Democratic State*, p. 204.
7 Cf. St Thomas, *Summa Theol.*, I-II, q. 10, a. 2.
8 Cf. St Thomas, *Summa Theol.*, I, q, 76, aa. 1-8.
9 *QQ. Disp. De Veritate.*, q. 25, a. 1.
10 The correlation between being and understandability will be examined in chapter thirteen.
11 *Preface to Metaphysics* (1945 printing), p. 24.

Chapter Eleven

A CLASSIFICATION OF THE PHILOSOPHIC SCIENCES

Our main purpose in this chapter is to divide philosophy into its parts, and indicate what each part deals with. This requires a consideration of the degrees of formal abstraction exercised by the human intellect. Formal abstraction is the starting point in a classification of philosophy, and indeed of all science.

1. Total and formal abstraction[1]

We must first see the difference between formal abstraction and the process called total abstraction.

The latter abstracts *away* from reality, rather than abstracting *something of* reality. It consists in prescinding from the determinations of things, to consider them at a less determinate level. Suppose we start with the concept of man, and progressively remove determinations. Man is defined *rational animal*. Now we remove the determination *rational*, which leaves us with *animal*. This is defined *sensitive living body*. Next we drop *sensitive* and are left with *living body*, which is applicable to man, brute and plant. By dropping *living* we are left with *body*, and this fits any corporeal entity.

In this abstractive process, the concepts become wider in their application – there is a progressive increase in the number of things named. But how is the amplification achieved? By reducing the content of the concepts. Each concept in the series says less: each is emptier or less determinate, and for that reason names an ever growing circle of beings. It can be illustrated by comparison with a torch having an adjustable focus: it can be focused to stab the darkness with a sharp pencil of light, or to spread its beam widely. As the area of illumination is widened the light becomes weaker. More things are seen by increasing the spread of light, but they are seen less distinctly. In the same way, *body* names more things than *rational animal*, but names them less distinctly. There is an increase in extension, but at the cost of a diminution in intelligibility.

This mode of abstraction is necessary, and is practiced in common sense thinking and in all the sciences. But, for that very reason, it does not distinguish one science from another. For the process that does this, we must look to formal abstraction.

Formal abstraction is *of reality*, not *away from* reality – some reality is abstracted for closer examination. It does not prescind from the determinations of things, but seizes determinations. There is greater distinctness here, just as the torch shows things more distinctly when focused to a powerful beam. However, at this point the illustration fails, for the torch shows less things when it shines more strongly, but this does not apply to formal abstraction, because the determinations in question may be widely distributed. The concept of *being* as understood by the metaphysician is not only the richest concept, but is verified in all things: all are being, although in diverse ways.[2] Through formal abstraction greater actuality, distinctness, intelligibility are attained, in contrast with the potentiality, confusion and dimness had by the intellect before achieving this abstraction. Think of the clarity of mind possessed by a specialist in his particular field, and contrast it with the obscurity of the man in the street: the penetration of the mathematician, for example, as he faces questions of higher mathematics, questions which to most people would be shrouded in obscurity.

Formal abstraction is possible because the intellect can penetrate into reality, to contemplate the formal without the material. Distinction between the sciences arises from the fact that each science has its own way of viewing reality, its own mode of formal abstraction.

2. Classification of the speculative sciences[3]

In his commentary on the *De Trinitate* of Boethius, St Thomas gives a superb classification of speculative science, based on the degrees of formal abstraction. We have already noted, in chapter five, that the term *science* means "certain knowledge through causes" and should not be restricted to the empirical sciences. Taking science according to this classical definition, St Thomas arrives at the following division.[4]

These are
according to existence
and understanding   ... natural things

depend on
matter

according to existence
but not understanding .....Mathematicals

Certain
speculables

whether never in matter

do not
depend on
matter

or not always in matter ... Metaphysical
being

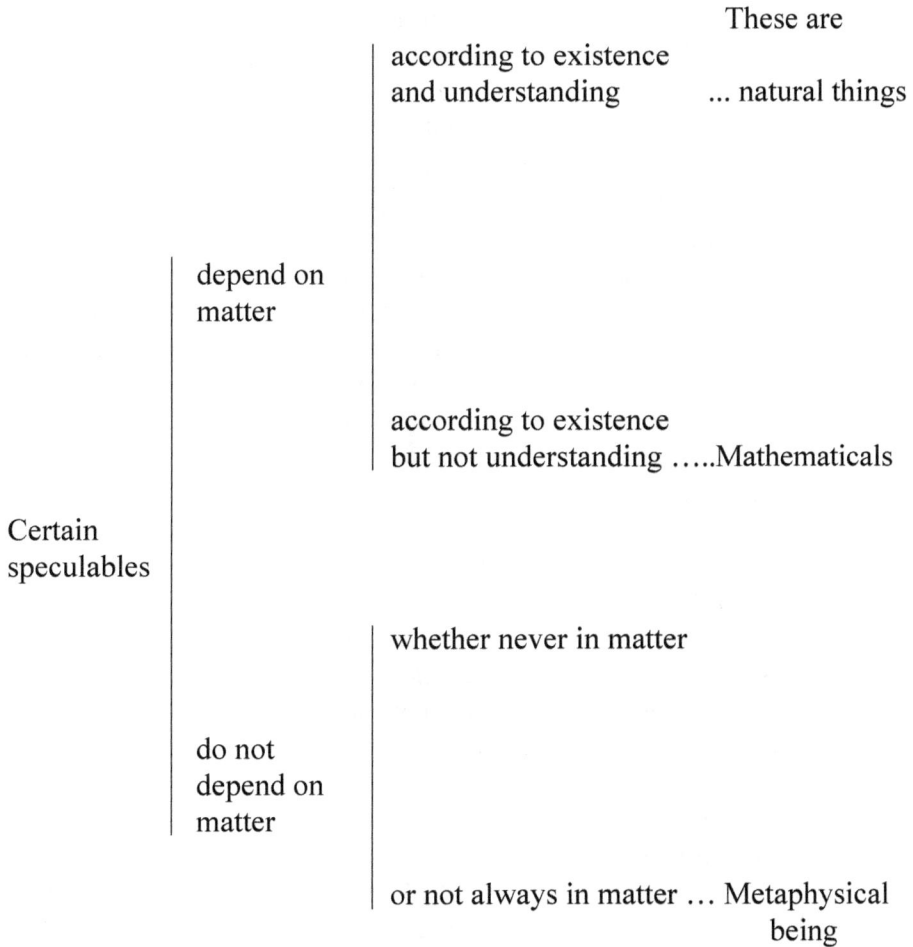

The first point to note about this classification is that it is concerned only with speculative, not with practical, sciences. With the latter, which are about actions to be done or things to be made, we shall deal in the next section.

Some things exist only in matter, others do not. The objects the physical sciences deal with cannot exist outside matter, and neither can those of natural philosophy, for these disciplines are about bodily realities. However, they deal with bodies from different standpoints. To recall what we said of the physical sciences in chapter five, they understand in terms of what is observed. The mineralogist knows silver in its observable properties: its malleability, its melting and boiling points, and similar phenomena. Empirical science is about phenomena.

Philosophy, on the other hand, is about the *being* of things. Natural philosophy is the study of the being of bodily things, living and non-living. It includes the treatise on the nature of knowledge; and from our examination of that question in previous chapters it is clear that it lies beyond the scope of physical science. Considerations of the two ways of having form, appropriative and non-appropriative; the degrees of immateriality; the distinction between sensitive and intellective knowledge – how could such considerations be dealt with by empirical science? Physics, chemistry and other sciences can investigate physical changes that take place in the knowing subject, but this does not tell us what knowledge is. Those sciences are confined to observable phenomena, as occultly indicative of essences, whereas an understanding of knowledge demands penetration into essences.

Formal abstraction, although it differs from one science to another, admits three general degrees. The first of these consists in dropping the individual characteristics of the corporeal things considered, and concentrating on their common nature. If the individual characteristics were retained, the knowledge would be of individuals, and would not be scientific knowledge. A physicist is not interested in the fact that *this* individual litre of water boils at a certain temperature, except as an instance of a general law. It is always the universal the scientist is interested in, not the particular instance. Science, whether philosophical or empirical, is not a collection of particulars. So at least the first degree of formal abstraction is necessary for any science: that is, abstraction from individuals.

Although a radical distinction exists between natural philosophy and physical science, both belong to the first degree of formal abstraction. Their distinction lies, as already said, in the manner in which they attain essences: penetratively in natural philosophy, phenomenally or in observable signs in empirical science. Both are about this sensible world, but the latter considers it sensibly, while the former considers it as being. And the objects studied depend on matter not only in their existence, but for their understanding. As St Thomas says: "They cannot be understood without sensible matter, as flesh and bones must be taken in the definition of man."[5]

The second division in the above schema is of those speculables which "depend on matter according to existence but not understanding." This brings us to the science of mathematics. In chapter one it was said mathematics is of quantity and its properties. Now we can see how the abstractive power of intellect makes this possible. The second degree of formal abstraction is not merely from individual matter, but from everything of matter except quantity. Quantity, continuous in geometry, discrete in arithmetic and algebra, is the determination the mathematician is interested in.

Quantity has a fundamental character: it underlies all the qualities of corporeal things, and is involved in all our sensations. Because it is so fundamental in things, it has been confused, by Descartes and others, with corporeal substance. This is an error, for there must be some substance which *has* quantity; however, quantity underlies all the other accidents. The intellect can abstract this most fundamental of all accidents, and consider it apart from the qualities that accompany it in reality. Quantity cannot exist without sensible matter, but it can be understood without it. But as thus understood it is not referred to sense perception as are the natural things of the positive sciences and natural philosophy. Yet it does not transcend the corporeal order, as do the objects of metaphysics. Mathematical being lies between the two, and is resolved in the imagination.

St Thomas says of mathematics: "Sensible conditions being removed, there still remains something imaginable; therefore in such things judgment should be made according to that which imagination manifests."[6] As an example, we could take the problem: Is a twelve inch ruler infinitely divisible? The answer is yes if we are speaking mathematically – that is, abstracting from the sensible matter of the ruler and judging it simply as extended. But the answer must be no if we are not making that abstraction, because there are physical limits to the division of a material thing.

The third division in the above schema is of speculables which "do not depend on matter, whether never in matter, or not always in matter." The science which deals with being on this level is metaphysics, the deepest of the philosophic disciplines. The abstraction required is the third degree of formal abstraction. In the first degree, individual matter was put aside, so that the universal could be attended to; in the second degree, all the sensible qualities were abstracted from, and matter as quantified was focused on.

In the third degree of abstraction, everything of matter is removed. The objects met here do not necessarily need matter in order to exist, and consequently matter must not be understood in the understanding of them – to attempt to do so would be to fail to understand them. Beauty, for example, is a perfection transcending the corporeal order, as Plato clearly saw. This does not mean that bodies lack beauty, but that it is not limited to them; and therefore the intellect, to understand beauty, must set aside the limitations of bodily being.

The proper object of metaphysics is being as being – not being as limited to bodies. This will become clearer in the following four chapters, devoted to metaphysics. Its concepts cannot be resolved in sense or imagination, but in intellect alone. Hence the abstraction required is the deepest, richest and most difficult of the three.

3. Practical science

We must now distinguish the speculative sciences from the practical. All science is of knowing – it is *knowledge* through causes. But knowing may be for its own sake; or it may be for the sake of operation: towards doing or making. The sciences we have so far viewed in this chapter are not directed to operation, but simply to attainment of truth. I am speaking of what they are *directly* occupied with. Indirectly they can be associated with operation – for example, when physics is applied to medical practice, or mathematics to measuring a field, or the insights of metaphysics to the leading of a morally good life. Speculative science studies an order it finds; practical science studies an essential, a quidditative, order which is to be brought into existence.

It is this direction towards human operation which diversifies practical science from speculative; a science whose knowing is ordered towards operation is practical. However, the order towards operation must be in the very structure and content of the science, diversifying it intrinsically, distinguishing it *from within* from the speculative sciences. If it were merely a question of the intention of the person pursuing a certain study, this would not distinguish the study.

Granted that a discipline is intrinsically ordered towards operation, it may be either remote from or proximate to operation. Moral philosophy is ordered to doing, but remotely. It is about the life that is fitting for man, investigating the guiding principles of that life, and seeing its various departments – personal, family, political, etc. – in the light of those principles. But it is remote from practice, for it does not apply its principles to concrete situations. A science that does so apply the principles is proximate to operation: jurisprudence and casuistry are examples.

4. The division of philosophy

From the explanation of formal abstraction and the distinction between speculative and practical science, we can proceed to an examination of the parts into which Thomistic philosophy is divided. The following schema shows a five-fold division; let us take each one separately.

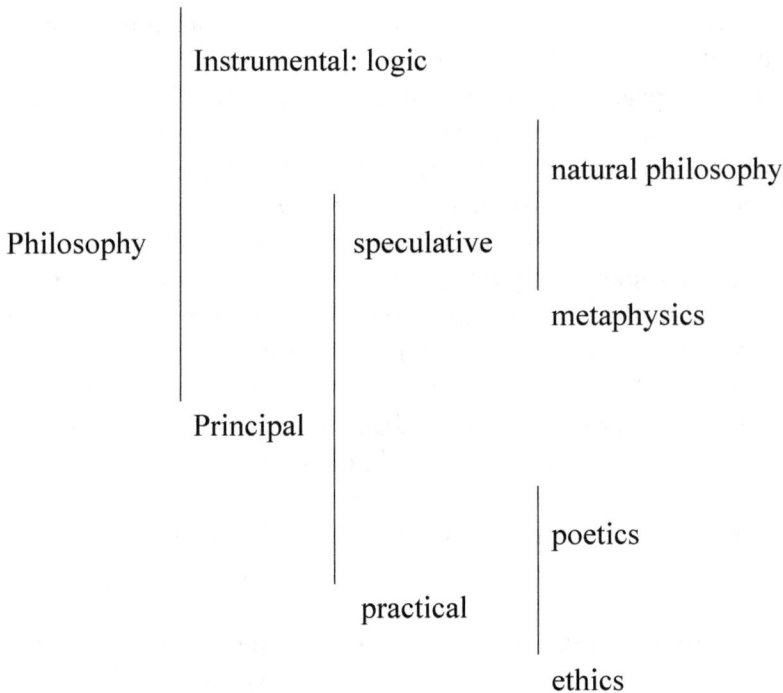

Philosophy
- Instrumental: logic
- Principal
  - speculative
    - natural philosophy
    - metaphysics
  - practical
    - poetics
    - ethics

Logic. Like psychology, logic studies mental acts; but from a different standpoint. The former investigates their psychological nature, whereas logic studies them as ordered to the attainment of truth. It studies the relations between subject and predicate in propositions, and the relations between propositions in argumentations; it exposes fallacious manners of arguing; it lays down the general principles of the various methods followed by different sciences – natural science, philosophy, sociology, etc.

All philosophy is a development of common sense knowledge,[7] and logic is a development of the common sense logic we naturally use. This everyday logic needs to be perfected: it is not clear and powerful enough to meet the demands of science, whether positive science, philosophy or sacred theology. Many people are incapable of close, orderly reasoning: they can't define their terms, they equivocate, and they become even more confused if faced with logical argumentation from someone else. These defects are due partly to unfamiliarity with the subject (politics, etc.) under discussion, but they are also due to a lack of education in logic.

What is the status of logic? It ranks as a science, for it studies causes – the causes of reasoning. But because it is about relations in reasoning, it is of mental being, not real being. Suppose a logician considers the sentence, "Caesar is crossing the Rubicon." His viewpoint is not that of the historian, or even that of the philosophical psychologist. The logician is interested in the relation between subject and predicate, which is a mental relation – something in the mind and incapable of existing outside the mind. To put it more generally, the order found within and between propositions is an order within the mind, and it is this mental order the logician studies. For this reason the other philosophic sciences have a better title to the name philosophy than logic has – they are about real being, not being which can exist only in the intellect.

Logic is essentially a speculative science, for it studies *an order we find* in our mental acts. But it has a practical role too, for it is concerned with showing us how to strengthen and perfect our reasoning.

Natural philosophy. Natural philosophy is the speculative science of sensible being. Like logic it belongs to the first degree of abstraction; unlike logic it deals with real being. It is distinguished from the positive sciences, as already noted, by the resolution of its concepts into being, not into the observable. This science comprises the whole philosophy of the sensible world. It is usually subdivided into cosmology, dealing with what pertains to bodies generally; and psychology, dealing with living bodies.

Cosmology investigates the nature of bodies. We have seen that crude attempts to answer this question were the beginning of Greek philosophy. Cosmology also deals with the meaning of quantity – real, not mathematical – and related questions, such as the continuum and the problem of infinite number. It investigates the nature of space, of time, of physical change.

The province of philosophical psychology is the living things of the world: their three grades – vegetative, sensible, intellective – their nature, powers and operations. Most of the topics of the previous five chapters belong to philosophical psychology.

It could be demurred that the study of the human soul and its powers of intellect and will belong to metaphysics, for these transcend the corporeal order and therefore pertain to the third degree of abstraction. This would be right if the soul were studied as separate from the total study of man. But it forms part of that total study. Just as the soul, in this life, exists as part of a compound which is man, it is through a study of the compound that we arrive at knowledge of the soul as something capable of existing apart from matter, as possessing two powers proper to itself – intellect and will. But the soul does not exist apart from matter in this life (what exists is the compound), and although understanding and willing are distinct from the organic acts, they are not separate from them. So it is through the proper object of psychology, sensible being – which "depends on matter according to existence and understanding" – that we know the rational soul. However, intellectual psychology borders on metaphysics; and questions about the soul after death are metaphysical questions.

Metaphysics. We now come to the third degree of formal abstraction. There is only one science on the second degree, namely, mathematics, because mathematics abstracts from everything of matter except quantity. And this abstraction distinguishes mathematics from the positive sciences on the one hand, and from philosophy on the other.

Metaphysics is the supreme philosophical science: it is philosophy in the fullest sense, because it penetrates most deeply into reality. And that deep penetration is possible only through the third degree of abstraction, for penetration into the depths of being involves setting aside the limitations of matter. Metaphysics unfolds what is contained in the concept of being – being simply, not being restricted to the corporeal order. It deals with act and potency; with essence and existence; with unity, truth, goodness and beauty. It studies the special modes, such as substance, in which being is realized. And because being is not static but dynamic, the four causes (material, formal, efficient, final) are examined in metaphysics. These topics are the central part of metaphysics.

But it also belongs to the supreme science to defend the principles of knowledge; and this is done in the treatise called epistemology. A third and final subdivision, theodicy or natural theology, deals with the supreme cause of all other being, God.

Poetics. Human activity is of two kinds: making and doing. The distinction is that in the first, some product results: the activity is a production, and terminates in something made. Doing, contrasted with making, is not unto a product: courage, for example, is a human act, but is not a production. Philosophy unfolds the deepest meanings of all things, so it must examine human making and doing. But these are practical, not speculative, and their study pertains to practical, not speculative, philosophy.

Poetics, or the philosophy of art, examines human making. It is not about *how to make* things, whether in the fine or the useful arts: that is the task of the artist or artisan. Philosophy, even when it deals with things as ordered towards operation, only deals with them from its own fundamental standpoint – otherwise it would cease to be philosophy. If a man who happens to be a philosopher designs an engine or composes a piece of music, he does so as a designer or a composer, not as a philosopher. As a philosopher he cannot even offer proximate advice about how the work is to be executed. Poetics deals with the nature, in general, of the arts, of their conditions and of the distinction between the fine arts, which are about beauty, and the useful arts, which are of products having utility.

Ethics. The scientific examination of the basic principles of human doing is ethics (or moral philosophy), which considers actions as ordered to an ultimate end. It shows what this is; it analyses the notion of morality and of the virtues and vices. In social ethics, the nature and functions of the various human societies (family, political, etc.) are studied, relatively to their ordination to man's ultimate end.

Conclusion. These five philosophic disciplines cover the whole range of being. The order of mental being is dealt with in logic; the order of real being in the other four: the speculative order in natural philosophy and metaphysics, the practical in poetics and ethics. All these sciences have the common character of understanding in terms of being, and therefore merit the name of philosophy. And because they understand in this way each gives the ultimate explanations within its own province. But because metaphysics alone understands in terms of being simply, that is, not being restricted to a particular order, metaphysics is the deepest of the five, and into it are resolved the principles of the other four.

Had God never made a Revelation to the human race, metaphysics would be the most profound scientific wisdom accessible to man. In fact, sacred theology is a greater wisdom, for it is a participation in knowledge proper to God.

Philosophy is a more perfect mode of knowledge than any of the empirical sciences, for they understand in terms of the observable. However, they are very important; not only, or chiefly, for the technology and numerous practical benefits they make possible, but for the speculative knowledge they give. The abstract character of man's reason, and the fact that he derives all his higher knowledge from sense experience, means that he can understand the natures of things only in a very inadequate way. This incompleteness is supplied for, to some extent, by the knowledge the empirical sciences give of the same realities on the level of phenomena. Physics and associated sciences should be closely linked with natural philosophy; experimental psychology and philosophical psychology should supplement each other; so should the positive social sciences and ethics. These various disciplines should be developed harmoniously, with each retaining its own character. In practice, they are too often confused with each other.

1   Cf. Cajetan, *prooemium in de Ente et Essentia,* conclusion.
2   See chapters twelve and thirteen.
3   Cf. Cajetan, *In I*, q. 1, a. 3, nn. 3-5.
4   *In Boethium de Trinitate*, q. 5, a. 1.
5   Ibid.
6   Ibid., q. 6, a. 2.
7   Chapter five, section one.

Chapter Twelve

FIRST PRINCIPLES

Metaphysics has the task of defending the fundamental principles. This cannot be done by inferior sciences, for they do not penetrate into the depths of being. In ontology, being is considered according to itself, and the following chapter will discuss this. In epistemology, being's knowability to us is examined. The proposition that being is in our minds through knowledge is critically vindicated. We have already seen this from a psychological viewpoint in discussing the nature of human knowledge. In this chapter, after a brief explanation of metaphysical being, we shall expound and defend the first principles, an understanding of which forms an essential part of epistemology, but is certainly not the whole of it.

1. Metaphysical being

References to "being as being" or "being forasmuch as it is being" or "being simply" as the object of metaphysics will convey only an obscure meaning. The meaning will become clearer, particularly in the next chapter, but a more explicit explanation is needed before we go any further.

Metaphysics considers the being which the mind sees when it has set aside the limitations of bodies. The being thus attained fits both bodily things and those above the bodily order;[1] the depth at which the metaphysician views things allows him to see in terms of what all reality has in common. It may be asked: But has all reality got anything in common? The answer must be that any commonness must be proportional, not univocal. For example, if beauty can be said of all things, it certainly cannot be said of all in exactly the same way: the beauty of a sunset is other than that of an opera. Similarly, the notion of being that we need here will have only a proportional commonness.

Another note will be its fundamental character. This almost goes without saying, for a notion that befits all is necessarily a fundamental notion. For the same reason there must be a simplicity about it: the complex, and especially the very complex, is analysed into simpler, and more fundamental, elements. Yet this notion of being will not be strictly simple: if it were it would not fit a host of diverse things.

Metaphysical being can be defined: *that which is or can be*; or *essence ordered to existence*. There is a distinction (which applies to all finite things, as will be seen later) between *what* something is and the *existence* whereby it is; that is, between the nature or essence and its existence. When we define it, existence is not put in the definition, yet the definition is not thus rendered incomplete. Man can be defined *rational animal* quite independently of whether anyone exists or not. This is because the nature, or what man essentially is, does not include existence.

But existence is important – uniquely important. There is an immense difference between something in the mind and the same thing really existing – and it is the act of existence that makes the difference. So the notion of being must include essence and existence – *what* receives the act of existence, and the *existence* it receives, or can receive.[2] I say "can receive" because a discussion of being is not necessarily about things as actually existing: it may be about things as "existable" although they have not, in fact, been actualised.

The above definition, *essence ordered to existence*, covers the two aspects of being: the essence and the existence. And it covers actually existing things and possibles, for the ordination to existence may be either fulfilled or not. The definition also involves the other points we have noted as necessary to any concept of being that fits both the corporeal and transcorporeal: proportional commonness; fundamentality; relative simplicity.

Firstly, this definition is common to all reality, but proportionally, not univocally. It fits both substance and accidents. A substance, like horse, is ordered to existence in self, not in another; an accident, like colour, is ordered to existence in another – in a substance. Taking a larger view, the definition fits the infinite and the finite, that is, God and creatures. The essence of God is identical with his existence; the essence of a creature is distinct from its existence.

Secondly, the definition is fundamental. Nothing is more fundamental to something than its essence and existence.

Thirdly, the relative simplicity of the concept of being appears from this definition. It will be shown in chapter fourteen that the only absolutely simple entity is God (so the order of essence and existence, in reference to him, does not pertain to him as he is in himself, but to our limited way of understanding him: we cannot form a concept of him in which his essence and existence would be seen as identical). But finite being is not strictly simple, for essence and existence are here distinct; and both must appear in its definition.

We use the word *being* with so many shades of meaning (in everyday speech as well as in philosophy) that attention must be paid to the context to see the exact sense intended. If we say, "The universe came into being from nothing", being signifies existence. The statement, "A new building has come into being", also refers to existence, but in a weaker sense, since the building was constructed from pre-existing materials and not created from nothing. When we say, "The centaur is a being which is part man and part horse", we are using the term being principally in the sense of essence or "kind of thing". Again, when logic is said to be about mental being, a considerable watering-down is had by comparison with real being. Discussing philosophy and empirical science, I have said that the former understands in terms of being, the latter in terms of the observable. This does not mean that the observable is non-being! The emphasis there was on the fact that philosophy penetrates into essences, while empirical science confines itself to the study of the surface level of reality revealed by the senses.

2. The basic principles[3]

The principle of contradiction.[4] Here as elsewhere in philosophy, the obscure notions of common sense are developed and clarified. Being is present in every act of intellection, as is the supreme principle of all reality and all thought. A dim and imperfect notion of being comes to the baby to initiate his intellectual life. The things he knows by his senses, but according to their phenomenal or appearance value, are dimly perceived by his intellect, but as being. This awareness of being is vague, yet concrete: vague because not yet clearly abstracted from the obscurity of matter, concrete because closely tied to the existing realities from which it derives. This first awareness is of something as opposed to nothing; and the intellectual vision of that *something* then grows clearer in itself and more clearly divided from nothingness. Thus are formed the concepts of being and its contradictory, nothingness. And from a comparison of these concepts arises the knowledge that being and nothingness are utterly opposed to each other.

It is a long journey from the primitive notion of being to the rich understanding that the great metaphysician has, and from the exercised awareness of the contradiction between being and non-being to a clear insight into the meaning and consequences of that position. We all start on that journey, but most of us stop somewhere on the way.

The supreme principle, or principle of contradiction, can be formulated: "It is impossible for the same thing at once to be and not to be in the same respect", or: "It is impossible to be and not be together", or: "Being is not non-being".

The principle is derived from an understanding of being, for being is understood to be the opposite of nothing, and the principle is an expression of that opposition. It is self-evident; that is, its truth is seen as soon as its terms are understood. The terms are *being* and *non-being*. When they are understood it is seen that they contradict each other, which is to understand the principle of contradiction.

Because it follows directly from the apprehension of being and nothing, it is the firmest of all principles, and all others presuppose it. Whatever judgment we make, we use this principle, for every judgment either affirms or denies something; but if this principle were not true, affirmation and negation would be the same – to deny would be to affirm. The statement, "It is raining" would not differ from "It is not raining". A person who would say, "The principle of contradiction is not true", would be using the principle in his claim to reject it, because his assertion, to mean anything, must imply that *is not* means the opposite of *is*.

As Aristotle points out, we can show that our defence of the principle is correct if our opponent will only speak; but if he refuses even to speak, "It is absurd to seek to give an account of our views to one who cannot give an account of anything, insofar as he cannot do so. For such a man, as such, is from the start no better than a vegetable."[5]

Some philosophers regard the supreme principle as a law of thought but not of things: it applies to our judgments, but not to external reality. This is at least logical for those who deny that our intellect knows real being. However, the first principle is a law of the mind – a law we employ in all our thinking – only because it is a law of external things. This follows from the truth of the realism of knowledge which we have already established. We apprehend being and judge about it. And our judgments are true insofar as they conform to reality, and false insofar as they conflict with reality. Reality is the standard. But if being were non-being, there would be no standard and no truth. Reality would contradict itself. What intelligible statement could be made about something that could both be and not be in the same respect? Such a "reality" would be meaningless. Consequently, any statement made about it would be meaningless.

Suppose I said to you: "I have a black and white dog." You would ask: "You mean, black in places and white in places?" And I replied: "No. Black all over and white all over." You would at once brand my statement as nonsense.

As a law of the mind the supreme principle can be formulated: "It is impossible together to affirm and deny the same of the same." But this is so only because being is not non-being. The stability of the principle as a law of logic derives from its stability in reality, and is unexplainable otherwise.

The principle of reason of being. This principle can be stated: "Whatever is has an explanation of its being"; or "No thing is without a reason". The expression "reason of being" is taken here in a wide sense, abstracting from whether the reason is in the thing itself or in something else. And reason here means explanation or foundation or ground. So the principle means that if something is, there is some reality that explains it. The principle is given in a logical form: "Every being is intelligible"; which means it can be understood by at least some intellect.

The principle of reason of being partly corresponds to what some philosophers call the principle of sufficient reason. However, the latter term is too restrictive, for it fails to distinguish between sufficient reason and efficacious reason.

The certainty of the principle derives, like that of the principle of contradiction, from the apprehension of being. Being is essence ordered towards existence. But order towards existence requires a reason or explanation, either in the very essence of the thing (God exists from himself, needing no external explanation) or in something else. If it were asserted that something might have no explanation (no ground for being rather than non-being), then this supposed thing would be both unintelligible and identical with nothingness. That which lacks an explanation is unintelligible: there is nothing for the intellect to grasp. That which has no reason for being is nothingness: this is precisely why it is nothingness. But being is the contradictory of nothing. So being must have a reason why it is.

This principle is not so immediate as the principle of contradiction, for it supposes the latter. That appears from the explanation just given, but may be clearer from the following reduction to the supreme principle. Reason of being is "that on account of which a thing is". Which means, "that without which the thing is not". So to assert that a thing *is* without a reason of being (a reason why it is) would be to assert that it *is* while lacking "that without which it is not". The assertion cancels itself out, contradicting the supreme principle.

It was said above that reason of being is taken in a wide sense, abstracting from whether it is in the thing under consideration or in something else. In the two principles to be examined next, efficient causality and finality, reason of being is considered as it is outside the things to be explained. They are caused things, having their explanation in another.

The principle of efficient causality. This can be formulated: "That which is not from itself is produced by another". Like the previous principles it is self-evident: its truth is seen when its terms are understood. It is of the nature of something "not from itself" to be produced by something else. The principle is explicated in the following syllogism. That which is not from itself is either from nothing, i.e., is without explanation, or is from another. But it cannot be from nothing, for this would violate the principle of reason of being. Therefore it is from another.

It would be a grave misunderstanding to think the principle of efficient causality means: "Everything has a cause." It is only applicable to things that are not self-explanatory; and in chapter fourteen the contingent realities subject to efficient causality will be shown to require a necessary being who is not subject to causality.

The principle of finality. This is formulated: "Every agent acts on account of an end." Agent means any operant, anything that acts, not necessarily an intelligent being. Acid is an agent which corrodes metal, for example. To say that an operant acts on account of an end is to take end as a final cause – that for the sake of which something is done.

An agent, in acting, is ordered towards its effect; it produces such an effect because it is such an agent. Acid corrodes metal and fire heats water because of their respective natures and the operative powers belonging to those natures.

An action is ordered towards a determinate effect. If it were not ordered towards its effect, it would not produce this rather than that. Nature would be full of surprises, anything resulting from any action. When you put the kettle on the fire, you would not know whether to expect hot water, a nuclear explosion or a musical composition. Strictly, there would be no reason for any effect to occur. Science would be impossible, for it is based on regularity. On the hypothesis that actions were not ordered to determinate effects, the existence of any effect, and the fact that an effect was this rather than that, would equally lack explanation or reason for being, So, as an efficient or productive cause, an action is the reason of being for its effect; the reason it *is* and the reason it is *this effect* rather than some other.

It follows that in the order of final causality, the effect is the reason of being of the action. For the action cannot be the reason its effect is, and is such, without the effect being that towards which the action tends – or that for the sake of which, or on account of which, the action takes place. The two – the efficient causality and the final causality – are like the convex and concave sides of a bowl: one is impossible without the other. The efficient cause is the producer of an effect; the final cause is the reason why the producer acts at all.

We are not naively taking finality that we find in human actions and transferring it to things in general. It is the analysis of action that forces on us the concept of finality, and causes us to see activity as bound up with finality, whether the activity is that of an intelligent being or not.

The principle of substance. There are two classes of things in the world: those that exist as independent realities, and those that exist only by adherence in something else. By an independent reality I do not mean totally independent, but "standing on its own feet", as it were, i.e., not a modification of something else. Water, grass, cats, people – these possess reality in their own right, and not as aspects of something deeper. Things of this class are called substances.

Think, by contrast, of beings like colour, size, thought, love: these are not entities capable of "standing on their own feet". They exist by inherence in something deeper, in whose existence they share. They are called accidents or (inasmuch as they are available to the senses) phenomena. An accident is not a being in its own right, but rather "a being of a being", or an aspect manifested by a substance; it "be-s in" a substance. Only in a restricted sense can it be called being or thing or reality; we must never think of an accident as a mini-substance.[6]

The principle of substance can be expressed in this formula: "Everything which simply speaking (*simpliciter*) *is*, is substance." That is, everything that is not a modification of something else.

Essence ordered to existence is the definition of being. But an essence may be order to be or exist either on its own or in something else. Now that which is apt to be on its own is a substance, e.g., a man or a horse. That which is apt to be in something else is an accident or phenomenon, e.g., the colour or shape of the man or the horse.

The assertion that only phenomena are real is self-contradictory. For something must either exist on its own or in another. But phenomena do not exist on their own: if they did they would be substances – colour, shape, etc., would be so many distinct substances. Therefore they exist in another. If that also existed in another, and so on indefinitely, an infinite regress would be involved. This is opposed to the principle of reason of being, for that which exists in another has the other as its reason of being. But to carry the process back to infinity would be to deny the existence of a reason of being. It would be like the islanders who lived by taking in each others' washing! The unavoidable conclusion is that substances are real.

Berkeley, while rejecting corporeal substance, at least saw that there cannot be unbased phenomena, and placed all sensible phenomena in spirits. Hume was more self-consistent in dispensing with all substances, including spirits; but his pure phenomenalism is even more repugnant to reason than Berkeley's position, because it presents a fleeting series of appearances with nothing underlying them: colours without anything coloured, shapes without anything shaped, thoughts without a thinker. It is the abolition of all independent existents, including man.

To deny substances is to contradict experience, both internal and external. Introspection shows me more than my mental states; it includes a perception – an intellectual perception – of the substance that has the states. As for external experience, this brings to the intellect more than a collection of sensible qualities: it brings an awareness of substances having sensible qualities. Of course, the substances are not sensed; but the same things known by the senses according to their appearance value are understood by the intellect according as they are substances. For this reason, words like man, horse, tree have a meaning for us that goes deeper than a collection of sense-data habitually found together.

In rejecting substances, many philosophers are really rejecting a false notion of substance deriving from Locke and Berkeley. Locke maintained that when we think of man, for example, all we have is an awareness of a combination of sensible qualities, together with a confused idea of an unknown something which supports them.[7] For Berkeley, material substance is a meaningless term; for it is supposed to be a support, but philosophers do not tell me, he says, what support would mean here. "It neither acts, nor perceives, nor is perceived; for this is all that is meant by saying it is an inert, senseless, unknown substance: which is a definition entirely made up of negatives, excepting only the relative notion of its standing under or supporting."[8]

The substance is the nature or essence of a thing that exists in its own right. It is not inert, but dynamic, for it is the source from which all powers and activities emanate. Although each kind of activity comes immediately from a particular power – for example, acts of vision from the power of sight, acts of touch from the power of touch – the radical source of all that is done is the substance. It is more correct to say that I see (meaning the substance) than to say that my sight sees (sight is rather that whereby I exercise vision).

Contrary to Locke, the idea of a particular substance is not the idea of a combination of sensible qualities, plus the vague notion of a hidden support. Since the substance of, say, an apple does not consist of a certain colour, shape, hardness, odour, flavour, etc., plus a support for all these, an idea that resolved itself into these would not be a true idea of an apple. An apple is a substance manifesting itself through these various accidents. The intellect does not stop at the manifestations but knows, through them, the manifested being. It is an imperfect knowledge, of course; but it is a knowledge of what is manifested, not of the accidents whereby it is manifested.

If only we were capable of a direct intellectual gaze into substances, we would have no need for imperfect, abstractive knowledge. We are not, so we have to get our knowledge through the senses; but we should not make the short-sighted mistake of denying intellectual perceptions, and reducing all knowledge to sense data. Here, as elsewhere in philosophy, our imagination sets traps for us. We try to picture what a substance looks like; and it is an impossible task because it doesn't look like anything. It is simply not imaginable. We feel that if only we could peel an onion fast enough, we would glimpse the substance! But the substance is not "beneath" the accidents in the sense of being situated in an area enclosed by them; and we cannot "glimpse" a substance with our eyes because it is not a possible object of the senses. It is worth pondering that even the most grossly corporeal things are sensible only in their manifesting accidents, while their essence or substance is accessible to the intellect alone.

The principle of change. This principle is enunciated: "Every change supposes a changeable subject." The denial of this would result in the doctrine that reality is a pure flow, or pure change, without any thing that changes. But this is to say there is change with nothing changed, or a change of nothing. Which is self-contradictory. Change requires an underlying something which has itself in one manner before the change and in another manner after it, as an animal which changes its position, or water which changes its temperature.

3. Difficulties proposed by empiricism and positivism

An empiricist would reject most of the foregoing as arbitrary, or meaningless, or tautological. To see his reason for this, consider Hume's criterion for discovering whether a philosophical term has any meaning. "When we entertain, therefore, any suspicion that a philosophical term is employed without any meaning or idea (as is but too frequent), we need but enquire, *from what impression is that supposed idea derived?* And if it is impossible to assign any, this will serve to confirm our suspicion. By bringing ideas into so clear a light, we may reasonably hope to remove all dispute, which may arise, concerning their nature and reality."[9]

This criterion is based on his position that "All our ideas or more feeble perceptions are copies of our impressions or more lively ones."[10] Since ideas are copies of sensible impressions, any possibility of supra-sensible knowledge, and of penetration into the natures of things, is ruled out. Hence, acceptance of being, of causality transcending phenomena, of substance, is illegitimate.

Philosophy has seen a gradual shift from reality to concepts (with Descartes and others), to sense impressions (with Hume), to language (with logical positivism). The last position is exemplified by A. J. Ayer.

Professor Ayer contends that philosophy is about language, and that many problems apparently about reality are actually linguistic. His point of view, if correct, would invalidate self-evident propositions as understood by Thomism. In chapter five, section one, we explained a self-evident (or analytic) proposition as one whose truth is seen as soon as its terms are understood. As examples we gave, "The whole is greater than the part", and "Good is to be sought and evil avoided". We also said that these principles are not arbitrary, but arise from the intelligibility seen in things. This realist understanding of analytic propositions is rejected by positivism. Let us look at the positivist alternative.

"A proposition is analytic," states Ayer, 'when its validity depends solely on the definitions of the symbols it contains."[11] But a language is constructed according to arbitrary conventions: grammatical rules and definitions of words come from custom; they are not something natural, and they vary from language to language, and even within the same language at different stages of its history. So the necessity of analytic propositions is not something grounded in reality – they are not made necessary by reality – but is due solely to the rules of our language.

Even the principle of contradiction is conventional, according to Professor Ayer. This was one of the points he discussed with Father F. C. Copleston in a BBC debate on logical positivism on June 13, 1949.[12] Father Copleston contended that one cannot admit the possibility of a piece of paper being both white and non-white at the same time. Professor Ayer replied that one cannot do so, given existing conventions about the use of the word "not". But a convention could be introduced according to which, when the paper was grey, it would be called "white and not-white".[13] In ordinary logic it is not allowable to violate the principle of contradiction; but it could be done in a different logic.[14]

Today deconstructionism expresses the same view. Criticizing it, Professor Peter Kreeft says: "The most fashionable philosophy in American universities today is Deconstructionism, and that's the explicit denial of the very essence of language: 'intentionality'. That's the technical, traditional term for the quality words have that makes them meaningful, significant, *signs* that point beyond themselves to objective reality."[15]

The extreme position is rejected by most philosophers, who realize that whatever status the primary principles should be accorded, they are certainly more than conventions found in some languages. Nevertheless, some who reject the uncompromising positivist and deconstructionist standpoint have been affected by it to the extent of doubting the fundamental existential importance of the principles.

We dealt in the previous section with the realism of the principles, showing how they are related to, and arise in our minds from, a perception of being. Here we need only add a couple of observations on the positivist position.

The claim that analytic propositions are only true because of linguistic conventions will not stand up to examination. It confuses the meaning of a proposition with the words through which the meaning is expressed. When an Englishman says: "This is my brother," he means the same as a Frenchman would by the completely different sounds: "*C'est mon frere.*" Every word is different, yet the meaning remains the same.

Three layers are present when we speak: on the superficial level are our words with their grammatical conventions; deeper down are the meanings, the concepts, they symbolize; deeper still are the realities presented in the concepts. The assertion that analytic propositions are true because of the conventions our language happens to have is an absurdity that ignores the symbolized to concentrate on the symbols – without asking what they are symbols of. Pressed to its logical conclusion it makes sentences meaningless, for it implies there is nothing for them to mean.

A piece of paper cannot be white and not white at the same time; and this has nothing to do with the conventions of our language. Suppose a language had the convention suggested by Professor Ayer of calling grey "white and not-white". In that case there would be a change in the words – a change in the first layer I mentioned in the previous paragraph. But what would the words "white and not-white" mean: what idea would they stand for? Exactly the same as the word grey stands for in our language. So the statement, "The paper is white and not-white", would mean, "The paper is grey". The principle of contradiction, far from being either bypassed or violated, would be exercised, because the subject "the paper" would be united to the predicate "white and not-white" by the copula "is". The statement would make sense precisely because an affirmation (symbolized by the word "is") is the opposite of a negation (symbolized by "is not").

Are the basic principles tautological? While rejecting the extreme stand of logical positivism, some philosophers nevertheless have grave doubts about the value of principles such as, "The whole is greater than the part", or "Being is not non-being". They object that the predicate of these propositions does no more than repeat the subject, and does not tell us anything new. Suppose I said: "Peter is Peter." This would be equivalent to saying: "Peter"; the additional words "is Peter" would convey no further information, but just repeat the subject. Similarly, it is argued, the sentence, "Being is not non-being," is a tautological utterance in which the predicate simply repeats what had been given in the subject, because "being" means "not non-being". So it appears that self-evident principles tell us nothing new; and if this is so, they cannot play the vitally important role in our understanding of reality that they are alleged to play.

In answer to the difficulty, it must be denied that self-evident propositions are tautological. Compare the above tautology, "Peter is Peter," with the sentence, "Man is a rational animal." The first tells us nothing; the second explicates something which was implicit in the subject "man". Certainly there is no difference in reality between "man" and "rational animal" – both terms name exactly the same thing. But the predicate advances our knowledge by making clear something that was veiled in the subject. And that is what the metaphysical principles do. Being is present in our minds, and has an inexhaustible richness of content. We see only a little of its richness at first, but our comprehension increases as we contemplate. The principle "being is not non-being" advances our knowledge by pointing out the dichotomy between reality and nothingness, and showing us the ultimate metaphysical and logical division.

Our verdict on the value of metaphysical principles, as on so much else in philosophy, depends on which position we hold regarding the nature of intellectual knowledge. Hume took a stand determined by his sensism; and positivism is built on the same foundation. Those with another concept of knowledge will inevitably view the principles in a different light. But one who finds himself dismissing them as tautologies should ponder the consequences of doing so, and decide whether to rethink his theory of knowledge.

[1]   Cf. St Thomas, *In Boeth. De Trinitate*, q. 5, a. 1.
[2]   St Thomas, *In I Periherm.*, lecture 5, n. 20.
[3]   Cf. R. Garrigou-Lagrange, *De Revelatione* (1925), pp. 253ff.
[4]   Aristotle, *Metaphysics*, book IV, chapter 3, 1005b 10 – chapter 7, 1012a 28.
[5]   Ibid., 1006a 13-15.
[6]   Cf. St Thomas, *QQ. Disp. de Veritate*, q. 27, a. 1, *ad* 8.
[7]   *An Essay Concerning Human Understanding*, book II, chapter 23, section 2.
[8]   *On the Principles of Human Knowledge*, section 68.
[9]   *An Enquiry Concerning Human Understanding*, section 2.
[10] Ibid.
[11] *Language, Truth and Logic* (1967 printing), p. 78.
[12] Published in *A Modern Introduction to Philosophy*, ed. Edwards and Pap, 1965 edition, pp. 726ff.
[13] P. 737.
[14] P. 740.
[15] Peter Kreeft, *A Refutation of Moral Relativism* (1999), p. 51.

Chapter Thirteen

SOME QUESTIONS OF ONTOLOGY

As was said earlier, ontology is the study of metaphysical being and the modes in which it is found. It is the central part of metaphysics, standing between epistemology, which vindicates our aptitude to know being, and natural theology, which studies the supreme cause. In this chapter we shall look at four very important questions of ontology: act and potency; essence and existence; the transcendentals ; analogy.

1. Act and potency

How are being and becoming reconcilable? In chapter one the extreme positions of Heraclitus and Parmenides were outlined. Heraclitus centred his attention on the changes in things, and made change or becoming the basic reality. For him, nature is a process, lacking all permanence. Parmenides went to the other extreme and claimed that being is fixed and absolute. Movement is an illusion.

Neither of these positions can explain reality. The claim that all nature, in its whole entity, is continually changing leaves no room for being, unity or rational principles. Implicitly it denies the principle of contradiction – and this makes all thinking impossible. If each thing, in its totality, is becoming, it lacks self-identity. It has no essence, and nothing can be affirmed or denied of it.

On the other hand, the principle of Parmenides that being *is*, without any change, equally leaves reality unexplainable for it reduces all things to one immobile being. What is needed is an understanding of being which accounts for the changes and multiplicity of things, and also for unity.

Parmenides thought he had reviewed all the possibilities. He said we can take as our first principle: It is (being is). Or we can take: It is not. Or we can take (or attempt to): It is and is not the same and not the same. He excluded the third way as nonsensical. And he excluded the second because "what is not" cannot affect or be the explanation of anything.

So the first principle must be: It is. He understood this to mean that there is only actually existing being, with no possibility of further things arising in the future; and that being is homogeneous. First, there is only actually existing being, because there is no source from which anything further could come: that which now is cannot become, for it already is; and being cannot arise from nothingness, for nothingness is not the source of anything. And this being must be homogeneous or undiversified, for a thing is not diversified by itself (since a thing is identical with itself); but being cannot be diversified by anything else, for there is nothing else.

The problem is insoluble if we understand being in a univocal sense; that is, as always meaning exactly the same. However, if being is not like that, but admits diversity *within itself*, the problem is soluble. The diversity must be *within* being; Parmenides was right in thinking that apart from being there is nothing, and that nothing cannot explain anything. Aristotle saw that the question is solved by the notions of act and potency, act explaining the perfections and unity of things, potency explaining their mutability and multiplicity.[1]

Suppose we are considering the perfection which consists in being a physicist, and want to know what is required to be a candidate for this perfection; or as Aristotle would say, to be in potency to this perfection. If we visited a university and found an actual physicist there, we could exclude him from our list of possibilities. He is already a physicist and is not in potency to becoming one. We could also exclude the office door, for a door is not only not a physicist, but cannot become one. What of a student at the university? He fulfils the requirements: he can become a physicist; he is in potency to that perfection.

This gives us an idea of what is meant by act and potency. A thing is in act regarding some perfection if it already has the perfection; it cannot become in that respect, for it already *is*. But if something lacks the perfection, it is not necessarily in potency to it. The door is an example: it cannot become a physicist. That which is in potency is that which is not, yet can be. Things have a real capacity to acquire what they do not yet possess, and it is this real capacity (potency) which makes possible the changes that take place, and also the fact of multiplicity. To understand this, we must look carefully at the two notions, act and potency, and compare them.

Act. The meaning of act, like that of being, is not univocal, but analogous. Further, because it is so basic, it cannot be defined by reference to something more basic. Descriptively, act means perfection; it names that which is the intrinsic perfection of something. It applies to "do" or operation, to form, to existence. So in ordinary speech, a doing is called activity or act: we speak of a kind act or say someone acted in a certain way. Secondly, form, or that whereby something is determined to be what it is, is called act: it is the actuality or essential perfection of the thing. Thirdly, existence is an act or perfection.

In general, act names only perfection, with no connotation of the imperfect; act, of itself, is not a defect: any defectiveness or imperfection found mingled in some act must be from another source. We are here taking the term act precisely according to its strict signification, and not in a loose and popular sense. If act were an intrinsic source or principle of defectiveness as well as a principle of perfection, the impossible situation would arise of the same principle making something better and worse in the same respect and at the same time. The perfection in which wisdom consists would make a philosopher more and less wise together, so that the more wisdom he had, the less he would have. The more perfect a saint became in goodness, the more fixed he would become in evil. The higher something was in the scale of existence, the lower it would be. But the same thing is not the explanation of opposites – of perfection and imperfection.

Potency. There is a correspondence between act and potency: each is analogous, each is a basic member of the division of actual being. While act names perfection, potency names imperfection – imperfectness, "unfinishedness", perfectibility. Something already existing may be a potency for a further act: sight is a potency for the act of vision; any appetitive power is a potency for its act. Substance is a potency in respect of accidents it can receive. An essence is a potency to the act of existence it receives, as will be shown in the following section. All these are mixed potencies; that is, they are actual in some respect, but in potency in another respect. Primary matter, on the other hand, is a pure potency. It is actuated by a substantial form, and with it constitutes a substance.

In general, the potential is the actualisable, the subject of perfection. Potency is not a mere absence of being, but is a real capacity for perfection. In the above example, the student has a real capacity to be a physicist. His intellect is in potency in that respect, and he thus differs from the physicist (who has the perfection in question), and from the office door (which cannot have it). Similarly, cold water is in potency to heat; hot water is not, but already has that perfection.

This does not mean, of course, that every change brings a greater perfection than was previously had. Perfections can be lost as well as gained; and if a perfection is lost, a lesser one may take its place.

Comparison. A potency and the act corresponding to it are really distinct from each other (the distinction is more than either a verbal or mental one). This is shown by the fact that they are separable: a man who is not actually seeing has not lost his power (potency) of sight. The distinction between them is also clear from their nature: potency is the determinable, while act is the determinant. So the same cannot be act and potency in the same respect. In diverse respects it can: an act can receive a further act to which it is in potency, as a substance which receives accidents – for example, water is actual, but is in potency to heat that it can receive. But to assert that the same thing can be potency and act in the same respect is to assert the contradictory. It would mean saying that to be heatable (not hot) and to be hot are identical.

So it cannot be said of being that "it is" in the Parmenidean sense. Change and multiplicity must be accounted for, and they can be explained only from the nature of being, not from an admixture of being and nothingness – for nothingness cannot enter into a mixture. Finite beings are never at the apex of actuality, but have within them the potential for further actualisation. But they are not pure becoming as the Heraclitean position supposes; that position destroys the actuality, the perfections, of things, melting them into a pure process without substance, without fixity, without meaning.

It is necessary to conclude that finite being cannot be either a pure oneness or a pure flow, but must embrace something of each. A principle of perfection or act is demanded; so is a principle of change and multiplicity, namely, potency. The proof can be set out as follows. Being not only *is*, but *can become*. But these require diverse explanations within being. Therefore, within being there is a principle or ground of what *is* and a principle or ground of becoming.

If we deny the first proposition, we must join either Heraclitus or Parmenides, and accept the impossible consequences of their positions. If we deny the second proposition, we must say that the explanation is outside being (which is to posit nothingness as an explanation) or else say that "the same thing is the reason of opposites" – that wisdom or heat is self-limiting, so that the wiser a man becomes the less wise he becomes, and the hotter something is the colder it is.

A similar argument can be proposed concerning unity and multiplicity. Being not only *is*, with a certain unity, but there is multiplicity – that is, there are many beings. But these truths require diverse explanations within being. Therefore, within being there is a principle of unity or oneness, and a principle of multiplicity or manyness.

It follows that two intrinsic principles are needed to account for any finite thing: a principle of act or perfection to explain its actuality, and a principle of potency to explain its limitations and becoming. "No act is found to be limited save by potency."[2] To say something is high in the scale of being is to say that it has greater actuality than lesser entities. We shall prove in the next chapter that there exists a being who is pure actuality, with no admixture of potency, namely, God.

Wherever something is found to be limited it is in potency in that respect. It might be asserted that a thing can be limited by its efficient cause – the cause, if defective, may produce a limited act. This is true, but an intrinsic cause of the limitation is still demanded – a potency in the product; and a defective producer will be one that only partially actualises this potency. So a candle will give less heat to a bucket of water than a furnace will. But the action of either heating agent presupposes in the water a potency for heat; without that intrinsic potency no heating, whether slight or great, could occur.

2. Essence and existence

Existence or be is an elusive yet vitally important aspect of the world. There is a big difference between an actually existing thing and the same thing in someone's mind: a gold mine on our property or a gold mine in our mind; an actually existing person or someone now dead. From one point of view existence makes all the difference. But from another point of view it makes no difference at all, for a thing can be understood without its existence necessarily being known. There are two aspects: the existence of the thing and its nature or essence; or to put it another way, *that* it is and *what* it is. The second does not imply the first (except in God, as we shall see). And to know what something is does not involve knowing that it exists. It may be something that existed once, but not now; or something (say, an invention) which will be brought into existence in the future.

I said above that existence is elusive. To see the point of this, reflect on your understanding of what it means. As noted, it does not mean the nature or *whatness* of a thing. We can enumerate all the parts of a man, and his existence won't be one of them, whether we take the essential definition of *rational animal*, or integral parts (legs, arms, head, etc.), or any other division we can devise. Existence adds to the nature; but what does it add? One is reminded of St Augustine's remark that he knows quite well what time is, provided no one asks him; but if he is asked for an explanation of time, it becomes clear that he does not know what it is. Similarly, we seem to know very well what existence is until we try to explain it; then its elusiveness, its mystery, forces itself upon us.

There is a tendency for philosophers to ignore existence and centre their attention on *what* things are. Existentialism is a reaction to this essentialist view of reality, and stresses the dynamism and the concrete being of man in the world. But the existentialists go to the other extreme, emptying out the nature of man, as though to make room for unimpeded existence. Nor do they see existence broadly enough. They centre their attention on man, and even then are interested in his behaviour more than his ontological existence. Their preoccupation is with what he does more than with the act whereby he is.

As noted, the essence or nature is what something is. It is what is expressed in the definition – e.g., of man or of triangle. It is that which constitutes a thing as one kind of thing rather than another.

There is a temptation to think of existence as an abstraction. But the existence of a thing is the most concrete or determined aspect of it. Things can have a common nature (e.g., man) with only individual differences, but they cannot have common existence. I exist by an existence proper to me, you by an existence proper to you – they are incommunicable. And the existence of a thing perfects the nature and all the attributes of that thing; as St Thomas says: "Be is the actuality of all acts, and on account of this it is the perfection of all perfections."[3]

This dynamic, concrete character is better signified by the word *be* than by *existence*, for the latter has a connotation of the static and abstract. Be corresponds to St Thomas' use of *esse*, which in his terminology signifies the act of existing, and not the infinitive *to exist*. So the translation *to be*, which is used by some Thomists, is inaccurate.

"Be is the most perfect of all, because it is compared to all as act; for nothing has actuality save inasmuch as it is; so be is the actuality of all things, and even of forms themselves."[4] Be names a perfection and actuality. It is the actuation of an essence, so that it no longer merely can be, but does be. It is an act of be-ing. And this actuating is a perfecting of the essence and all its attributes. Without be a thing would have only mental existence – it could be only an object in some mind. When that thing receives be it gains a place in the real world.

Be is difficult to conceive because it is not an essence, but rather something that happens to an essence. We are more at ease in thinking about what things are than in trying to grasp the be whereby they are. It is easy enough to drop the be and consider the essence – to think of man without his act of existence – but it is another matter when we attempt to drop the essence and reflect on the act of existence. An abstract notion of existence indeterminately taken arises in the mind – and this is just what it is not, for nothing else is so concrete and determined as the act of existing. The very words we use in speaking of existence have an essential, as opposed to existential, ring about them.

I said just above that be is "something that happens to an essence". But it is not "something" in the usual sense; it simply does not belong to the essential order. However, we all have a deep awareness of be, and see more than we can say.

Proof of the real distinction between essence and existence. When some essence exists, is there a real distinction between the essence and the existence whereby it is? By a real distinction is not meant a separation. Distinction names lack of identity. Two real aspects of the one thing are distinct, although not separate: a power of acting, such as sight, and the act of seeing; or the shape and colour of an apple. The power is really distinct from the activity – we retain our power of sight when our eyes are closed; and the shape and colour of the apple are distinct from each other, and not simply two words with the same meaning, or two ideas of exactly the same reality.

From the description just given of essence and existence, it follows that they are distinct. But this is a conclusion many philosophers have rejected, notably Suarezians; while many others have ignored the question completely. St Thomas teaches the real distinction in numerous places, and the thesis is of supreme importance in his philosophy.[5]

He gives one argument for the real distinction in the *De Ente et Essentia*, chapter IV. It can be expressed as follows. An essence cannot be understood without what belongs to it. But finite things can be understood without their be. Therefore their be is other than their essence.

The major premise means if any of the constituents of an essence are omitted a clear understanding of it cannot be had; e.g., if we leave out part of the definition of a geometrical figure, or leave *rational* out of man, defining him as *an animal*. The minor premise points out that such obscurity or ambiguity does not arise when we leave out *existence*.

We may have great difficulty in defining something clearly; in fact, we cannot give an essential definition of any physical substance except man: we can distinguish him from the lower animals by the difference *rational*, but how do we define horse so as to distinguish it from lion? We are forced to give a descriptive definition, not one that delineates the essential marks of horse, for we do not know what they are.

But in the search for definitions we are not impeded by leaving be out of consideration. It would not help in the slightest to include it. It is totally irrelevant to the nature or essence of the thing defined: it is, as we have said, something that happens to the essence, not something that belongs to it as a constituent part, nor is it the whole essence considered in a particular way.

A second proof proceeds from the concepts of act and potency, and can be formulated as follows. Anything whose be is its essence is pure act. But no being except God is pure act. Therefore no being except God has its be and essence identical.

In dealing with act and potency it was shown that act cannot be self-limiting, but can be limited only by reception in potency. But be is act. So when it is found to be limited this must be because it is not pure be, but is received in potency. A stone, a potato, a dog each has be, but not equally: the dog "be-s" more than the potato, and the potato than the stone. Why? Because the nature of each determines the degree of existence it can have.

This can be illustrated by three jars of different sizes; the amount of water that can be poured into each depends on the capacity of the jar.

Similarly, the degree of existence a nature – stone, potato or dog – can receive depends on the capacity of the nature. Now, suppose the nature and existence of something are identical. The existence will not be received in a nature, for it cannot be received in itself – receiver (potency) and received (act) are necessarily distinct. Such an existence will be unreceived. But act is not self-limiting. Therefore such an existence will be unlimited, i.e., pure act. And that means it will be unique; there cannot be two beings which are pure act, for there is no principle of diversity or differentiation in pure act: act is multiplied only by reception in potency. So it follows that the finite and multiplex things of our experience, and anything beyond our experience but less than the Supreme Being, have their essence and existence distinct.

An understanding of the real distinction is extremely important, for it reveals a fundamental composition in all finite actual being. We are thus enabled to prove creation, to avoid pantheism and refute agnosticism.

Immanuel Kant exemplifies the tendency, mentioned above, to ignore existence and concentrate on the essences of things. He states: "Existence is obviously not a real predicate, that is, it is not the concept of something which could be added to the concept of a thing. It is merely the positing of a thing, or of certain determinations, as existing in themselves."[6] Again: "The real contains no more than the merely possible. A hundred real thalers do not contain the least coin more than a hundred possible thalers."[7] He adds that we do not make the least addition to a thing when we declare that it *is*. If we did, "It would not be exactly the same thing that exists, but something more than we had thought in the concept."[8]

Kant saw that existence is not part of the nature of a thing. When we say, "Tigers are ferocious" or "Tigers are strong", we are asserting a real quality possessed by tigers. But existence is different: it is not one of the attributes, along with ferocity, strength, etc., possessed by tigers. Kant was right, and was in agreement with St Thomas, in excluding existence from attributes that make up what a thing is; he was wrong in treating existence as though it were not real. Existence is not the mere positing of a thing; and the real does contain more than the merely possible. An actually existing thing contains no more *essentially*, but its very existence is a perfection – the greatest of all perfections.

Reality has two aspects: *what* things are, and the be whereby they are, and these two merge only in God. Kant made the fatal mistake of treating the first aspect as though it were the whole; since existence would not fit into the concept of what a thing is, he dismissed it as irrelevant to thought. And his essentialist outlook has haunted philosophy to the present day.

3. Transcendental properties of being

Transcendental, as used here, means lacking restriction to a particular sphere, transcending this or that order and having application to all reality whatever. Property, as used here, means a transcendental which is more than a synonym of being, and which applies immediately to being. The words *thing* and *beauty* express transcendentals, for they apply to all reality; but they are not properties of being. Thing is excluded because it is a synonym of being: it says the same as being. And beauty is not a property because it is not *immediately* predicated of being, but only through the properties of truth and goodness. If being lacked truth and goodness it would consequently lack beauty, as we shall show in chapter sixteen.

It may be argued that being cannot have properties, on the grounds that a property is really distinct from its subject. For example, sight is a property or attribute of man, but it is a quality belonging to his nature, not something identical with his nature. If a man loses his sight he does not cease to have human nature. On this analogy, it seems that a property of being would be something additional to it, some added perfection. But this is impossible, because apart from being there is nothing.

This reasoning would be right if we were asserting physical properties of being. But those of which we are speaking are called metaphysical properties. A metaphysical property is the explication of something that was previously implicit. If we examine being we find certain characteristics necessarily implied, characteristics immediately consequent on the notion of being, but not expressly stated: these are the properties of being.

Firstly, being must be understood to negate division, for it necessarily has a certain unity; secondly, being is opposed to non-being, so it is "something" in the sense of "opposite to nothing"; thirdly, being is related to intellect, so it has the character of true; fourthly, it is related to appetite, or has the character of good. The properties in question – one (or unity), something, true, good – add nothing extraneous to being, but each is real being considered from a different standpoint.

One.[9] Every being has a certain unity. It is not a pure flow, although it is not necessarily perfectly simple or uncomposed . At least it is undivided from itself. It may be divisible, but if the division takes place it ceases to be what it was: a man is a unity, despite his complexity and changeability; if he gets cut in two he ceases to be a man. Loss of essential unity causes loss of existence. Transcendental unity applies to all things, not just bodies, for being is "essence ordered towards be", and a pure disunity is not an essence, nor is it apt for the perfection which is be.

Something. As was said in the previous chapter, the understanding that being is opposed to nothingness is the basis for formulating the principle of contradiction. The explicit understanding that being is the negation of non-entity gives us the metaphysical property named *something*. It is not something in the sense of "some reality", but in the sense of "other than non-being", or "opposite of nothingness". The placing of *something* as a property depends on a positive notion of being as essence ordered towards be. If being were thought of in a negative fashion as "non-nothing" it would mean exactly the same as something, which therefore would not explicate it. But granted that the concept of being is positive, a further clarification is had when it is understood as the opposite of nothingness, a clarification in which we see the absolute distance between being and nothingness.

True. We are concerned here with truth in its most fundamental sense: true, in this acceptation, is coextensive with being – it would not be transcendental otherwise. When we say that someone is truthful we mean that his statements are in conformity with his thought: what he says is what he thinks. In this sense a primitive tribesman may be a truthful man in saying that the earth is flat. But this truth leaves the possibility of error: in the example given the statement is not in conformity with reality. Again, when we call a judgment true, we mean it is in conformity with things – with the reality judged of. But the concept of transcendental truth is deeper than either of these meanings. It is not the conformity of our speech to our judgments, nor the conformity of our judgments to the reality judged about.

Ontological (or transcendental) truth has two aspects. Firstly, things are true in the sense that they are apt to cause a true judgment. Being, as we have seen, is the formal object of the intellect; the intellect's ordination to being is comparable to sight's ordination to colour. And this ordination means that things are apt to be truly known by the intellect. Any falling short will be on the part of the knower, not of the thing.

But why are things apt to cause true apprehensions and judgments about themselves? This brings us to the second aspect of ontological or transcendental truth. The very being or entity of things is true in itself, and is therefore apt to cause a true apprehension of itself in the intellect. The foundation of this truth-of-things is in their supreme cause, God, as will be considered in more detail in chapter fifteen. A thing is true because it conforms to the standard which determines what it must be. To take an instance from artificial things, the measurements of a house are true if they conform to the architect's blueprint, false if they deviate from it. Now, the blueprint, so to speak, of natural things – man, trees, water, etc. – is the idea of these in the divine mind. God understands himself as imitable in an infinity of ways, and each of these imitations of the divine nature is a possible being, an essence.

Truth has been defined classically as "conformity of intellect and reality".[10] St Thomas points out that there are two ways in which a reality can be referred to an intellect: the intellect may cause it, or it may cause knowledge of itself in the intellect. Operating practically, the intellect causes things; the example just given of an architect's design is an instance of this: he causes the house insofar as he formulates the plan of what it is to be. In that respect the resulting reality is from, and is measured by, his intellect. On the other hand, when the mind operates speculatively – that is, understanding things but not constructing them – the realities cause knowledge. My knowledge that the earth is spherical is caused by the reality, and the reality is the standard that measures the knowledge.

The measuring function my intellect has regarding the things I construct is had by God regarding all finite things. The reason will be developed in chapter fifteen. For the present, we can say this. Every cause produces something resembling itself; but God is the supreme cause of all things; therefore all resemble him. The very condition for a thing to be creatable is that it be an imitation (a very remote one, of course) of the Creator. So the foundation of the intelligibility of things, the ultimate reason they are what they are, is their conformity to their exemplar, God. And God understands his own nature as imitable in this or that way; which is to understand the finite essence which is such an imitation.

The transcendental notion of true fits the definition of truth as "conformity of intellect and reality", whether being is considered in its relation to the human intellect or to the divine. In relation to the human intellect, being is true because it is apt to cause a true estimation of itself: the conformity is at least aptitudinal, although not always actual, because we sometimes make mistakes. In relation to God's intellect being is true because always actually conformed to his understanding of it.[11]

Natural things measure our intellect in the sense that it must conform to them or it will lack truth: my intellect is conformed to reality in understanding that the earth is spherical; it would be disconformed from reality if it judged the earth to be flat. The divine intellect, on the contrary, is not a measured intellect, but a measuring one, for things must conform to it; and it is primarily in this that all things have transcendental truth: finite things because they are properly measured by God's intellect, God himself because he is improperly measured in the sense that he fully understands himself to be what he is.

Transcendental truth is not other than being itself, but is being or entity in its relation to intellect (whether a measuring or measured intellect). As St Thomas says, this truth is "entity: adequated to intellect, or adequating intellect to itself."[12]

Good.[13] The notion of good, like all primary notions, must be described rather than defined, because it cannot be resolved into more basic realities. It can be called the desirable or the object of appetite: whatever can be appetised is good in that respect. And what does appetite mean? We are not restricting it to sensible inclination, although it includes this. In general, appetite means an inclination, tendency or leaning towards something suitable; and this has three levels.

The first is a purely physical tendency – that is, without knowledge in the inclined thing – such as the tendency of a seed to grow into a tree. The second is the inclination that follows sensitive knowledge, and is called sensitive appetite. The third is the inclination that follows an understood good: and this is will. Anything is good that fits appetite (taking appetite in this quite general way).

It follows that all being is good. For being is essence ordered towards existence. But existence is a good: it is a perfection which actualises all the other perfections of a thing, as we have seen. And so self-preservation is a fundamental urge in all things, an urge that we see working most powerfully in irrational animals and in man. Every essence is good, too, for it reflects God, the supremely desirable and utterly perfect being; we have noted something of this in considering the truth of finite things. Even primary matter is good, for it is ordered towards form, which is a perfection.

As already said, the transcendental properties add nothing to being, but explicate it in some way. The very being of each thing is good, that is, apt to be appetised; in other words, its perfection and be constitute it desirable or related to appetite (whether to physical, sensitive or intellectual appetite). But the notion of being does not express this relation to appetite, whereas good does. So good is a transcendental property of being.

It may be thought that this is an abstract and rather uninspiring view of good. Where, for instance, does moral goodness come in?

In the first place, we can tend, erroneously, to think of being as something flat and uninteresting; if we do, the idea of transcendental good, or being as good, will seem equally flat and uninteresting. Secondly, the degree of goodness of a thing depends on the degree of being the thing has. Thirdly, as regards moral goodness, this is included in transcendental good, because the latter is analogous, extending itself over the whole range of goodness, whether physical, moral, etc.

The analogous character of transcendental goodness is seen not only in the fact that it embraces the various modes of good, but also in its division into fitting, pleasant and useful. Suppose we consider some good, say health. How is it good? First of all, it is good in its very being. Health is said of an organic constitution which is functioning normally. Now this normally functioning organic constitution is a good *thing* because it conserves the existence and increases the perfection of the plant, animal or man possessing it. It is not just good for something else, but is itself a perfection. Similarly, moral goodness is itself a perfection: it is not just good for the sake of something else. Intrinsic goodness is the fundamental goodness. In Scholastic terminology it is called the *bonum honestum*, which can be translated fitting good. It is something which is fit to be possessed because of its own perfection; so when possessed, it perfects the possessor. It is not only intrinsically fitting, but "enfits", or makes suitable, other things.

This can be illustrated by such examples of fitting goods as physical health, wisdom, moral rectitude. Various means must be taken towards the acquisition and conservation of these goods, and some of the requisite means may be difficult and unpleasant. To gain and conserve health, it may be necessary to take bitter medicine, to diet, etc. Arduous study is necessary for the attainment of wisdom. Moral struggles and the renunciation of selfishness are necessary for the attainment of a good moral life.

Bitter medicine, dieting, arduous study, moral struggling – does one find these good? Intrinsically, no. They are only "good for" something; they are means towards an end, and are good only through relation to the end they serve. In this sense, it is true that the end justifies the means. End is the only thing that can justify means; the character of order towards some end is of the definition of means – unless means were directed to something beyond themselves, they would not be means.

In a third sense, good means pleasant, or subjectively satisfying. Examples are the sensible pleasure consequent on good health, the intellectual pleasure (pleasure of will) found in the contemplation of objects of wisdom, the pleasure found by good people in their way of life. The good that is pleasure is found, of course, only in beings having knowledge: one must know before one can know something as pleasant. The pleasant good is closely linked with the fitting, because the possession of something fitting causes pleasure to arise in us. It is also possible, obviously, to derive pleasure from things that are unfitting.

To sum up. The being of each thing is a perfection, and this perfection of being when considered in its relation to appetite – or in its power to draw appetite – is called good. "The character of good," St Thomas says, "consists in this, that something is perfective of another through the manner of an end."[14] The very thing as perfecting something is called the fitting good (*bonum honestum*); the pleasure, whether sensitive or intellectual, found in something apprehended as good is the pleasant good (*bonum delectabile*); a mere means towards the attainment of a fitting or pleasant object is the useful good (*bonum utile*).

It might seem excessively, even naively, optimistic to claim that all things are good. Has philosophy no explanation of evil? Actually, there are three philosophical treatises on evil: one in ontology, dealing with the nature of evil; a second in natural theology, dealing with evil in relation to God's providence; and a third in ethics, dealing with moral evil. Let us now look at the nature of evil.

Evil is the opposite of good. But a thing is good because it is (actually or possibly) an object of desire; and it is this because of its perfection.

Evil, then, is a certain negation of perfection. There can be no such thing as transcendental evil existing alongside transcendental good. All being is essentially good, in the sense explained above, and this is incompatible with the existence of being which would be essentially evil.

In what way are things said to be evil? The answer must be: not in their entity, but privatively. The classic definition of evil is *Privation of good*.[15] A privation is more than a mere lack; it is the lack of something due. Sightlessness in a stone is not the same sort of lack as blindness in a man. The first is only a lack, for sight is not due to stones – they get on quite well without it. The second is a privation, for sight is due to a man, and in lacking it he suffers a deficiency. If a bird cannot fly, that is a privation and an evil; if a man cannot fly, that is a mere lack, for flying ability is not due to human nature.

When we think about it, we can see that we never call something evil because of its entity, but because of the adjoined privation of some good. A painting is bad because it fails to come up to the standard a work of art should have. Cancer is bad because it deprives the sufferer of the good which is health, or the greater good which is life. Immorality, such as an act of injustice, is bad because it takes away goodness (justice) that should be present. But would we call these evil if their opposites were not good? Suppose we had no artistic standards, no conception of health or life as good, no preference for justice over injustice. Then we would have no reason to give the name evil (bad) to poor paintings, cancer or acts of injustice. The very character of evil, or evil taken precisely as such, is privation of good. And consequently, the magnitude of an evil depends on the greatness of the good removed. For example, if I lose a finger, that is an evil because it is the privation of a good; but if I lose an arm, that is a greater evil because the privation of a greater good.

What of pain: surely it is both evil and positive? It is certainly positive; a toothache is not a mere negation of pleasure or comfort. But the sensation of pain does not imply *an evil being*. Just as the basic good is the fitting good – the *thing* which is good – and the possession of this by a knower results in pleasure, so there is something more basic than pain, namely a privation of what should be present, a disorder in the organism. This disorder gives rise to the pain. But the disorder or privation is not an evil entity: a decayed tooth is not evil as a being, but in its privation of due integrity.

4. Analogy[16]

At the beginning of chapter twelve it was pointed out that being is not univocal, but that there is flexibility in its meaning. A substance is being and so is an accident; God is being and so are creatures. Clearly the term being is not used in exactly the same sense in these diverse cases. The same applies to many other terms, such as goodness and beauty. To treat them as always saying exactly the same would be to run a steam-roller over reality, flattening all the differences into one monistic plain.

An equally untenable position is reached if we claim that these terms have utterly diverse meanings in different contexts; that there is no more resemblance between the beauty of a rose and that of an opera than there is between the word tick as used of an insect and of the sound of a clock. That view would cut the world into unrelated pieces.

When a predicate is said of two or more things in the same sense, it is called univocal; for example *man* predicated of Peter and Paul, or *animal* predicated of horse and tiger. A predicate said of two things in utterly diverse senses is called equivocal; for example, the word tick as used just above, or pupil said of a student and of part of the eye. Analogous predicates come between these extremes. However this can happen in three different manners, which gives rise to three modes of analogy, called analogy of attribution, analogy of metaphorical proportionality and analogy of proper proportionality. Let us examine each.

Three modes of analogy. An example of the first is the predicate *human* said of Peter, of his emotions, of his shape and of a footprint he leaves in the sand. When we say, "Peter is human", we are not naming some attribute he possesses, or something related to him. We are saying what he is: there is no distinction between Peter and his humanity. But when we speak of human emotions, or a human shape, or a human footprint, we are not speaking of something identical with human but of something related to it. Peter's emotions proceed from one of his powers; his shape is what it is because he is a man and not some other creature; his footprint is the kind left by a human, not by a dog or horse.

From this appears the reason for the name, analogy of attribution. The principal subject or analogate, Peter, is identical with human, while all the others are secondary analogates to which the name human is attributed because they bear some relation to the principal. They are not identical with the analogous character (human) but related to it.

The other two modes of analogy differ from the first because each analogate is identical with the analogous character. Being, said of God and creatures, or of substance and accidents, is an example. In naming each of these *being*, we are saying what it is, not what it is related to. Similarly, when the term anger is given to the passion of an animal and to the storminess of the sea, it says what the thing is, not what it is related to. But there is this great difference: in the first case, the analogous term (being) is used *properly* of each subject; in the second case, the term (anger) is used metaphorically of one. The first is called analogy of proper proportionality, the second analogy of metaphoric proportionality. By examining each we should be able to see their distinction.

God and creatures, substance and accidents are called being because they literally are being: the character of *essence ordered towards be* is true of each, without metaphor. But in the other example, anger is literally in only one analogate. An animal can be angry; a sea, strictly speaking, can't be. Anger is a passion, and is found only in sentient things, not in a lifeless ocean. Why, then, do we say, "The sea is angry"? The turbulence of the sea is called anger because it produces effects similar to those caused by an angry animal. That wild sea is menacing and destructive, just as an angry animal. The sea's turbulence is called anger because of what it is, not what it is related to; however, it is not *formally* anger, but *virtually*: i.e., it is a menacing and destructive power with effects like those of an angry animal.

What does proportionality mean? the diversity found among analogates retains a certain proportionality. Take the analogy of being. Being is always essence ordered towards be, or proportioned to be, but there is vast diversity in the manners in which this is realized: God does not be in the same manner as a creature, or a substance in the manner of an accident. But there is a proportionality between the essence of God and the subsistent be with which it is identified, and the essence of a creature and its received be; as between a substantial essence (such as tree) and the be-in-self which it has, and an accidental essence (such as shape) and the be-in-another – in a substance – which it has. However, it is important to see that the resemblance between the terms of analogues – substantial essence, substantial be; accidental essence, accidental be – is only a secondary resemblance, and consequently the proportionality between two analogues is not like mathematical equality, e.g., three-sixths equals four-eights. Each of these fractions is univocally a half; and a single proportion exists between them. But being is not simply, only secondarily, the same in its diverse modes; and a secondary proportionality, not a simply proportion, exists between them. Three is related to six in exactly the same proportion as four is related to eight; but the essence of a substance is not related to its be in exactly the same fashion as the essence of an accident to its be.

It should be stressed that analogy of proper proportionality is often found together with analogy of attribution. Failure to see this can lead to a misunderstanding of various texts of St Thomas where he speaks of both.[17] Being can be defined, from an existential standpoint, as being which is actual by its very essence – pure being without potency, and without dependence on anything else. God alone is being in this sense; and all other things are called being because they are related to him as effects to their cause. They exist by participation, but he by essence. And this is analogy of attribution. It is like calling a footprint human because it is related to that which *is* human, namely, a man.

Schematic summary:

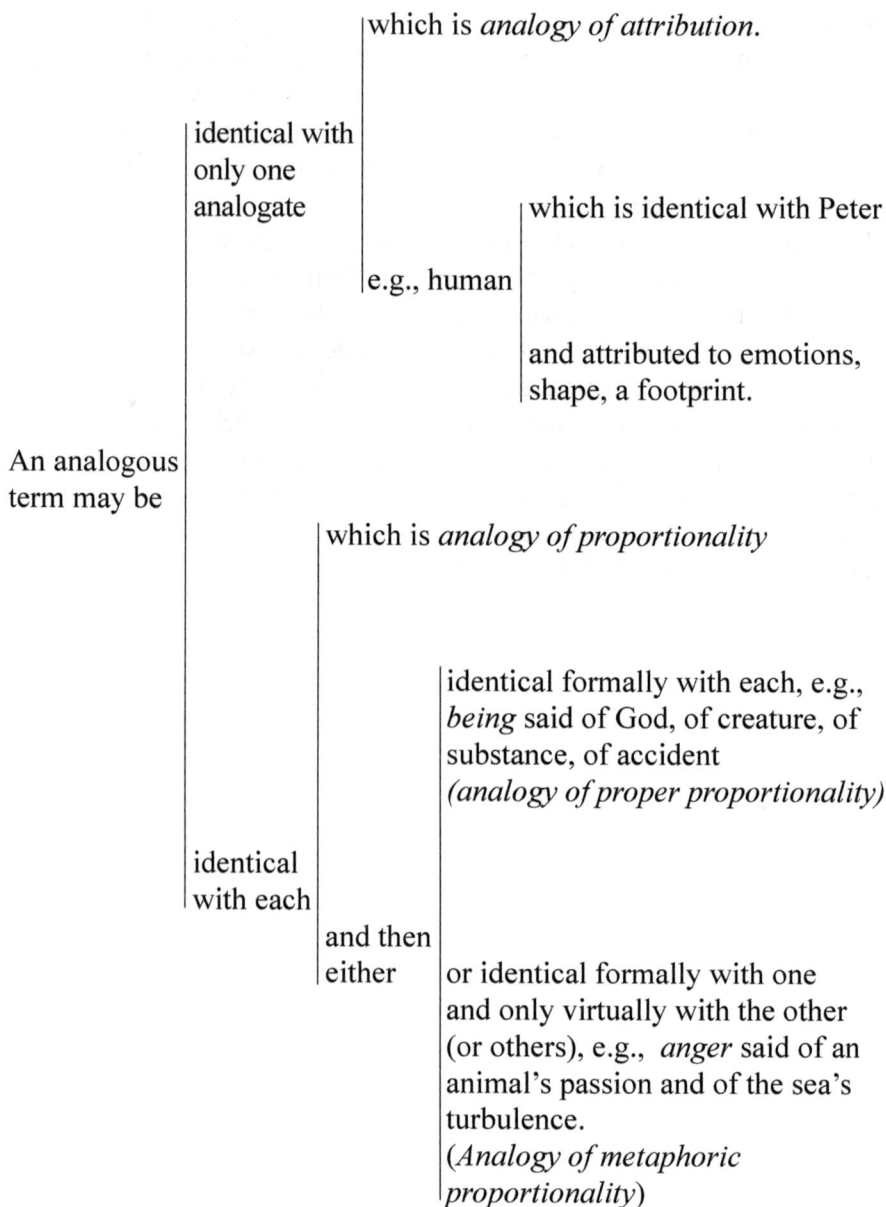

which is *analogy of attribution.*

identical with
only one
analogate

which is identical with Peter

e.g., human

and attributed to emotions,
shape, a footprint.

An analogous
term may be

which is *analogy of proportionality*

identical formally with each, e.g.,
being said of God, of creature, of
substance, of accident
(analogy of proper proportionality)

identical
with each

and then
either

or identical formally with one
and only virtually with the other
(or others), e.g., *anger* said of an
animal's passion and of the sea's
turbulence.
(*Analogy of metaphoric
proportionality*)

1   Aristotle undertakes a detailed examination of act and potency in his *Metaphysics*, book IX.

2   St Thomas, *Comp. Theol.*, chapter 18.

3   *QQ. Disp. de Pot.*, q. 7, a. 2, *ad* 9.

4   *Summa Theol.*, I, q. 4, a. 1, *ad* 3.

5   *Cf. In Boeth. De Hebdomadibus*, chapter 2; *QQ. Disp. de Verit.*, q. 27, a. 1, *ad* 8; *Con. Gent.*, I, 22, nn. 8, 9; *Summa Theol* I, q. 6, a. 3, *ad* 2.

6   *Critique of Pure Reason*, B 626.

7   B 627.

8   B 628.

9   Cf. St Thomas, *Summa Theol.*, I, q. 11, a. 1; *In X Meta.*, lecture 4.

10   Cf. *Summa Theol.*, I, q. 16, a. 1.

11   Cf. *QQ. Disp. de Verit.*, q. 1, a. 2.

12   Ibid. , a. 4.

13   *Summa Theol.*, I, q. 5, aa. 1-6.

14   *QQ. Disp. de Verit.*, q. 21, a. 2.

15   For the history of this definition, see Charles Journet, *The Meaning of Evil* (1963), chapter 2, section 2.

16   John of St Thomas, *Logic*, part 2, q. 13, aa. 3-5.

17   Cf. *QQ. Disp. de Verit.*, q. 2, a. 11; *In I Ethics.*, lecture 7.

Chapter Fourteen

THE EXISTENCE OF GOD

Now we come to the final subdivision of metaphysics, theodicy or natural theology. This is the most sublime part of philosophy, the highest peak the philosophic reason can reach. In this treatise the existence of God is proved, atheism and agnosticism are answered, and human reason explores, as far as it can, the nature of the Supreme Being (his perfection, eternity and transcendence, his understanding and life, his will and power, etc.) and his creation, conservation and government of the world.

1. Preliminary

Status of natural theology. The question arises: How can natural theology be a part of metaphysics since it deals with the Supreme Being, whereas metaphysics deals with being in common? The answer must be that God is not studied directly in natural theology, for we attain knowledge of him through the study of metaphysical being.

The method will be seen more clearly as we proceed, but can be outlined as follows. We take the things that fall under our senses, the things of our experience, and look at them in the light of metaphysical principles and at the level of formal abstraction proper to metaphysics. We see that these things are dependent, that they demand an explanation beyond themselves. In the light of the principles we seek that first cause, and develop proofs of its existence. Then, still under the light of metaphysical principles, we learn what we can of the nature and activities of the first cause.

God cannot be the subject-matter of natural theology, for he is known only through his effects. He is reached as a predicate, not as a subject: we argue *to him* from other things, not *from him* to other things. Certainly natural theology is partly deductive, for after showing the existence of the first cause we go on to deduce conclusions about his nature; but as he is reached only through his effects, the deductions are from God as thus known.

Before examining St Thomas' proofs we must grasp the notion of a proper cause and also the principle of limited regression.

Proper cause. A proper cause is one that cannot be dispensed with, if the effect is to take place. If this cause operates, the effect *necessarily* occurs; if it does not operate, the effect cannot occur. So if the effect is "a man generated" the cause must be "a man generating". If the cause given was "an animal generating" this would be true, for man is an animal – a rational animal – but it would not assign the *proper* cause, for there are other animals besides man. So the cause assigned would be too wide, too indefinite. But if the cause were given as "Socrates generating" this would be too narrow, for the *proper* effect of Socrates generating is "son of Socrates generated"; but for the generation of a man it is not necessary that Socrates be the generant. The proper cause is neither wider nor narrower than is required for the effect.

In arguing to the existence of God, we must argue from effects to their proper cause. Suppose I found a broken stick lying on a path, and argued that it had been broken by a person stepping on it. This would have a certain probability, but would be inconclusive, because the cause assigned is not the proper cause of a broken stick. Many other agents can achieve the same effect – a horse, a falling rock, etc. Likewise if I put forward some effect as evidence of God, and on examination it turns out to be an effect a being other than God could achieve, I have failed to prove my case. A conclusive proof of God's existence must be based on proper effects of God – on effects he alone could produce.

The principle of limited regression. Some people, attempting to prove there is a God, argue from the premise that everything in the world must have had a beginning. They say that if we went back far enough, even if it were trillions of years, we would eventually reach a beginning. Certainly, we cannot make this trip through time; but there is no need to, they assert, for the notion of a universe without a beginning is absurd. But nothing can't turn its non-existent self into something; so there must be an eternal being who made the world.

Agnostics usually reply that a universe without a beginning is not absurd. And they often assume that all theists disagree with them. But St Thomas expressly states: "It is held by faith alone, and cannot be demonstratively proved, that the world has not been always."[1] The arguments he gives for the existence of God do not depend on the premise that the world had a beginning. This truth, taught by the Bible, is simply abstracted from, and God's existence is established independently of it.

But there is a principle, common to all five of St Thomas' ways, called the principle of limited regression. This can be formulated: In causes essentially subordinated there can be no infinite regression.

A series of causes may be either of two kinds. It may be a series where each member – each individual cause – does not depend on the preceding ones; and this is called accidental subordination. Or it may be a series where each cause, precisely as it causes, depends on a preceding one; and this is called essential subordination, or subordination *per se*. To give an example of the first kind, suppose a carpenter successively breaks each hammer he is using. Each new hammer acts after the preceding one, and when it breaks a further hammer acts in its stead. But the very activity of each hammer is independent of those that preceded it. This is called accidental subordination because although there is a series of causes, each is independent of the others in the causing it does.[2] St Thomas held that there is no absurdity in such a series stretching back forever into the past.

As an example of the other kind of subordination among causes, take the activity exercised in driving nails into wood. The hammer causes the nail to penetrate the wood, but dependently on the carpenter's hand which moves the hammer. And his hand moves dependently on his arm, and his arm dependently on motor nerves, and so on. These causes are subordinated precisely as causes: the causal efficacy passes from one to another. And in this they differ from the series of hammers.

But essentially subordinated causes cannot explain the causality they exercise; they are conveyers of causality, not originators, and its ultimate explanation must be sought elsewhere. That which is subordinated in causing, i.e., causes dependently on something else, supposes something unsubordinated in causing. Otherwise causality would be without a reason of being, which involves a contradiction.[3] The objection that the series might be infinite is irrelevant, for a series of subordinated causes, even if it could be infinite, necessarily leaves causality unexplained.

The five ways.[4] St Thomas' procedure starts with the observation of an aspect of finite things in which some deficiency is found. He first shows that this demands a cause which is free from that deficiency. Later he shows that this prime cause is absolutely perfect.

In the progressive consideration of things, five deficiencies appear. Things need to be acted upon before they can act; the very causality they exercise is itself caused; their existence is contingent; their perfections are mingled with imperfection; they depend on an end towards which they are ordered. Each of these deficiencies gives the starting point for a proof of God's existence. The fact – the deficiency – is examined under the light of two principles: the principle of limited regression and another principle, different for each proof, which constitutes the *proper* principle of each way.

The criticism is often made that the first three ways are really three formulations of one argument. However, this is impossible because each (a) proceeds from a different fact, i.e., movement, caused causality, contingent existence; (b) uses a different principle; (c) issues in a different immediate conclusion.

The following schema shows the architecture of the five ways.

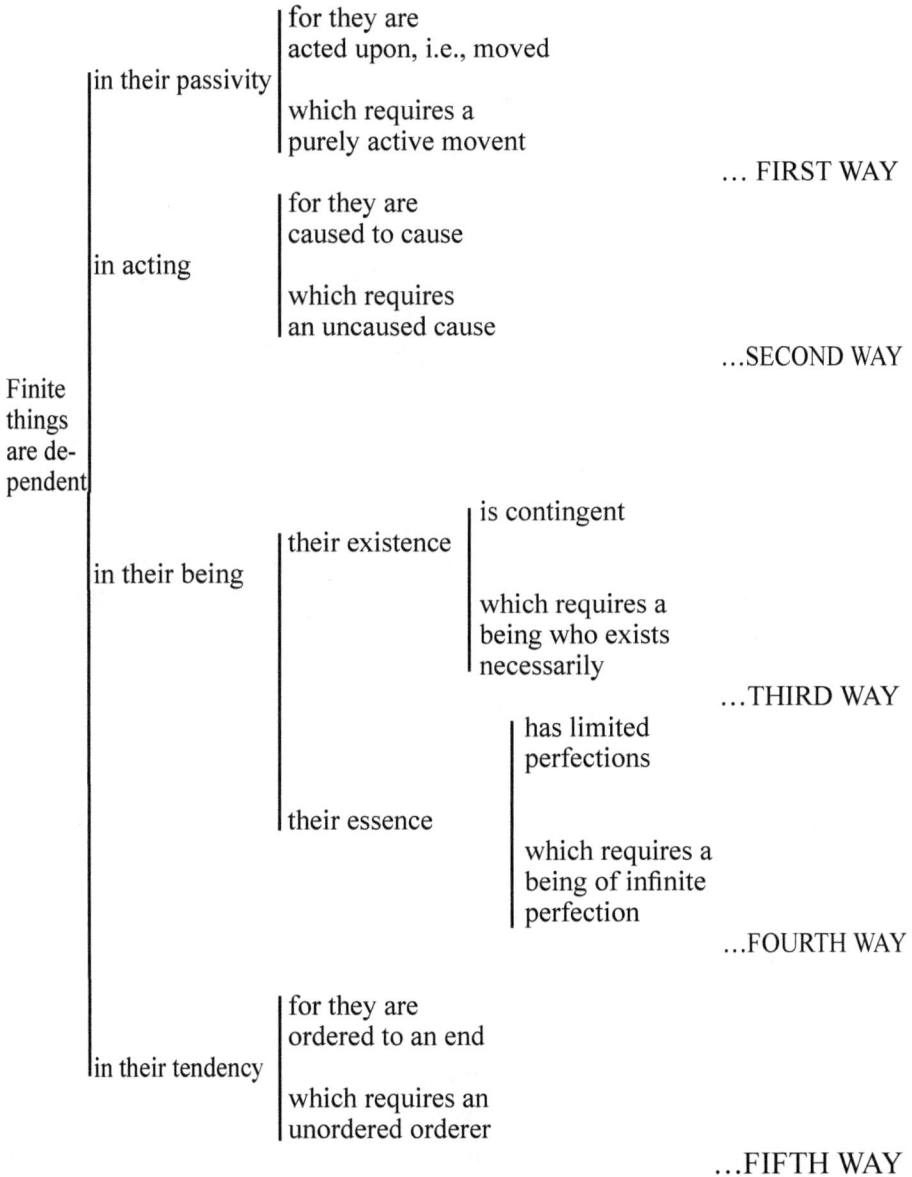

in their passivity — for they are acted upon, i.e., moved

which requires a purely active movent

... FIRST WAY

in acting — for they are caused to cause

which requires an uncaused cause

...SECOND WAY

Finite things are dependent

in their being — their existence — is contingent

which requires a being who exists necessarily

...THIRD WAY

their essence — has limited perfections

which requires a being of infinite perfection

...FOURTH WAY

in their tendency — for they are ordered to an end

which requires an unordered orderer

...FIFTH WAY

In this necessarily brief treatment of natural theology we shall concentrate on the third, fourth and fifth ways; then discuss the nature of God.

2. The third way

This way is called the proof from contingency, or the proof from the distinction between necessary and contingent being. First we must clarify our terms. A thing is contingent if it is such that it can either exist or not exist: existence is not inseparably bound up with it. And it is a fact of experience that there are contingent beings, for experience shows that some things come into and pass out of existence. The never ceasing changes in the universe reveal this constantly. Now this instability is a deficiency, because a being having such instability is dependent on something else for its existence. A necessary being, on the contrary, is one which is such that it cannot lack existence.

The argument starts from contingent things – which we know to exist, for we experience them – and argues that a necessary being must exist as their cause. The proper principle of the argument is: Every contingent being that exists has an efficient cause of its existence. This principle is self-evident – its denial involves a contradiction. For to say that something is contingent is to say that it is indifferent from itself to existence and non-existence; that if it has existence, this must come to it from elsewhere. The only alternative would be to assert that its existence came from nowhere at all – that the thing just was, without any reason why it was. But this is to violate the principle of reason of being; which involves violation of the supreme principle of all thought and reality, as was shown in chapter twelve, section two.

So we have this unshakable truth: every contingent being is caused. But caused by what? Not by something contingent, for all these are equally in need of a cause. So their ultimate cause is something non-contingent, something necessary. To put it another way: if everything without exception were contingent, i.e., neutral from itself as regards existing, there would be no reason why anything should be rather than not be. So all things would be without a reason. But to be without a reason of being is contradictory. If we are logical, we are forced to either admit a non-contingent being as the explanation of all other things, or else opt for the self-contradictory. And if we try to take the latter alternative we are not really free to say anything at all, for any sentence supposes that "is" and "is not" are opposites – which is to invoke the principle of contradiction.[5]

The proof can be approached from another angle. We showed in chapter thirteen that essence and be are distinct from each other in all finite things. To repeat what was said there, we never include be in our definitions of these things, for it is totally irrelevant to *what* a thing is; it is something that happens to an essence, not the essence itself, or any part of it. The argument from contingency can be formulated as follows.

1. The things of our experience receive existence, i.e., their existence is caused.

2. But it is impossible that the existence of all things whatever be caused, for this would involve something causing itself.

3. So there must be something whose existence is uncaused.

It comes to this: if all things were havers of existence, but not identical with their existence, existence would be unexplainable, because there would be no source from which it could come to these havers.

We must look more closely at the concept of a necessary being. We have said it is one that cannot lack existence. Why? Because in it essence and existence are identical. If they were not, this being would have the same need as all others, the need to receive be. It is only something identical with its act of existence, a pure existent, which can be uncaused in being. To cause something is to make it be. But the self-existent "be-s" from itself: it is by definition something which is not made to be by another. That which is identical with its own act of be, and is not a mere haver of be, cannot be united with its be, for a thing can't be united with itself.

The necessary being is infinitely perfect. For existence, as shown in chapter thirteen, section two, is the ultimate perfection of a thing. And no perfection is self-limiting. When perfection is found in a limited degree, this is because something else limits it. If some perfection could limit itself, it would be at once and in the same respect a perfection and a defect. The perfection which is wisdom would make a philosopher more and less wise together, so that the more wise he became, the less wise he would become. If existence made something more and less together, the higher it was in the scale of being, the lower it would be; the more it was, the less it would be.[6] Existence is found limited only when received in a limited nature. But in the necessary being there is no distinction between nature and existence – between what he is and the act of existence whereby he is. His existence is not received in anything; he is pure actuality.

He is the original and continuing source of all other things: not just the cause of their coming into being, but of their continuance in being. If someone makes a table, how does it depend on the maker? Only in becoming. If he stops working, the partially built table remains in that incomplete state. But once he puts the finishing touches to it, it depends on him no longer. He can go away and forget about it, and it will continue existing; he can die and it will continue. His causality was only in making the table become; he exercises no influence at all on the continued being of the table. For its being it depends on the materials of which it is constructed – wood, nails, etc. Because of the stability of these it may last a hundred years, or a thousand. If it were made of ice, it would have a very short existence. The wood, in turn, depends on its molecular structure.

So it is one thing to depend on a cause as regards becoming, quite another to depend on it as regards being. And dependence in being may be considered in relation to the secondary causes just illustrated, or the fundamental cause which is God. For however much we analyse a table to find the causes on which it depends, all the elements involved will themselves be in need of a cause of their being. They are all havers of be. That which exists necessarily, or by essence, is the cause of the existence of all other things, for they exist only by participation. God did not simply bring things into being like a carpenter making a table; he holds them in being at every instant. If he ceased to do so they would cease to exist: this follows necessarily from the fact that their existence is dependent.

The notion of a proper cause was explained above. It is a cause which cannot be dispensed with if the effect is to take place. We said that an argument for God's existence must proceed from effects to God as their proper cause. Otherwise doubt would remain as to whether it was really God we had proved the existence of, or some lesser agent.

Clearly, the argument from contingency leads to the proper cause of contingent things. For the proper cause of things dependent in being is something independent in being. And this cause is required wherever the dependence is found. But the dependence is common to all things other than God. Therefore all depend on him for their be.

We also explained the principle of limited regression: in causes essentially subordinated there can be no infinite regression. This principle applies in the present argument, as in all of St Thomas' proofs of God. The question of whether there was a first moment in the history of the universe does not enter the argument. We are not arguing that each thing existing now owes its origin to something prior, and that to something earlier still, until we come to God as the one who started the whole process. We are arguing that the present causes of being with which we are familiar are secondary causes which leave being radically unexplained, because each of them is contingent. And therefore the primary cause is operating *at every moment*, maintaining all things. This is no remote deistic conception, but shows God as intimately present to his creation.

3. Objections to the third way

Arguments given against the five ways are generally due to misunderstandings of them or vagueness about the principles involved. Once the third way, for example, is correctly understood most of the objections to it are seen to be irrelevant. To test this, let us take some commonly urged difficulties.

Objection. Even a materialist need have no hesitation in admitting necessary being. He would say that this is the matter of which things are composed – the subatomic particles which constitute the building blocks of the universe. They are permanently present throughout the constant changes that cause the rise and dissolution of the bodies we observe. The water and grass and cattle and people of our experience can be called contingent because they come into existence and pass away again; but the particles of which they are composed remain always. Nor is it rationally repugnant that the particles should have existed without a beginning, as Aquinas agreed. So the question of God is not solved by positing necessary being; it is gratuitous to assert that God and necessary being are identical.

Reply. The objection is based on a superficial view of things and shows unawareness of what is involved in the notion of necessary being. What we are seeking is an adequate explanation of the existing things of our experience, and we can find this only in a being in which essence and be are one. And that means a being which is subsistent be, and therefore without any imperfection. If we met a being that fitted that description, we would certainly not mistake it for a universe of subatomic particles!

Objection. According to Kant, the identification of a necessary being with the most real being (*ens realissimum*) involves the mistake of trying to derive God's existence from a mere concept. "If I say, the concept of the *ens realissimum* is a concept, and indeed the only concept, which is appropriate and adequate to necessary existence, I must also admit that necessary existence can be inferred from this concept. Thus the so-called cosmological proof really owes any cogency which it may have to the ontological proof from mere concepts."[7]

Reply. The fact that we have a concept of something, even of God, never justifies us in accepting that the thing exists. Nor do we covertly do so in this proof. The argument proceeds from contingent things whose existence we experience, and which force us to conclude to a necessarily existing being. We then see that this being could not be necessary unless essence and existence were identical in it, and therefore that it is pure actuality and the *ens realissimum*. Certainly the concepts of necessary being and the *ens realissimum* imply each other – a reality could not be one without being the other. But whether any reality exists which is identical with these concepts is a question that needs proof and cannot be assumed – and the third way proves it from experience.

Objection. Regarding the above it may be further insisted: a necessary being is, by definition, one that must exist – it wouldn't be necessary otherwise. It could no more lack existence than a triangle could lack the property of having its internal angles equal to two right angles. If we understand what a triangle is, we are compelled to admit that it has this property. Similarly, if God is defined to be a necessary being (if this is what the name God means), the definition implies that he exists. But this is the ontological argument of St Anselm and Descartes, an argument rejected by most philosophers, including Aquinas. So it seems that Aquinas and his followers are inconsistent in accepting and utilizing the concept of a necessarily existing being, yet rejecting the ontological argument.

Reply. The notion of God as a necessarily existing being does not imply that we should accept the ontological argument. Whether there is really a being in which essence and be are one is something we need to establish, not something we can know just by our idea of it. When we say (before having proved his existence), "God is a necessary being", we mean *if* he exists, he exists necessarily. A proof is needed to eliminate the if.

Objection. Why assume there has to be an ultimate cause? For all we know the universe might just be there, without any cause. As Bertrand Russell put is: "The whole concept of cause is one we derive from our observation of particular things; I see no reason whatsoever to suppose that the total has any cause whatsoever."[8]

Reply. We have already pointed out that this assertion violates the principle of reason of being, and indirectly the principle of contradiction. The reason empiricists so often make this assertion is that empiricism is necessarily confined to the examination of sensible phenomena, and cannot admit anything beyond. One consequence is that a cause is looked upon as a phenomenon producing a further phenomenon, and the notion of a cause transcending all phenomena becomes meaningless. It would be like talking about a pink pain; which does not make sense because colour is irrelevant to pain. Another consequence of empiricism is the impossibility of showing that every event has a cause. All we can do is to examine each case as it comes along and then infer that cases we have not experienced will resemble those we have experienced in having a cause. But we cannot be sure, because our minds cannot penetrate into the nature of causality to give us certainty that every event (or every entity we experience) requires a cause. We cannot be sure this law applies unfailingly throughout the universe, so it would be very rash to argue that it applies to everything in the universe in relation to a transcendent cause, even supposing the term "transcendent cause" to be meaningful.

The argument stands or falls with the empiricist theory of knowledge. If that theory were true, knowledge of God's existence – and of his nature – would be utterly unattainable. Since we have dealt in earlier chapters with knowledge and with the deficiencies of empiricism, it is unnecessary to do so here.

Objection. The argument from contingency is inconsistent. For it claims as a premise that everything needs a cause of its existence. Then it concludes from this that something exists (namely, God) which does not need a cause of its existence! Schopenhauer remarks very aptly that advocates of the cosmological argument treat the law of causation as "a hired cab which we dismiss when we have reached our destination". Again, this procedure has been compared to the argument, "Every crow is black. Therefore a white crow exists."

Reply. Scholasticism certainly does not claim that everything needs a cause. The principle of causality is applicable only to contingent things, and an attempt to apply it to absolutely everything leads to an absurdity. It is for this reason that we conclude to the existence of a being who is uncaused. And he does not require a cause, as already explained, because his essence and be are identical – so there is no need for a cause to unite them.

4. The fourth way

St Thomas takes his fourth proof from the varying degrees of perfection found in sensible things. It is the most beautiful of the five ways, but people often fail to see its force, due to failure to grasp the proper principle on which it is based.

Such perfections as truth, goodness and nobility are found among things, as St Thomas points out in stating this proof.[9] These and similar perfections are not equally in all things; some possess greater goodness, etc., than others. Here we have the factual data of the proof.

At this point we need to clarify the class of perfections we are concerned with. Some perfections imply a limitation, others do not. Colour and shape are perfections; so are truth and goodness. But the first two can be found only in very limited beings, for they presuppose matter: only a body can be coloured or shaped. An understanding of what colour is, or what shape is, involves understanding that things possessing these characteristics are limited; and these perfections themselves are restricted in their entity. It is otherwise with truth or goodness; no limitation is implied here. Matter is not always needed as their subject: corporeal things have truth and goodness, but these perfections are not tied down to matter, or to anything limited. They are perfections which, considered in themselves, do not imply any limitation. A thing may be too perfect to be coloured or shaped; nothing is too perfect to be true, good or beautiful. The pure perfections are found wherever being is found.

To prove God's existence from the transcendental perfections we experience in the world, we must see them in the light of the proper principle of the fourth way. Let us examine that principle.

It can be formulated: *When the diverse are united, there is a cause of their union.*[10] This principle, like all those used in St Thomas' proofs of God, is self-evident. For diversity means dividedness of being, whereas unitedness means oneness of being. So two things (not necessarily two substances, but any two real principles, for instance act and potency) are unable to account for their union insofar as they are different from each other. We do not need to invoke a cause to explain why a triangle has certain properties, but we do need to do so in order to explain why it is composed of wood. Triangularity does not demand wood rather than metal, chalk, ink, etc. And composition of the diverse requires an efficient cause of their combination.

Our experience shows us things having transcendental perfections like goodness and beauty. But all things do not have equal perfections. A human being, a rose and a noble deed each has beauty, but in different ways and degrees. So experience tells us that (a) there are *many things* having transcendental perfections; (b) the perfections are had *unequally*. These are the data which, seen in the light of metaphysical principles, lead to the conclusion that an infinitely perfect being exists.

"When something is found participated in diverse manners by many," says St Thomas, "it is necessary that from that in which it is most perfectly found, it be attributed to all those in which it is found less perfectly."[11] We have here an application of the truth that act is not self-limiting, but is limited only by reception in potency.[12] Beauty and other pure perfections do not imply a limitation, so when they are found to be limited this is due to the limitations of the subject which possesses them. The beauty of sensible things is not beauty pure and simple, but is beauty received in limited natures, and therefore diluted and mingled with imperfection. If it were all that beauty can be, it would be one (not scattered among many things), and would not have varying degrees. An entity having limited beauty is necessarily composite: both act and potency are involved in it – act to account for its perfection, potency to account for the fact that the perfection is less than infinite.

Now, that which only *has* beauty, but is not identical with infinite beauty, is not the explanation of beauty. For *the diverse do not unite themselves, but there must be a cause of their union*. And the cause must lack the composition or diversity or duality found in its effects: otherwise it too would need a cause. Whereas they are compounds, participating in perfection, it is simple, and is essentially perfection. They are beautiful; it is beauty.

A transcendental perfection – a perfection extending to all being – is not something extraneous to being, but is being viewed from a certain standpoint. And being implies all such perfections; it cannot be true yet not good, for example.[13] Clearly, then, an infinite or limitless perfection must be identical with an infinite being; and this being must be perfect by all the transcendental perfections. He is pure entity, truth, goodness, beauty. He is God.

The fourth way can be expressed briefly as follows. *Proper principle.* When the diverse are united, there is a cause of their union. *Observed data.* But there exist things in which there is a unity of the diverse. For some things have more or less of pure perfections than others do. And the same perfection, say beauty, is found in many things. *Conclusion.* So a cause must exist of these observed perfections. And the ultimate cause must lack the diversity found in these effects; otherwise it would not be an adequate cause, and an infinite regress would result, leaving perfections without a reason of being.

St Thomas' brief expositions of this proof in the *Summa Theologiae* and the *Summa Contra Gentiles*, expositions which can be puzzling because of their brevity, are clarified by other passages in his works, where he enunciates and employs the principles used here. In the *QQ. De Potentia*, q. 3, a. 5, he states: "If something *one* is found commonly in many, it is caused in them by a single cause; for that common attribute cannot befit each from itself, since each, according to what it is properly, is distinguished from the others, and diversity of causes produces diversity of effects." Elsewhere he says: "What befits something from its nature, and not from some cause, cannot be in it in a lower degree and falling short."[14] And again: "If something is found in a thing by participation, it must be caused in it by him whom it befits essentially."[15]

The fourth way explicates something that has always caused a fascination, whether in poets, philosophers, saints or ordinary people: the transcendental perfections experienced in the world have always been seen as a dim mirroring of the divine, as a reflection of God. Philosophy shows this is not poetic fancy, but a glorious truth. The beauty we find shining in human nature and throughout the physical world is derived from the subsistent beauty that caused it. The perfections of the world are able to bring us closer to God because they are from God. When philosophers like Plato and Plotinus contemplated goodness and beauty and traced them to their awesome source, they showed a profound intellectual perception.

5. The fifth way

The argument to the existence of God from the order we find in the universe has always attracted many minds, although it has encountered a great deal of criticism in modern times. When it is expounded and understood in a merely "popular" way, without penetration into its full significance, that formulation can be subjected to a shattering attack. As always, we first need to get the principles clear, then the full force of the proof appears, and we are in a position to answer objections.

Its proper principle is the principle of finality, explained in chapter twelve, section two. Things do not act haphazardly, but produce effects in an orderly way. Each thing acts according to what it is: fire heats, acid corrodes metal, etc. Since each action is ordered to a certain effect (otherwise there would be no reason why this effect rather than that would occur), the effect is the final cause of the action: it is that to which the action tends.

A complicated organization is required in things that they be able to attain a determinate end. Think of the intricacies of any living body, or even a part of the body, such as the eye. The whole of nature manifests an immense network of parts coordinated into an orderly system. It is not a totality of inert things fitted into an orderly design, like a mosaic. But each thing is itself apt to produce determinate effects; and it is from this intrinsic order of each to a determinate end that the design of the totality arises: there could be no total design if the parts were indeterminate in their operations.

It is an obvious fact of experience that things act in a determinate way – not just at random, and producing all sorts of startling results. And it is clear that nature considered as a whole has a harmony of operation. This order or harmony makes science possible; there cannot be a science of chaos. But the marvellous order of the universe must have a proportionate cause. To say that it occurs without any cause, or to posit some cause insufficient to account for it, is to deny the principle of reason of being, and to say that something happens without an explanation. Order, on the contrary, requires an orderer as its explanation. For order involves each part tending to a determinate end, and a convergence of parts tending to a harmonious and intelligible whole.

But this supposes something that knows the end to be attained and the means thereto: something that has insight into all that is required for the completed system to be the harmony it is. That is, it supposes an intelligence. And not merely an intelligence coordinating externally, like someone fitting a prepared framework together, but which knows and brings into existence all the natures in the universe, each with its intelligible structure – otherwise those intelligible structures have no reason of being.

Some people agree that the order manifest in the world shows the existence of an intelligent orderer, but they cannot see how it can be proved that this being is an infinite God. After all, they say, the order of things, although very impressive, is still finite. So how do you know an infinite being is the cause? Could it not be some spirit of immense, yet limited, intelligence?

The answer must be that order is unexplainable without an infinite orderer. To see why this is so, we can note first that while some things are merely ordered to their end in a passive fashion, others cooperate by knowledge. Inanimate things and vegetation are passively ordered, having no knowledge of the process taking place; they are active, but without any knowledge of their own activity. Brute animals, by contrast, have a rudimentary share in the ordering of their activities, for they are guided by sense knowledge and appetition, as when a dog chases a rabbit which he sees and wants. But they have no knowledge of an end precisely as such, for this cannot be sensed but only understood.

Man cooperates much more intimately in the ordering of his life, because he understands means and ends, and can adjust the former to the latter. For the same reason, he can pervert his nature by acting in an irrational manner. Man is an ordered orderer, whereas beings below him are merely ordered (with the above qualification concerning brute animals). What is implied in man being an ordered orderer? He has a determinate nature of whose intrinsic order he is not the cause. He has powers with a natural ordination independently of his will. He lives in a world he did not design. All this means he orders in only a very subordinate way. But subordinated orderers do not explain order, since they themselves are subject to it. Again we meet the principle of limited regress. Outside the series of those who are ordered to order, there must be an unordered orderer.

To order without being ordered implies complete actuality, utterly without potency. For to order supposes an act of understanding. But something which is only able to understand, or in potency to an act of understanding – someone about to think of something – must be brought over from that indeterminacy to an actual understanding. And this process of coming over requires a cause. So if an alleged primary orderer underwent this process, it would not really be primary, but would be a subordinated orderer subject to the cause that made it understand.

It follows that the supreme ordering cause – the absolutely unordered orderer – must be eternally understanding. Further, he must be identical with his act of understanding: otherwise he would only *have* understanding as a quality distinct from what he is. And this would imply that he is ordered to his act of understanding; which passive ordination – even though eternally actualised – would need an ordering cause. Just as the divine essence is identical with its be and with its essential perfections, so it is identical with its act of understanding. In all other things a gap is found between what they are and what they do. In God this gap does not exist: he is his act of doing – he is his activity. This conclusion, necessitated by the fact of order and by the principles of finality and limited regress, implies that he is infinite. For that which is its act of understanding is its act of existence; in other words, that which is its understand is its be. Otherwise its understanding would be naturally prior to its existence; which is impossible. But since be is the ultimate perfection,[16] that which is its be is infinite.

The fifth way can be condensed as follows. It is an observed fact that order exists in the world. But order supposes an orderer, and subordinated orderers suppose one that is not subordinated. This orderer, since he is not ordered to his act of ordering, is identical with that act. He is an infinite intelligence.

6. Difficulties regarding order

Objection. A commonly raised criticism of the fifth way is that it rashly assumes that the purpose we find in human actions is paralleled in nature. A man wears clothing for warmth, and he does this deliberately, adopting appropriate means to the attainment of the end he has chosen. It is easy to assume that nature does the same sort of thing; that a bear has thick fur *for the purpose* of keeping it warm in cold weather. Likewise, a civilized man fashions false teeth for the purpose of chewing his food more efficiently after having lost his natural teeth. One can easily jump to the conclusion that nature provides man with teeth *for the purpose* of chewing food.

Reply. The principle of finality is not an anthropomorphic carry-over from human actions to things in general, as is clear from its analysis in chapter twelve, section two. Nevertheless, we can readily concede (although not in the instances given in this objection) that the designs of nature are hard to diagnose correctly. This does not affect the fact that order, not chaos, is a very obvious reality. Nor is it simply a question of the overall design found in the universe, but more particularly the ordination of each entity to the production of a determinate effect. Denial of order involves rejection of the principle of finality, and consequently of the principle of reason of being and the principle of contradiction.

Objection. However plausible the conception of a universe directed by an intelligence may once have been, Darwinism and neo-Darwinism have now shown it to be untenable. Evolution explains the facts without recourse to a directing mind. To refer to the above illustration, the bear's thick fur is not *meant* to protect it from the cold; the real explanation is that only those animals survive which are fitted to do so, and therefore those we find living in a particular environment are the species fortunate enough to have possessed favourable characteristics. The rest have either died out or migrated to more congenial environments. Similarly, teeth are not intelligently designed for biting and chewing food; but species which, in the struggle for existence, were able to develop such advantages had a better chance of survival than their less fortunate neighbours.

Reply. Imagine two men on a desert island who thought they were the only intelligent beings in the universe. Then one day they found a large box containing the pieces of a jigsaw puzzle. This might not cause them to suspect an intelligent designer as the maker of the puzzle, because they could easily fail to see any order in the jumble of irregular pieces lying before them. Next, suppose they invented a game which consisted in shaking the box violently back and forth and from side to side. And after a lot of shaking, a remarkable thing happened: the pieces gradually assembled themselves into their right places in the puzzle, until eventually the castaways were gazing in awe at a painted scene of animals and people and houses and forest and blue sky. They would conclude that the jigsaw puzzle could not have just happened, but must be the work of an intelligent designer.

One of the two, however, proceeding to investigate further, made an interesting discovery. Each piece of the puzzle, along the edge where it joined its partner, was studded with tiny magnets, interspersed with patches of material attracted by magnetism and others of an antimagnetic nature. The arrangement was such that each jigsaw piece would combine with its right partner, but wrongly matched pieces would lack sufficient attraction on each other and would fall away. Now, the investigating castaway argued like this: "We were wrong in assuming design and a designer. The truth is that the random tossing about of the pieces resulted at last in the picture we see before us, and no design was involved. It was all a matter of natural selection: only those combinations survived which were fitted to do so."

His friend, seeing the inadequacy of the alleged solution, answered: "You've accounted for the method by which the picture got assembled. But you've utterly failed to explain the following: (a) each piece is suited to a particular place; (b) after the series of combinations occurs, an intelligible harmony results."

That story is a very imperfection comparison, but it does have a certain illustrative value. Take (a) above: each piece of the puzzle is suited to a fixed place. In nature each thing acts in a determinate manner, i.e., towards a definite effect and not in a random fashion. If this internal finality were absent, there would be no foundation from which natural selection could operate. And it must be emphasized that it is with this basic finality that the fifth way is mainly concerned.

Next take the other point made by the second castaway: an overall harmony results from the conjunction of numerous individual things. The universe, too, is a harmony of diverse parts. No matter what the mechanics of it (natural selection or something else) the overall harmony refers us back to the support on which it rests: the determinateness of each particular thing, and the suitability of each to contribute to the perfection of the whole. Just as the intelligibility of the jigsaw puzzle could not be explained by showing how it came to be assembled, the intelligibility evident in the universe would not be explained even if it could be shown that natural selection operated to bring things to their present state. In the case of the jigsaw puzzle, the ordination of each part to the totality requires explanation; and in the world an explanation is needed of the ordination of each entity towards the harmony of the whole.

We can add these further observations.

A. Natural selection through favourable variations is ruled out as the explanation of apparent design by the sheer complexity of the things it is supposed to explain. The digestive system, the eye, the brain – to say that any of these could have occurred in that way is to refuse to face the facts and assess them rationally.

B. Why should there be a trend towards intricate rather than simpler bodies? Rocks have a greater fitness for survival than trees, and trees than animals.

C. Many organs, such as wings, would be a hindrance to survival until well developed. So they are not explained through natural selection, but would be contrary to its exigencies during most of their long formative period. And a very long time indeed must be allowed for their formation if a guiding intelligence is excluded. Chance mutations could not accomplish the result in a short time, because of the enormous number of genetic modifications required for an organ as complicated as a wing.

D. The fossil record is against the theory that all animal life evolved from one or a few primitive species. Douglas Dewar, after years of careful investigation, made the following points, which remain as valid today as they were sixty years ago, when he wrote. The earliest animals are "as sharply differentiated into species, genera, families, orders and phyla as they are today."[17] "So far it has been found impossible to produce a series of fossils showing that one family has gradually become converted into another family, or an order, class or phylum into another."[18] As for the assumption that the fossil record would tell a different story if it were more complete, it is far more complete than Darwin supposed, or his followers admit.[19]

1   *Summa Theol.*, I, q. 46, a. 2; cf. *Con. Gent.*, II, 38; *QQ. Disp de Pot.*, q. 3, a. 14.
2   Cf. *Summa Theol.*, I, q. 46, a. 2, *ad* 7.
3   chapter twelve, section two.
4   For St Thomas' explanations of his proofs, see *Summa Theol.*, I, q. 2, a. 3; *Con. Gent.*, I, 13; I, 15, n. 5; *De Ente et Essentia*, chapter 5.
5   Chapter twelve, section two.
6   Cf. chapter thirteen, section one, dealing with act and potency.
7   *Critique of Pure Reason*, B 635.
8   BBC debate on the existence of God between Bertrand Russell and Father F. C. Copleston, published in *A Modern Introduction to Philosophy*, ed. Edwards and Pap, 1965 edition. The quotation is from p. 478.
9   *Summa Theol.*, I, q. 2, a. 3.
10 Cf. I, q. 65, a. 1.
11 *QQ. Disp. de Pot.*, q. 3, a. 3.
12 Chapter thirteen, section one.
13 Chapter thirteen, section three.
14 *Con. Gent.*, II, 15.
15 *Summa Theol.*, I, q. 11, a. 3.
16 Chapter thirteen, section two.
17 *Is Evolution Proved?* A debate conducted by letter between Douglas Dewar and H. S. Shelton, published by Hollis and Carter, London (1947), P. 120.
18 P. 119.
19 Cf. pp. 58ff.

Chapter Fifteen

GOD'S NATURE AND ACTIVITY

1. The Divine perfections

Each of the proofs gives us an insight into perfections of God. A different immediate conclusion is reached in each: a being who is his be in the third; undiluted perfection in the fourth; subsistent and infinite understanding in the fifth. But each of these direct conclusions implies the others. For each shows God to be pure actuality in some respect; but this implies that he is purely actual in every respect. This is particularly evident from the identification of essence and be in him; an identification that rules out all potency, that leaves no foothold for any defect. God is reality in its fullness.

In deciding whether some attribute befits God, we can ask: does it suppose an imperfection? If it does, the attribute in question is unbefitting to him, and therefore absent from him. Matter and all its properties imply imperfection. A thing is less than infinite if it has colour, shape, hardness and similar properties; if it is composed of molecules; if it is restricted to a particular time and location in the universe. All these limitations must be excluded from God.

He cannot be attained by any external sense – sight, hearing, touch, taste or smell – and consequently cannot be known in any image in the imagination. He is not corporeal, but spiritual. And his spirituality immeasurably exceeds that of man's soul or any created spirit. For all creatures, however exalted, are a mixture of the diverse. All have that fundamental composition of essence and be; all have powers distinct from their essence and from each other: intellect and will are powers of the soul, but are not the soul, and each of these powers is distinct from the other. And the knowledge in the intellect and love in the will are not identical with these faculties themselves – if they were, the knowledge and love could not be lost without the faculties lapsing into nothingness. But one who is sheer actuality lacks all potency, including potency of essence for be, of the nature for its faculties, of the faculties for the activity that perfects them.

His lack is not a loss, however. He lacks all limited perfections because he transcends them in the one perfect act of infinite existence which is himself. In him all are together in complete identity: essence and existence, powers and activity. This is what is meant by the simplicity of God. An amoeba is relatively simple, and a molecule is simpler still. But the absence of complexity in these things denotes poorness of being: they don't *be* very much. God's simplicity is at the other end of the scale, so to speak. He "be-s" so perfectly that every shadow of potency is excluded from him. The imperfect actuality of other things makes necessary a multiplicity in them, as the eye needs great complexity of parts in order to see. The perfect actuality of God makes an apparatus of parts unnecessary. And his actuality is utter simplicity, because complexity implies potency, since one part has a perfection which is lacking to other parts, and one depends on another.

It follows also that he is changeless, for any change would mean either the gaining of something previously lacking, or the loss of something previously had. Imperfection would be involved in either case. Besides, the absolute simplicity of his nature means he can neither gain nor lose, for an addition or subtraction supposes composition of the being which gains or loses with that which is gained or lost.

Because he is immutable or changeless, he is eternal. Time arises from movement. Without a flow or succession there could be no past, present and future, and without these there could be no time. But if a thing is completely changeless it can have no past or future. Our present bears a resemblance – a faint one – to God's eternity. The present is the indivisible instant between the immense reaches of the past and the ever approaching future. Even as we try to reflect on it, it vanishes into our past. It is like a line too fine to be measured, yet it is all we have of our life at once. Even the shortest syllable takes a space of time to be uttered, and that fraction of time has past and future and the indivisible present between them. One is reminded of the total becoming of Heraclitus; and perhaps the seductiveness of his teaching for many minds is partly explained by their constant awareness of the flow of time.

How are we to conceive God's eternity? That he must be eternal is rationally certain from his perfection. What eternity is we cannot clearly grasp, for we have never experienced it. But we can have some notion of it. As just said, it must be faintly like our present. All God's life is had together. Our lives are spread out thin, and the present is all we have at once. God's life is concentrated, as it were, into one indivisible act, and exists all together, with nothing fading into a dead past and nothing emerging from a nameless future. Boethius summed it up in his famous definition of eternity: "Perfect possession, all at once, of interminable life."[1]

The divine perfections we have just considered are in contrast with imperfections of creatures: God is simple, creatures are composed; he is immutable, they are mutable; he is eternal, they are in time. But we saw in the previous two chapters that some perfections befit God and creatures. This is true of those transcendental perfections which are found wherever being is found.[2] From the existence of such perfections in the things of our experience it was shown, in St Thomas' fourth proof, that a being must exist who has them to infinity and in strict simplicity, so that he is absolute entity, truth, goodness, beauty, etc. The same applies to certain other perfections which, although not possessed by all things, are had by the highest things. Intelligence is possessed by God, as the fifth proof shows. He also has will. And since beings of intelligence and will are persons, God is personal. Such perfections must be affirmed of an infinite God, for their lack would be a great imperfection. A God who (or rather which) was without intelligence and will and was non-personal would be inferior to us, for we enjoy those perfections.

2. Our knowledge of God is analogical

How much can philosophy tell us of God? It can tell us what creation reveals of him – and no more. His existence can be proved because the world requires him as its ultimate explanation. The conclusions of the various proofs are so many predicates about God: he is subsistent existence, infinite understanding, etc. From these primary conclusions others must be inferred, as we have just done.

The human intellect first knows bodily things, and can understand higher things only through this knowledge. Consequently, we are liable to two contrary extremes in thinking about God.

One is anthropomorphism, that is, investing God with typically human attributes. No one is naïve enough to conceive him as an old man with a long beard hovering above the clouds. But that image, or something vaguely like it, often accompanies people's thoughts about him, and can have a powerful, although indirect, effect on their understanding of him. It is difficult enough to make progress in understanding him, without inane images blocking and diverting us.

I read an account where someone, criticizing the idea of God, said that he could not imagine *even a man* so conceited that he would crave adoration and praise from all over the globe twenty-four hours a day. But that's just what he was imagining! That anthropomorphic image, perverting God to our level, can prevent a true understanding of his nature, of our relation to him, and of the whole question of his providence. In a most real sense he is benevolent and a father – but he is not a benevolent father-figure.

The opposite extreme is agnosticism regarding the nature of God, the claim that he is so different from us that we can have no notion of what he is. The basis for this is the doctrine of knowledge accepted by its proponents. However, granted that human knowledge is not confined to corporeal manifestations, but reaches metaphysical being, the way lies open to some understanding of God.

It might be noted first that if we had no knowledge of his nature we could not have established his existence. For proof of his existence requires an inference to him as the necessary cause of some effect. But if nothing whatever could be said of what he is, there could be no reason to ascribe certain effects to him – to say that he is that which causes certain effects. For example, if the predicate subsistent be meant nothing to us, it would make no sense to argue that subsistent be is the cause of contingent be.

In the perfections attributed to God a distinction is necessary between what is signified and the human way in which it is signified. The perfection signified, in the case of a transcendental perfection, befits God; it is more befitting to him than to lesser things: goodness or beauty, for instance. But we have experience of these perfections only in creatures; and in creatures they are limited by the subject possessing them: a sunset has beauty, but is incapable of the greatest beauty because of its limited entity. It is likewise with all the things of our experience; their perfections are limited by reception in potency. We know the perfections and we know their limited modes. And we know (the proofs of his existence make it certain) that God has the perfections without the limitations. So we affirm the perfections of him and deny the limitations. Doing this gives us true knowledge of him, but falling infinitely short of the full reality.

It falls short in two ways. Firstly, there are things about him philosophy can never know, because all philosophical knowledge of him is of what his creation tells us about him; but it does not tell us everything. Secondly, although we know perfections that he has, we cannot know them as he has them. We know beauty; but what is that beauty which subsists pure and simple, and is identical with all the other divine perfections? The necessity that it be so has been shown; a mental grasp of the thing itself escapes us. As St Thomas states of names said of God: "As regards what these names signify, they properly befit God, and more properly than they befit creatures themselves; and of him they are said by priority. But as regards the manner of signifying, they are not said properly of God; for they have that manner of signifying which befits creatures."[3]

What of those attributes which God has and creatures lack, such as simplicity, immutability and eternity? Have we any positive notion here, or do we just deny certain deficiencies found in creatures, and leave it at that? On examination, these notions are seen to have some positive content for us, derived from what we positively find in the things we experience. Take simplicity. The things we experience are not utterly complex, but various degrees of relative simplicity are found among them. Nor are they in a state of pure change, but have a degree of stability: so from them we can get a notion of immutability. As for eternity, an inkling of its nature is obtained from the present in time.

From the above paragraphs it is clear that analogy of proper proportionality is the most important mode of analogy in our understanding of God. But analogy of attribution appears also, as when perfections are considered from the viewpoint of possession by essence (not by participation). God is identical with infinite be, truth, beauty, etc. Other things are endowed with these, in a limited way, by God. It is as though one wealthy man supported ten penniless relatives; all the wealth they used would come from him as its source and they would have none in their own right. Somewhat similarly, all existence, goodness and so forth have their source in God, and are in us only by participation. Considered in their subsistent state, they are intrinsic to him alone, and are predicated of other things by analogy of attribution. It was in this sense that Christ said: "God is good, and he only."[4]

Analogy of metaphoric proportionality is employed too, as when God is called angry. It is something like calling the sea angry: that property (the passion of anger) which is proper to sentient beings is said of the sea because the effects of a turbulent sea are similar to those of an angry animal or man. And God is called angry because of effects, such as the punishment of evildoers and opposition to evil, which would be associated with the passion of anger in a man. Metaphorical expressions of this kind are very common in the Bible, which speaks of God's anger, his repentance, etc. There is no reason to avoid these expressions; they have a concreteness and vividness which are very necessary if our thinking about God is not to become too remote. But we should also strive to deepen our metaphysical penetration into divine things, a penetration that becomes more real to us as it progresses, and which guards us against anthropomorphism.

3. God and the world

God is cause of the world in three senses: he is the efficient cause of all things; their exemplary cause; and their final cause.

Efficient causality. St Thomas' third proof brings out sharply the total dependence on God of everything created. He alone has be necessarily; other things exist only because he makes them be. It is not simply that he has to get them started, and they could then continue independently. Each thing depends as totally on the divine will now as things did at the instant of creation. If he should cease holding something in being, it would just stop existing. This follows from the truth that independence in being is proper to him, creatures having being only as it is bestowed by him. And since their existence hangs on his will, so does their activity: they could not be and they could not do unless he gave them the power.

Exemplary causality. God is the exemplary cause of things: all are made resembling him. Every effect bears some resemblance to its cause, because what the cause is accounts for the effect being what it is. Some proportion exists between a dry leaf and the sun that caused the dryness, although the two are immensely different. The whole entity of each thing is basically from God, and is a faint imitation of its cause.

When we think about the truth that God is the supreme cause of all else, we see that he must be the source of the essence as well as the existence of things. He depends on no other. He is not like an artist who, in producing a painting, subjects himself to something external, e.g., a mountain. God is self-sufficient; and in any case, apart from him there is nothing on which creation could be patterned, for apart from God and his creation there is nothing at all.

The conclusion that God is the exemplar of all things appears from St Thomas' fourth proof of his existence, which shows that the transcendental perfections found in lesser things are derived from his infinite perfection. Without subsistent truth, there could be no truth in other things; without subsistent goodness, no other goodness, and so forth. Even the mixed perfections, such as shape or heat, must derive from him: otherwise they would lack any cause. In their own way they manifest him, although not found in him according to their proper character.

The same conclusion comes from the proof from order, which shows a subsistent intellect as the source of all order. This intellect, because independent, must understand others in knowing himself: otherwise he would depend on something else for his ideas, and would not be independent in understanding. This means that in knowing himself God knows all things. He knows himself as imitable in one way by a man, in another by a palm tree, and so on. His understanding of himself as imitable in this or that way constitutes the essence of each thing in the divine mind. Each of these imitations of God is a possible being.

However, they may never exist in the world, any more than the ideas of an inventor. God understands the natures of things whether he wills them ever to exist or not; they are necessarily and eternally possible ways in which he could be imitated, and he eternally knows that this is so. This is why intelligible principles have everlasting stability and reliability. The principles of mathematics must be forever true; so must those of speculative reason (the principle of contradiction, etc.); so must the practical principles (e.g., that good is to be done and evil avoided).

I was told of a nun who asked her class whether God could draw a square circle. The girls decided after some discussion that he could – provided he first created it! The truth is that God could not create a square circle; not because of any deficiency in him – as though he could accomplish it if he were a bit more powerful – but because of a deficiency in it: a square circle lacks capacity to imitate God because it lacks intelligibility.

It is important to see that the essential order (*what* things are) is

271

independent of whether things are. The essential order is based on God's own nature, and is as immutable as he is. What he is determines what other things essentially are. As was said in chapter thirteen, section three, a thing is true (ontologically) because it conforms to the measure which determines it; but God's understanding of himself as imitable is the measure of all natural things. But it is otherwise with the existence of things. Whether they exist depends on whether he chooses to will their existence. So their nature depends on his nature, their existence on his willing that they should be.

If we mix up these two orders, we either make creation necessary (as Spinoza did), or make essences arbitrary (as Descartes did). The first takes away God's freedom and ultimately our own, for it makes creation a fatalistic flow of necessary events. The second takes away God's truth and goodness, and ultimately all truth and goodness, for it supposes he could have willed contradictories to be equally true: circles to be square; and that he could have made kindness immoral and cruelty moral, or the love of him the worst vice and the hatred of him the highest virtue.

Descartes writes: "It is my opinion that one cannot say of anything that it cannot be done by God; in fact, the essence of the true and the good depends upon his omnipotence, and I should not dare to say that God cannot make mountains without valleys or one plus two not be equal to three. All I say is that he gave me a mind of such a kind that a mountain without a valley or a sum of one plus two not equal to three is inconceivable by me."[5] Again: "The truths that are called eternal, e.g., that the whole is greater than its part, etc., would not be truths at all had not God established it so."[6]

To say that the very nature of things depends on God's choice, so that their being this rather than that (e.g., an act of love for him being good rather than bad) is from his willing it so, is to make all law completely arbitrary.[7] That position abolishes all intrinsic necessity, setting voluntary decrees in its place. It would not be a valid objection to say that God's goodness would prevent him making bad decrees. If essences had no basis in God's nature, decrees could only be arbitrary; one thing would not be intrinsically better than another, and therefore would not be a more worthy choice, even for God.

Final causality. God is the final cause of all things: all exist for his sake. If he could have some ultimate reason apart from himself for creating he would not be infinite, because this reason, whatever it was, would be influencing him: he would be subjecting himself to it. Again, everything acts for the sake of some good. But God is the subsistent good from which all others derive. So he could not act ultimately for these lesser goods without bypassing the greater good – himself – from which they come.

This may seem, at first glance, sheer egoism. Imagine a man acting ultimately for himself. But that anthropomorphic fancy distorts the truth. It is not egoism to act for the greatest good. If a man puts himself first, he is egoistic; but God is not a man. A man who would act in the way mentioned would be acting as though he were God, which would be monstrous. But it is not monstrous for God to act as God.

Part of the difficulty some feel about this comes from a misunderstanding. When someone possesses a good, he tends to share it, to diffuse it more widely. Take knowledge. If someone possesses great truths, he wants to propagate them. In doing so he does not lose them himself, and he enables others to share them. God, in creating, shared being, truth, goodness with his creation. He lost nothing of them himself, but enabled the world to participate in them. Love of his own goodness was the reason for creation. However, that does not exclude love for his creation, but requires it, for since the goodness of created things is a participation of his own goodness, his love for himself embraces them; he loves all things as they resemble him.

To sum up what we have been saying about God's causality. He is intimately present to all things; his will alone keeps them in being from moment to moment; their nature and attributes are a reflection, as it were, of him; he is the end for whom they exist. Thus from created things knowledge of God can be gained; the cause is known through his effects. However, he is infinitely greater than the effects, so the knowledge attained will not show him as he is in himself, but only so far as effects manifest him and the human mind can grasp what is manifested.

Evil. How is the existence of evil compatible with God's universal causality? This perennial question cannot be fully answered in the present life. But that is no reason to ignore it. We can get much light on it.

Basic to a solution is the ontological treatment of evil outlined in chapter thirteen, section three. Evil, precisely taken, is a privation of being, not some positive entity. So the problem does not arise of how it could be created by a good God. It is not created at all: it is a parasite on created things.

How do these privations happen? God is not imperfect, but other things are. Their imperfections give a foothold to evil. For instance, bodies are very complex and therefore subject to dissolution: they can be broken up, burnt, corroded, etc. Dissolution is a physical evil. Sentient beings are exposed, from their nature, to suffering. Intelligent creatures are able to misuse their free will, thus bringing about moral evil.

Although God is the supreme cause of all, he is not the sole cause. Created things are not puppets, with God pulling the strings. Fire burns because of its nature and not because God arbitrarily wills that it should burn rather than have some other effect. All things are subject to God and depend utterly on him for their existence and activity, but they remain true operants; they are not occasions of the divine activity, but genuine causes. Now, it would be against his infinite wisdom to create a world of beings apt for operation, and then constantly intervene when their limitations led them to the brink of evil. If even physical evils like the destruction of chemical combinations or of plant and animal life were prevented by God's special intervention, the universe that we know simply could not be.

It would be a different matter if evil were ultimately triumphant. St Augustine says that God "would never allow any evil to exist in his works unless his omnipotence and goodness were such that he could make good come out of evil."[8] Evil is allowed for the sake of a greater good. If we could see this clearly and in its full amplitude, the problem would cease for us. Unfortunately we cannot; but we can see obscurely and in a limited field how this works out.

The part is for the sake of the whole, and the advancement of the whole sometimes involves evil afflicting a part. The continuance and functioning of the physical world involves chemical corruption and the death of plants and animals. Human suffering is a greater mystery. But even here it is evident that good can be occasioned by evil. Character can be purified and strengthened by suffering. People can become more closely united – families, larger social groups, even whole communities. This is very noticeable in time of war and persecution. The person who escapes nearly all suffering and effort, or the community that leads a soft and easy existence, are likely to be shallow and selfish.

The immortality of the human soul helps solve the problem of human misery. Our sojourn in the present world is but the briefest beginning of our existence, and sufferings endured must be seen in the context of eternity if they are to be seen rightly. The innocent baby who dies miserably after months spent in pain will find itself enjoying everlasting bliss, a bliss beyond comparison with those early sufferings.

If a vision of the whole universe in time and space lay before us, the place of evil and its subordination to good would be manifest. But what we have is like a view through a narrow window on to a misty landscape. Only a part is seen and it is not seen well. How can we expect to judge the whole and understand where each part fits in? All we can do is explore the principles involved, such as the privative nature of evil, and apply them cautiously.

4. Difficulties

In this final section, let us consider a number of objections regarding God's nature and activity.

Objection. If an infinite God existed, nothing else could exist. The reason is that an infinite being means one containing every perfection: if it lacked a perfection this would constitute a limitation, thus making it finite. But if other things exist, the perfections they have – existence, goodness and so on – are their own, not God's. Suppose a multimillionaire is reputed to own all the money in the world. Then we discover that many other people also own some money, although their total finances equal only a small percentage of the multimillionaire's wealth. No matter how tiny the percentage, we have disproved the assertion that he has all the money in the world. Similarly, the existence of things other than God shows that not all perfection is contained in him, and therefore he is not infinite.

Reply. This objection would be right if finite things did not owe their whole being to God's causality. But since their being and all their possessions are from him, they subtract nothing from his infinite perfection. After creation there are more beings, but not more being: more things enjoy perfection, but there is no greater perfection than before. The objection treats the concept of being as though it were used in the same way of God and creatures. When we reflect on the analogy of attribution that holds between the existence of God and that of everything else, the position is clarified. God is identical with pure existence, and other things exist only by derivation from him.

If an explorer found a strange new animal in the depths of Africa, an animal no one had ever seen before, then returned and wrote a description of it, his article would be full of original information. No doubt it would occasion a flood of books and articles from other writers. But (granted they gained their knowledge entirely from him) would there be any more knowledge of this animal as a result of these secondary writings? There would be no more knowledge; there would only be more knowers – because of the wider dissemination of the knowledge.

Objection. A totally self-sufficient God, enjoying perfect happiness in contemplating himself, would have no reason to create anything. To say he experienced an urge to create is to imply that his happiness was not complete. Even supposing he created a universe, it seems very far-fetched to hold that he takes a personal interest in each thing he made; that would be like a grown man spending his life absorbed in playing with toy soldiers in the nursery.

Reply. God's happiness is not affected one way or the other by the creation of the world. He did not create to provide himself with something he lacked. He is infinite being, and therefore infinite goodness; so it is impossible that he could stand in need of anything outside himself. Why then did he create? Because he chose to give other things a share in his goodness. We can get some appreciation of this reason by reflecting on our own attitude when we find ourselves in possession of something good: we feel inclined to spread this goodness more widely.

In our case there are often inhibiting factors, like the fear of losing what we have gained; in fact, some possessions, e.g., money, cannot be shared without the donor losing part of them. This is not the case with everything: our knowledge, for instance, is not diminished when we share it. The inclination to diffuse goodness more widely is not a peculiarity of human nature, but derives from the nature of goodness, which signifies something attractive, something worth having, and therefore worth extending to others.

God is not faced with the various disadvantages that we meet when we think of diffusing some good possession more generously. He cannot lose through the diffusion of his goodness; nor does he experience any toil or strain in creating, sustaining and directing things.

Is it below God to take an interest in each element of his creation? On the contrary, if his knowledge, love and power did not extend to each one, he would be imperfect because the individuals in question would be independent of him. Nor is it any trouble for him to know each thing through and through. He is not like the managing director of a large company, who finds it hard enough to keep abreast of all the top-level matters in his province, and would go mad if he tried to follow the activities of every employee and to take a detailed interest in the problems of each one. God works, but he does not labour.

Objection. From what you have just said about the yearning we have to spread goodness, it seems to follow that God would desire infinitely to communicate his goodness to others. This would mean, firstly, that creation is necessary, not a free act of God; and secondly, that ours is the best of all possible worlds. Theologians will call the first point heresy, and anyone of common sense and sympathy for his fellowmen will see the second point as nonsense.

Reply. God loves himself necessarily, and other things only in relation to himself. Loving his own goodness, he chose to extend it by creating the universe, but there was no necessity that he should do so, because his goodness was not increased by creation.

When an end is willed, does this demand that we will something else connected with the end? That depends on how the two are connected. If I will to be in London, that involves willing suitable means of getting there. But it does not involve willing to travel first class rather than economy. Nor does it compel me to use one particular form of transport rather than another, e. g., a plane rather than a ship.

God does not strive after happiness, but possesses it from eternity. And the object of his happiness is himself, the infinite good. Nothing can add to it, so nothing is required by it. His relation to the world is not like my relation to suitable means of reaching London, because the attainment of my object would be frustrated by lack of transport, whereas his happiness does not depend on the world. There is a closer resemblance between my freedom about the specific means to choose, or about which class to travel in, and God's freedom about whether to communicate his goodness or not, and if he chooses to do so, about which possible world to bring into existence.

There is a fitness that goodness should be communicated, and this provides a reason for creation; but God is self-sufficient, and so is under no compulsion to communicate his goodness.

Objection. According to Scholastics, the divine nature must be absolutely simple. However, they do not seem to see the consequences of this. One is that God would be incapable of thinking; another is that he could not love. These activities involve duality: thought supposes an object which is thought about; love supposes an object loved. Also, a life of thought and volition implies a multiplicity of acts. As Hume puts it: "A mind, whose acts and sentiments and ideas are not distinct and successive; one, that is wholly simple, and totally immutable; is a mind which has no thought, no reason, no will, no sentiment, no love, no hatred; or in a word, is no mind at all. It is an abuse of terms to give it that appellation; and we may as well speak of limited extension without figure, or of number without composition."[9]

Reply. The difficulty arises from taking a characteristic of finite beings and wrongly assuming it belongs also to God. In us, knowledge and love involve duality, but this is because they are finite, not because they are knowledge and love. The problem is an ancient one, and led Plotinus to conclude that God lacks knowledge and volition because he is too perfect for them. In fact, these are perfections whose absence would make God less perfect than we are.

In understanding something, we become the understood object; our intellect is a potency for receiving the forms of other things, and when actualised, it is these forms. However, duality is necessarily bound up with this. The human mind first understands things other than itself, after immaterialising them by an abstractive process. And when one reflects on one's own knowledge, one has to form a fresh concept, because the knowledge in one's mind is only ready to be reflected upon, but is not identical with the act of reflection. Further, many ideas are needed of a thing before it can be well understood: the human mind is too weak to hold very much in a single concept.

God's knowledge is vastly different. He knows himself primarily. But all other things derive from him, so through understanding himself, and in the same act of knowledge, he understands everything else. God, unlike man, does not understand himself by an act of reflection distinct from the object reflected upon. God and his knowledge are strictly identical.

Nor does he form a multiplicity of concepts. In one infinite and eternal concept he perfectly understands himself and everything else; and that concept is himself.

His love, too, is primarily about himself, and extends to other things according as they resemble him. And it is an infinite act identified with his knowledge and with himself.

Objection. A being which is simultaneously changeless and active is self-contradictory, because activity implies the actualisation of a potency, i.e., the realization of one's possibilities. An immutable God would be eternally static and inactive – not thinking or loving or creating. If a supposed cause remains exactly the same during and after the event it is alleged to have brought about, this can only mean it was not really the cause. So the idea of a changeless God acting to bring about changes in the world, and yet remaining changeless, is repugnant to reason.

Reply. Movement means the actualising of a potency, but movement and activity are not synonymous. God differs from all other things in being pure actuality, without any admixture of potency; he cannot become because he already is. Parmenides, with rare metaphysical insight, glimpsed the significance of pure being, but failed to understand that potency is mixed with actuality in the things of our experience.

Free from potency, God acts without movement; that is, he does not pass into activity from a passive state, like someone awaking from sleep; nor does his activity become more perfect with practice, like someone learning tennis. Activity is a perfection, whereas movement is a transit from potency to perfection. In our lives activity is always mingled with imperfection and bound up with movement; hence the difficulty we find in grasping that it can be free from movement, and that it will then be the most perfect activity. Custom and imagination impede our understanding of this. Even in our experience, though, we see that a great deal of bustle and movement often indicates inefficiency, while a quiet economy of movement is a sign of power and competence.

God causes the world by an eternal act, identical with himself, and involving no expenditure of energy. His effect, the created world, comes into existence in time. He has no dependence on the world, and suffers no alteration from it; but it depends entirely on him at every moment of its existence.

Objection. God is said to have qualities such as justice and mercy. But his absolute simplicity implies that these are both the same – and that both are identical with the divine essence. This destroys the ordinary meaning of the words justice and mercy, and leaves them meaningless.

Reply. Justice means rendering to each person what is due to him. But God does this; therefore he is just. Mercy means aiding others in their misfortune, and doing more for them than justice demands. God also does this, and therefore is merciful.

Virtue in God, however, differs greatly from virtue in us. For one thing, when he acts virtuously he is not obeying a moral law superior to himself. He is the source of morality, and is acting in accordance with his wisdom and goodness when, for example, he renders us our due. He gave us our human nature, and owes it to his own wisdom to deal with us in a way befitting our nature.

Again, our virtues are so many distinct qualities in us, whereas God's virtues, as the objection points out, are a unity identical with his essence. But this does not make the terms justice and mercy meaningless in relation to him. We name things according to the mode in which we experience and understand them. In us justice and mercy are qualities distinct from each other. Reason tells us they are not distinct in God, but our minds are unable to form a concept showing us God as he is in himself. All we can do is to form many concepts, each one showing some aspect of his perfection.

We are on the receiving end of the divine mercy, and know it in its effects. When someone receives what is due to him, that is justice; when someone is aided in his misery, that is mercy.

1. *De Consolatione Philosophiae,* V, prose 6; P. L. 63, 858.
2. Chapter thirteen, sections three and four.
3. *Summa Theol.*, I, q. 13, a. 3.
4. Matt 19:17.
5. Answer for Arnauld, July 29, 1648. Adam and Tannery, V, 223-224.
6. To Mersenne, May 27, 1638. Adam and Tannery, II, 138.
7. Cf. *QQ. Disp. de Verit.*, q. 23, a. 6, where St Thomas brands this voluntarist view as blasphemy.
8. *Enchiridion*, chapter 11, n. 3.
9. Spoken by Cleanthes in *Dialogues Concerning Natural Religion*, part IV.

Chapter Sixteen

BEAUTY AND ART

Dealing with the division of philosophy, in chapter eleven, it was said that poetics, or the philosophy of art, examines the nature of human making, explaining the general conditions of the arts and the distinction between the fine and the useful arts. We will not attempt a sketch of the subject here, but will concentrate on the question of beauty and the fine arts. In the first section the nature of beauty will be discussed; in the second, its expression in art.

1. Beauty

The treatment of beauty belongs to metaphysics, for it is one of the transcendentals. Its consideration has been reserved for now because I wish to say something of its bearing on the philosophy of art.

Discussing ontological truth and goodness in chapter thirteen, section three, we saw that truth is being as related to the intellect, and goodness is being as related to appetite. Now, what are we to say about beauty? Clearly it is synonymous with neither truth nor goodness. Yet it owes something to each of them. When we are captivated by a beautiful object – scenery, literature, music or whatever it may be – we find ourselves in the mysterious presence of something both true and good. There is a kinship between our intelligence and the beautiful object, and so we are drawn to the contemplation of it; and a kinship between our will and the object, and so it delights us. If a reality lacked truth and goodness it would lack beauty, while the possession of these constitutes it beautiful.

Beauty has been defined: "The splendour of form."[1] And St Thomas says: "Three things are required for beauty: first, integrity or perfection, since impaired things are by the very fact ugly; due proportion or harmony; and radiance, whence things are called beautiful which are brightly coloured."[2]

These three constitute the splendour of form, and we can gain an understanding of that definition by considering them. Integrity names the wholeness, the fullness of being, due to each thing. It is marred by stunting or weakness or falling short of the perfection appropriate to the thing in question. Proportion (or harmony) is the balance and relationship of the various parts of the beautiful thing to one another: for example, the arrangement of words and ideas in a poem, or the symmetry of members in the human body, or the due exercise of intelligence and will in harmony with man's rational nature. The third element, radiance, is the manifestation or shining forth of the form of the beautiful thing. The form of a thing (the human soul, for example) specifies it to be what it is, and is the source of its perfections. It is the source of the integrity and harmony the thing enjoys, and it is revealed by this integrity and harmony. They show forth the form to those who contemplate the beautiful object, and the shining forth, or manifestation, or radiance, of the form is the principal requirement for beauty. Hence the definition of beauty as *the splendour of form*. To the extent that a form or actuality manifests its perfection, beauty is had, although we often fail to see it, at times because we are not attuned to the beauty surrounding us.

While beauty is coextensive with being, it is especially the beauty of sensible things that moves us, and when we wish to understand beauty we naturally turn to the sensible world for illustrations. The above explanation, for example, refers to beauty in music, points out that the radiance of form is shown through bright colours, and illustrates harmony through the kind of harmony found in bodies.

There is a special reason why the beauty of sensible things attracts us, a reason indicated by St Thomas when, defining the beautiful through its effect, he says it is, "That which, being seen, pleases."[3] It is a vision bringing delight. The knowledge that figures in aesthetic appreciation is concrete, not distant and abstract, because sense and intellect are closely united: the sounds and colours and shapes of things come to us through the senses, and the intellect benefits from this intuitive sensitive knowledge.

It is particularly through sight and hearing that beauty is most powerfully conveyed to us; touch, taste and smell are poor instruments of aesthetic perception. With some people, the scent of flowers or of incense are instances of the beautiful perceived through smell. I was told of a man who, when asked what the word beautiful brought to mind, replied: "A meat pie!" Perhaps he had his own definition of beautiful; most of us would use other adjectives to describe food.

Why is it that sight and hearing mediate beauty so strongly, whereas the other senses mediate it weakly? Suppose someone were created with his powers fully developed, and they came instantly into use. He would find himself seeing, hearing, touching, tasting and smelling the things about him. Would he know the location of his various external senses? There would be no difficulty regarding three of them. He would be aware of taste in his mouth, of scent in his nostrils, of touch in his fingers or whatever part of his body was involved at the time in this sensation. The same would not apply to sight and hearing; further investigation would be needed to establish the location of those senses.

Why the difference? Because the three senses first mentioned not only give awareness of an object, but also of the contact with the object; whereas the objects of sight and hearing are had without any awareness of the very contact of the thing with the sense. Certainly we may have a painful sensation as the result of a very bright light or a very loud sound, but that sensation – when it does occur – is of touch, not sight or hearing. It is because sight and hearing have their object purely, unmingled with possessive contact, that they are especially fitted to bring beauty to our understanding. When a sense experiences the possession, the physical contact, of its object, the pleasure that results (in the case of a congenial object) is an interested, or egoistic, pleasure: a pleasure of possession. Using words strictly, we do not speak of a tasty meal as beautiful; we experience a qualitative difference between the taste of the meal and the pleasure arising from the scenery we view, or music we hear, while eating the meal.

Because of the objective or disinterested character of these two senses, they readily convey to the intellect a perception of beauty. And thereby a delight in the beautiful thing arises in the will. The will's enjoyment of beauty is not a possessive and egocentric pleasure, but a disinterested delight in the object for its own sake; not a pleasure of appropriating, but a joy of beholding. It pertains to the beautiful, as St Thomas says, "that in the sight or knowledge of it appetite is allayed."[4] And he continues: "That is called beautiful whereof the very apprehension pleases."

Intuition is utilized in aesthetic perception. By intuition I mean a knowledge that directly encounters a thing in its real existence, and not as mediated through a previous knowledge.[5] The beauty connatural to man is that of sensible things. His external senses immediately contact things, and his intelligence benefits from this intuition; the perception, by intellect, of beauty is mediated to it by the instrumentality of the senses.

Inseparably linked with this perception is a delight of the will in the beauty perceived, for the will loves good found existing in reality.

When a person is captivated by a beautiful object, both intellective and sensitive powers of cognition and appetition are involved. His sense knowledge ministers to the intellect in a more intimate way than is the case when he is thinking more abstractly. We wish for an intellectual intuition of reality, and it is a wish we cannot fulfil; but in aesthetic appreciation we approach closer to it than in either our ordinary humdrum experience or our abstract scientific thinking. Yet the experience of beauty is in the powers of intellect and will, not in the senses and emotional powers. It is in the intellect because beauty is transcendental, and therefore above sense knowledge; and it is in the will because the will alone is proportionate to rejoice in intellectual knowledge. But a redundance of that disinterested spiritual pleasure moves our emotions, so that they respond in their own way to the appreciation of beauty.

Note that beauty cannot consist in being as related only to the intellect, for then it would not differ from transcendental truth; nor is it being as related to the will alone, for then it would not differ from transcendental goodness. Beauty consists essentially in being as related to both powers together, through the medium of truth and goodness.

It is often said that beauty is in the eye of the beholder. Nothing is beautiful in itself, according to this point of view. Music or scenery or literature that makes one person thrill with aesthetic pleasure leaves another cold. So beauty is subjective, not objective: it is a feeling generated within us by something with which we happen to have a certain kind of rapport, whether because of sentimental memories, or psychological needs, or social conditioning, or other factors.

Acceptance or rejection of subjectivism in regard to beauty is related to our theory of knowledge. If we hold that knowledge contacts realities existing independently of us, we will be prepared to maintain that beauty is not reducible to our psychical states; whereas if our theory of knowledge is subjectivist, the subjectivity of beauty will be a necessary corollary.

A problem remains, though. How is it that people differ so much in their estimation of whether something is beautiful? Why are we sometimes sure a thing is beautiful without being able to give any reasoned justification of our certainty? The explanation to these queries appears when we look closely at aesthetic appreciation. It is one thing to say that beauty belongs to reality independently of every percipient; it would be quite another to assert that every percipient appreciates all the beauty objectively there. We referred above to the kinship or connaturality found between our intellect and will and the beautiful object. A thing is apprehended as beautiful because it is "in tune" with the percipient: a congeniality, a sympathy, arises. And when one is captivated by beauty, the whole person is involved. All this supposes a readiness, a facility, on the part of the person in question to respond to the objectively existing beauty. But sometimes one lacks this readiness and is "out of tune" with the beautiful thing, whether because one has never cultivated a taste for beauty expressed in that manner, or because the object is associated with unpleasant memories, or for some other reason. Beauty is objective; but the appreciation of beauty varies from person to person because it depends on the degree of sympathy in each of us.

2. Beauty and the fine arts

When we think of the word art it often brings to mind man-made products. And products of the fine arts, especially painting, are most often thought of. But the word has a wider meaning, as already indicated at the beginning of the chapter. As regards the products, not only those of the fine arts but all those of the useful arts – aeroplanes, computers, etc. – are works of art. However, the word art as used here refers primarily to the productive ability of the maker or artist, not to the thing produced. In common speech the word is sometimes used in this sense, as when we say that someone has the art of doing a certain thing. But in that context we usually think of the manual dexterity he exercises; which is not what artistic ability essentially consists in. A bird or spider may have wonderful dexterity, and construct a well-designed nest or web; but man is a maker in a sense shared by no other animal.

The difference stems from the possession of intellect. Human constructions proceed from understanding; there is an order "which reasoning by considering makes in exterior things of which it is the cause, as in a box or a house."[6] This ability to order exterior things makes one an artist, whether in the useful or fine arts. The artist is concerned with truth as ordered to a work. Hence art is defined: "Right reason about things to be made."[7] It is an intellectual quality, a habit, ordered towards making.

All art is creative, a bringing of something into being. This explains the feeling of release, of achievement, experienced by the artist. In fine art he brings new beauty into existence. His task is to show forth the splendour of form in the works he produces. This is not done by a slavish copying of external reality. As Arp says: "We do not want to reproduce, we want to produce."[8] A painter does not exert himself to reproduce a face or a landscape exactly as it looks in reality – a painting is not a photograph. Rather, he seizes on an intelligibility, a meaning, and tries to express it; and the more successful he is, the more the intelligible form will shine through the matter (the variously coloured paints on the canvas) that he is using.

The musician has another medium (sound), and his genius is exerted in manifesting through that medium what he wishes to convey. Each medium has its own exigencies, and these must be respected if the desired result is to be achieved. A painted canvas stands complete but motionless before the viewer, whereas a musical composition meets the listener successively and fluidly; and these differences affect the way in which each art-form reaches its results. Some things can be conveyed more easily in one than in the other, and they are always conveyed differently in each. Music, because of its fluidity, can be employed very readily to evoke a sense of movement; whereas painting is a very apt instrument for conveying a sense of stillness to the viewer, and can only with difficulty give a powerful impression of movement. It can depict a still-life more perfectly than a battle.[9]

The fine arts have the noble aim of creating and expressing beauty. But beauty is transcendental, and so cannot be fully captured in any finite thing, and certainly not in any work of man. Several consequences follow for the artist.

Firstly, he has a wide freedom concerning the manner in which he chooses to make form shine forth from the matter of his art. Jacques Maritain says: "There is not just one but a thousand or ten thousand ways in which the notion of *integrity* or perfection or completion can be realized."[10] If a futurist gives only a quarter of an eye to the lady in his painting, he cannot be denied the right – "One asks only (here is the whole problem) that the quarter of an eye is precisely all the eye this lady needs *in the given case*."[11] Likewise, as Maritain explains, proportion can be realized in many ways; e.g., "Figures constructed according to the Greek or Egyptian canons are perfectly proportioned in their genre." Moreover, limitless ways are possible in which the radiance of forms can appear in a work of art, and reveal to us some facet of beauty.

Secondly, the artist often feels himself frustrated as, in spite of all his labour, he sees that the completed work falls hopelessly short of the glorious ideal he had set up as his goal. This happens partly because of the severe limitations imposed by the inert materials he is forced to employ: paint or sounds or words are poor means for bringing into being the splendour he yearns to create. His frustration arises partly also from his own imperfect talents; he longs for greater dexterity, more penetrating insight, finer sensitivity.

Thirdly, since no one can give what he hasn't got, the artist needs a certain nobility, a greatness of soul, if he is to produce an enduring masterpiece of beauty. Artistic talent is not isolated from the rest of the person, and his life will inevitably affect his art, to a greater or less degree.

Fourthly, the culture of the time exerts a powerful influence, whether beneficial or harmful, on the artists immersed in it. Affinity with a work of art is essential to a real appreciation of it, so an artist who offers something that the people of his time are "out of tune" with will find his achievement rejected; and no artist wants to be rejected. His reaction may be to persist in his chosen way despite having his work shunned; but while he thus preserves his integrity, the burden of rejection will weigh down his talent. Or he may adapt his methods and themes so that they are more pleasing to potential admirers. This can be at the expense of truth; although on the other hand, the public attitude to his early work may be a sane one that will help him overcome his defects and develop his art in healthier ways.

The art of any historical period is a reflection of its hopes and fears, its customs, its economic and political life, its philosophy, its religion. Is not this the explanation of the hostility to truth found in much modern art? When people are oppressed by a sense of the meaninglessness of reality, they will gravitate to art that mirrors their mood rather than art that manifests meaning. And hostility to truth causes hostility to beauty, so that we get the monstrous paradox of "art" ordained to the expression of ugliness. I do not mean that the artist should not depict ugly things – that a painter should not produce a scene of squalor or a portrait of an ugly face. Certainly this should be done, and an aesthetic masterpiece may result, for the intelligibility manifested will have its own splendour. What I am criticizing is the depiction of ugliness *for its own sake*, as though this were the purpose of art. And associated with these aberrations, especially in the theatre and on television and the internet, is a delight in the depiction of moral evil.

Our culture is technology-oriented, and this is reflected in art, v.g., in sculpture. Attempts are even made to produce paintings and music by computer. Subjectivism is another factor – more than a factor; it is a root cause of today's trends in art. If truth, goodness and beauty were not objective, we could not enter into communication with them; we could only plunge into our own psychic states and respond to what we found there. Works of art – a sculptured figure, a play, a poem, a song, a painting – these would be but springboards and focus points for our inner vibrations, and need have no meaning other than the meaning we chose to give them.

Art critic Suzy Gablik commented that "In the multidimensional and slippery slope of Postmodernism anything goes with anything, like a game without rules. Floating images such as those we see in the painting of David Salle maintain no relationship with anything at all, and meaning becomes detachable like the keys on a key ring."[12]

Fifthly, the true artist, meeting beauty in the works he creates, gains entrance to a limitless world, for beauty extends as far as being does. The beauty of one thing suggests that of others, and the beauty of lower things is like the reflection of a higher beauty. It is not surprising that artists at times speak of their vocation in a quasi-religious way, and that some have dedicated their lives so utterly to their work (work in which the detached observer often sees little merit) that the result may be their financial, physical and social ruin. Such excesses are explained when we see the strength of the motivation.

1   *De Pulchro et Bono*, sol. 2. Authorship disputed; probably St Albert the Great.
2   *Summa Theol.*, I, q. 39, a. 8.
3   Ibid., q. 5, a. 1, *ad* 1.
4   I-II, q. 27, a. 1, *ad* 3.
5   Cf. chapter seven, section two.
6   St Thomas, *In I Ethics*, lecture 1.
7   *Summa Theol.*, I-II, q. 57, a. 4.
8   Hans Arp, *On My Way* (1948), p.70.
9   Cf. E. Gilson, *Painting and Reality* (1958), pp. 19ff.
10 *Art and Scholasticism*, p. 27, The Scribner Library, 1962.
11 Ibid.
12 Suzy Gablik, in a talk published in *Art and Design* 3, 7/8 (1987), p. 36.

Chapter Seventeen

ETHICS

In this chapter, our ultimate end and the meaning of morality will be considered. Then in the light of the conclusions established, some specific moral problems will be glanced at.

1. Human destiny

To learn the end towards which anything should be directed, it is necessary to know the nature of the thing. Members of a society without technology, faced with a complicated machine, would be at a complete loss as to how it should be used. Their ignorance would hardly be a disaster; but ignorance by man as to what he is, and therefore how he should act, is a very serious matter. Philosophy shows truths about man and his place in the universe without which life cannot be lived intelligently, because it cannot be understood.

Man is not a merely corporeal organism, destined to perish utterly after seventy or eighty years. His soul is spiritual and naturally fitted to live forever.[1] He is not determined in his activities, like the beings below him. His will is free, enabling him to choose his actions and be personally responsible. His knowledge is not confined to sense-data, like that of the lower animals. Through his intellect he transcends sensible things and has a kinship with being in its full amplitude. Questions about human destiny must be asked in the light of these truths about human nature; otherwise efforts to find the answers will resemble the feeble attempts of the non-technical society to see the purpose of the machine. What would give man complete fulfilment? What is his true destiny? His highest powers are intellect and will; by these he dwarfs the rest of the corporeal world. To be most truly and fully himself, he must operate through these powers in the highest and most intense manner of which they are capable.

He must choose the most suitable object.[2] But this cannot be money, fame or sensual pleasure, or a combination of these. Money is good only for the sake of something else – what one can buy with it, or the feeling of security its possession gives. To live for money is to degrade oneself.

The ambition to be famous and honoured is degrading; a really able person who sets this as his goal may end up a tyrant; a less able person as

293

a petty domestic tyrant, or as a social snob. Well deserved honours may bring satisfaction to the person concerned – which is natural and right; but it would be contemptible to set up fame as the goal of one's life.

Nor is sensual pleasure a worthy goal, because pleasure is ordered towards a further good, as pleasure of eating towards health. So a person who chose pleasure as the highest good would be perverting the natural order and acting irrationally. Wealth, fame or sensual pleasure, chosen as an ultimate end, necessarily degrade man; they bind him to something below him, and they make him egocentric.

Is the true end to be found in knowledge? This is certainly nobler than the ends just considered. Knowledge perfects man in his highest faculty, intellect. But the degree of perfection varies with the things known, and the manner in which they are known. If one person devotes his time to studying forms of sport, and another to physics, the second has chosen a worthier object. Or if someone studies in an academic way, while another puts his whole self into it, the second perfects himself more fully (assuming the goodness of the topic chosen). Man's true end could not consist in knowledge of anything less than God, because any lesser knowledge would leave something greater to be known, namely, God. Nor could it be an academic knowledge: it would need to be knowledge that drew the will with it.

Some place man's end in service to others. His true happiness, they think, is found when he shuns all self-centredness, and spends himself in love and service of his fellowmen. However, it is impossible that other people should be the ultimate end. Each has essential equality with others, for all are of the same nature. And while the individual is part of human society, and in that respect inferior to society, he is also a person, and in that respect transcends society. If he were simply a part, he would be totally subject to the whole, and a totalitarian society would be the right one.

What of the Stoic emphasis on virtue? The good man is the virtuous man – courageous, patient, generous, etc., thereby living in accordance with his rational nature. It is true that man should live rationally, and therefore virtuously; but this does not go far enough. The question still remains: what is the ultimate end towards which virtue itself, and man's rational nature, should be directed? Action is always towards an end, and unless we act for the right end we are not behaving rationally.

Man differs sharply from the lower animals because of the possession of intellect and will. They lack his yearning for the infinite. Their knowledge extends only to sensible things superficially known; their desires are confined to the organic level. Man is different. He apprehends, dimly but surely, being surpassing all earthly realities. He is drawn by goodness without a limit, without an admixture of evil. Imperfect things attract him because they have some perfection; but they leave him unsatisfied because there is so much perfection they lack. He is free about them, as we saw earlier,[3] because of the admixture of perfection and imperfection in them. He could be completely satisfied only by the possession of being in its fullness. But God alone is being in its fullness. So only the possession of God could satisfy man completely.

It might be objected: you may be right in arguing that the possession of God is needed to completely satisfy man. But how do we know he is meant to be completely satisfied? Surely people often desire things beyond their powers of attainment.

To answer this difficulty we must again see man realistically and in his total context. The desire we are here concerned with is not something trifling and accidental. It is a desire for that which the highest human faculties are bent towards; that which is reflected in everything true, good and beautiful met with in life; that which, if unattainable, would leave man frustrated forever, eternally reaching for the impossible. This would be literally forever, because the human soul is everlasting. But the universe is ruled by an all-wise God, and it is impossible that he would give man such a nature and not provide for its fulfilment. It would be like creating eyes marvellously adapted for sight, but without the possibility of light existing. Not only the saint and the theologian, but also the philosopher, can say with St Augustine: "Thou hast made us for thyself, O Lord, and our heart is restless until it rest in thee."[4]

Further, man can know that God created him and holds him continually in being. He can know that God is the Supreme Being, infinite in perfection. Hence, a man acts against reason if he gives some lesser being preference over God.

The conclusion is inevitable that God is the end to which human life should be directed, and that subjective happiness or fulfilment consists in the most perfect possible knowledge of God, a knowledge from which flows perfect love and delight. Each person is meant to set out on the road to that destiny, but the end can be attained only after death.

During this life man, if he is to act in accordance with his rational nature, must choose God above all else. For God is the end in which he is to find everlasting happiness. But he cannot know and love God in this life with the intensity and fullness which are proper to the soul after death. He must, however, choose God in preference to lesser things. If a choice arises between a created good and the supreme good which is God, the lesser good must be rejected. This applies no matter what that lesser good may be – money, pleasure, friends, etc. This love for God is preferential, not necessarily more intense than the love of other things. The tangible things present to our senses draw us with an intensity we do not usually experience for something not so tangibly present. A mother will have a more ardent feeling of love for her baby than for God, because the baby is sensibly present to her, and God, by comparison, seems remote. But she has preferential love for God if she would obey his law even at the cost of the child's life.

We must have a true hierarchy in our scale of values. We dealt, in chapter thirteen, section three, with the division of goods into fitting, pleasant and useful. Fitting goods are apt to be chosen for their own sake, i.e., for their inherent goodness, as knowledge or friendship. Among these due order should be observed, as in the example of the mother's choice between God and the baby. On the other hand, it is not to be forgotten that fitting goods are intrinsically worthy of love: it would be sheer perversity, even were it possible, to regard other things – friends, knowledge – as mere means, mere stepping stones, to God. In making things, God makes them good; and that real goodness of theirs is worthy of love. To say otherwise is, implicitly, to deny their goodness and to regard, e.g., the goodness of friendship as of the same kind as that of money, i.e., something merely useful for an end beyond itself. That would be a wildly irrational equation. Friendship is intrinsically good, a fitting good. An integrated life is one in which each thing has its due place.

Useful goods, like money, are regarded as means to something beyond themselves, and not perverted into ends to be sought for their own sake. Pleasures are given their due value – which is an important one, for a life without pleasure would soon become unliveable – but while pleasure itself is good, it is also ordered to something else: as the pleasure of eating is ordered to bodily health. Insofar as true fulfilment or happiness can be had in this life, it is had by harmonizing one's powers and actions, and steadfastly choosing God as the supreme good. But our weaknesses – bodily, mental, moral – make our happiness imperfect and precarious. Only after death can it attain its perfection and stability.

Here we must make an important distinction: the distinction between the natural destiny of man and the supernatural destiny which God has, in fact, given him. By man's natural destiny I mean the possession of God in the highest, most complete way possible to the human intellect and will, without any elevation to a higher order. In fact, man is meant for something greater still: for a destiny transcending his nature.[5] So the question we are about to look at – the character of man's *natural* ultimate end – is, in a sense, hypothetical.

Dealing with intellectual knowledge[6] we saw that the proper object of the human intellect, when in union with the body, is the essence of corporeal things. After death the soul no longer has this formal object, because it lacks the sensible powers on which abstractive knowledge extrinsically depends. What is the formal object of the intellect in the separated soul? That is, what is the object it knows primarily, and in virtue of which it knows others things? St Thomas answers: "The soul when separated from the body will understand itself through itself."[7]

The reason is this: the proper formal object of the intellect is that which it is immediately apt to know. In the case of the separated soul this must be the substance of the soul itself, because soul and intellect are on the same level of immateriality, and the intellect is immediately united with the substance of the soul. Direct insight is impossible in this life because the intellect knows through the instrumentality of the senses. But with the body removed, the soul will intuit itself; in fact, will know itself perfectly, for nothing will stand in the way,

As the soul is much more perfect than corporeal things, the analogical knowledge gained through direct intuition of the soul will be much more perfect than that laboriously gained in the present life. "Separated substances know God through their own substances, as a cause is known through its effect, inasmuch as each of them sees God in itself."[8] We now know God through bodily things; then the soul will know him through itself, and this knowledge will be far more perfect, both because the soul is much more perfect than bodies, and because it will be better known than bodies are: it will be known intuitively and fully.

Knowing itself thus, it will understand clearly its utter dependence on God's power sustaining it in being. And it will know his perfections – his truth, goodness and beauty, etc. – as they are reflected in the soul. Even in this life all things mirror God, as appears very powerfully to us sometimes in the presence of magnificent scenery; however, this is but a shadow of the awareness of his presence, power and glory had by the soul as it sees itself through and through. Imagine someone who had lived a noble life and striven to love and serve God above all things. After death (we are speaking of the natural order alone, of course) he would know the object of his desire in the most perfect way naturally possible to a created intellect, and the love he used to have for God on earth would be perfected and immutably stabilized through that clear knowledge. This would be the consummation and the apex of the natural order: the best and clearest knowledge of the highest being, together with the purest and most intense love. Here man's highest powers would be operating at their peak.

What of the man who had turned his will against God in this life, deliberately preferring lesser goods? Having rejected God in this life, he will reject him forever. Commitment to an ultimate end is from itself irrevocable. The reason is that the ultimate end is that which is loved above all else, and which dominates other volitions. So if a person switches from one ultimate end to another – say, from pleasure to God – this must be from another source: the love of pleasure does not account for the subordination of pleasure to God. In the present life we are very illogical much of the time, and are worked on by all sorts of outside influences; which leaves the possibility of a change for either the better or the worse.

The separated soul is strictly single-minded: the state of will at the time of death seems to be fixed forever; there is no longer a changeable body to influence it, and no longer the possibility of acting inconsistently. It has chosen itself in preference to God – in preference to the one good that could truly satisfy it. And the clarity of its new knowledge adds immensely to its frustration; it knows so much better what God is, yet is set resolutely against him.

The Beatific Vision. We spoke above of a destiny transcending human nature, and said that the question of man's ultimate *natural* end is hypothetical. In explanation, we must first note that the end just examined leaves a certain desire unfulfilled. We have mentioned the drive for intuitive knowledge – not just sensitive, but intellectual. Now the knowledge of God just discussed is gained through an intuition of the soul, not of God: in other words, it is a knowledge of God through the (intuitively seen) essence of the soul, but is not an intuition of God himself. But man has a desire to know God intuitively – to have a direct intellectual vision of him. "However well we know that God exists, we do not rest from desire, but still desire to know God through his essence."[9] "Every intellect naturally desires vision of the divine substance."[10]

This may seem at first sight to be a contradiction of what has just been said about man's end; it seems now that the ultimate natural end would be the vision of God. We must examine this desire to see God. Is it something demanded by our nature, something essential for our fulfilment, so that without it we would be frustrated? Or is it a mere wish, something man would like if it were attainable?

Man has no positive capacity to see God. For he is naturally apt only for knowledge that can be gained through the proper formal object of the intellect. However, even in the separated soul this object is but the essence of the soul, which is infinitely below God, and manifests him only analogically. So that is the highest knowledge of God for which we are naturally apt.

By way of illustration: human eyes are suited for vision, but not for X-ray vision. And our power of locomotion enables us to walk, but not to fly. A person unable to see or walk would be naturally frustrated in these respects: would lack due fulfilment. But we cannot reasonably complain about being unable to see X-rays or to fly. The vision of God is beyond any positive capacity of human powers, and therefore its absence would not be a frustration of human nature. The natural desire for the vision is for something to which human nature is not necessitated.

Nevertheless, the desire exists, and the philosopher may well ask whether there is any possibility of its realization. It can be reasoned, philosophically, that the desire indicates an openness to receive some special divine gift which would make it possible to intuit God. This would consist in an elevation so tremendous that we would become apt for a vision for which no creatable being could be naturally apt.

Reason alone, without Revelation, cannot know whether this would even be possible, much less whether God has chosen to offer such a precious gift. The answer must be obtained from sacred theology, which teaches that man is offered grace which elevates him to a supernatural life whose consummation is the eternal and immediate vision of God. The sharing by man in the life of God is the heart of Christianity. For this the human race was destined from the beginning; by original sin the gift was lost; Christ's redeeming sacrifice restored it; the life of grace unites its possessors to God and to one another in a sacred friendship; its end is an eternal happiness far surpassing the natural end which we have been considering; its rejection brings everlasting suffering greater than that which would result from the loss of a merely natural end.

We noted in chapter five, section five that sacred theology is a higher knowledge than philosophy. This has a special relevance in regard to philosophical ethics, which is subordinate to moral theology. Theology sees man in a new and higher light, and gives knowledge philosophy could never attain. But although philosophy is transcended it is not contradicted. All truths harmonize. The soul will still know God in knowing itself. But this will not be the ultimate; it will be excelled by the realization of man's highest wish: the vision of God. Nor are the precepts of ethics annulled by theology: they are the foundation of Christian morality. Grace does not contradict nature, but perfects it. Philosophical ethics is right as far as it goes, but it does not go all the way, for man, in actual fact, has a supernatural destiny and the Christian Revelation to guide and support him. But because of the harmony between nature and grace, and between reason and Revelation, any attempt to construct a Christian moral theology while ignoring or depreciating natural ethics would result in an inhuman system.

2. The meaning of morality

By the morality of acts is meant that quality which distinguishes them from acts considered psychologically, sociologically, or in some other way, and gives them a unique value of befittingness or unbefittingness. Our first task is to vindicate the existence of morality in this sense, for many philosophers doubt or deny it.

Proof from consciousness of moral values. We are confronted, in our experience, with moral values irreducible to psychology or sociology.

We judge necessarily that good should be done and evil avoided. But certain actions have a special goodness or badness related to the exercise of personal responsibility. An act of kindness is good. An act of cruelty is bad. These are not good or bad because society approves or disapproves of them, or because they bring us some advantage. The goodness and badness involved here retain their character even when social pressure tempts us to reverse those values.

In wartime, for example, numerous atrocities are perpetrated and tremendous group pressure is exerted on individuals to force their compliance. Many who succumb do so knowing they are behaving in an unworthy manner; and some refuse to conform. There is in man a sense of right and wrong, of the worthy and the unworthy, of the noble and the base, of actions befitting man and others perverting him.

This is a consciousness of the peculiar goodness and badness attaching to human actions. Such goodness and badness are not inferred, but experienced. I do not mean, of course, that concrete judgments about the morality of actions are necessarily right. People are often mistaken about which actions are good and which are bad. But the distinctive character of morality is evident to the understanding. People are aware of themselves as responsible agents, and of an obligation to choose befitting actions and shun the unbefitting.

This is very obvious when someone sees that the moral thing to do is something opposed to what society approves of, or to his own psychological inclinations. He knows his awful responsibility to choose the right course regardless of every enticement to abandon it. It is the human experience of irreducible moral values that gives meaning and nobility to the lives of those who heroically stand firm and refuse to betray their standards. But once the uniqueness of moral values is denied, those heroes should be regarded as ignorant or stubborn or mentally unbalanced; if they had any sense, it should be contended, they would take the easy way out.

Proof deriving from human freedom. A second argument comes from a consideration of human acts relatively to goodness and badness. In general, something is good if it has the fullness of being that is due to it. A fruit tree is good if it is well-formed and healthy, and produces fruit plentifully and with the due nutritive elements. It is bad if defective in these respects. Restricting the question to actions, an action is good if appropriate to the attainment of its end, whether the action is a skilful tennis stroke, expert surgery or anything else. It is bad if inapt to attain the end.

Now when we come to that class of human actions called moral, we find ourselves in the presence of a value other than those just mentioned. And the difference arises from the truth that man is a free agent with an ultimate end befitting his nature. Granted that truth, a peculiar value must necessarily belong to certain actions. The actions in question are those which are (a) free; (b) either in harmony with or opposed to his rational nature; (c) and consequently, either directing him to or deflecting him from his ultimate end. These characteristics combine to differentiate the acts called moral from those of a non-moral kind, and therefore give them a value of a higher order than that of a good tennis stroke or a skilful surgical operation.

The nature of morality. We sometimes tend to think of actions as morally indifferent in themselves, but extrinsically related to moral laws. But if this were so, all actions would be intrinsically equal: kindness and cruelty would not be morally differentiated according to themselves. Closer inspection shows that the morality of an action *is the whole action* as related to a moral standard. Goodness or badness is intrinsic to the action, not related to it from outside. (The denial of this will be critically examined in section four.)

Suppose I have lent you a computer, and you later tell me you no longer need it because you have now bought one yourself. I then remove my machine from your house to mine – which, physically considered, is an act of transportation. While doing so I resolve to return and steal your new computer, because it is better than mine. So I go through the same process again, transporting a computer from your house to mine. Were the two acts specifically the same? Physically they were: each was an act of transportation. But morally they were diverse: the second was theft.

Actions are specified or determined, i.e., made this kind of action rather than some other, by the object to which they are directed. The act of extending one's leg may be a kick, a signal or a dance step – its nature is fixed by its object. The two actions of transporting computers are determined likewise: hence in reference to one object (the physical) they are identical; in reference to another (the moral) they are diverse.

What is the standard, the rule, in reference to which acts have moral value? St Thomas says: "The proximate rule is human reason; but the supreme rule is the eternal law."[11] We will consider the proximate rule first, then see how it is related to the eternal law in God. Human reason in this context means reason operating practically, not theoretically,[12] and operating rightly, not erroneously.[13] In other words, the immediate guide in acting morally is a true understanding of what should be done. This follows from the premise that acts having a moral character are those which proceed from the use of intelligence and free will. While human reason is the immediate guide, or proximate rule, human nature itself, together with the natural order in which man is placed, constitutes the proximate foundation of the rule. That is, his reason does not operate in a vacuum but operates *about* his nature and that of the things affecting him, finding that certain actions befit him while others are unbefitting. Thus certain actions are reasonable, others unreasonable.

But man is not the ultimate source of the truth of things and the rightness of actions. He *finds* these, he doesn't originate them. This brings us to God as the fount of morality.

Dealing with the existence and nature of God, we showed that he is the exemplar and orderer of all other things. In knowing himself, he knows all things, eternally and completely. His ordinance (or blueprint, as it were) of his creation is called the eternal law. It is, "The very ordering (*ratio*) of the government of things, existing in God as in the ruler of the universe..."[14] The divine understanding is the ultimate measure of the rightness of acts. This does not imply that God acts arbitrarily. The meaning is this. He understands himself as imitable in a multitude of ways by created things. But he is infinite and subsistent goodness; and no action of a creature can be moral which does not imitate that goodness. Just as our reason, to be morally right, must act in harmony with human nature, God's understanding of what man should do is in harmony with the divine nature. The absolutely ultimate reason why some act is moral or immoral is because God is what he is. An act of cruelty could never be good except on the impossible assumption that God became something else.

When man thinks about himself and the world in which he is, he can understand something of that God-given order according to which he is constituted, and in accordance with which he is morally bound to act.

Thus by his reason he participates in the eternal understanding of God.

Morality is unconditional. Kant rightly insisted that moral laws are bidden categorically. It is not a case of act morally *if* you wish to be successful, or happy, or attain some other advantage. The moral bid is imperative: act morally, come what may. A builder has to construct a house in a certain way *if* he wishes it to endure; but the art of building does not impose on him an obligation to wish this. If it *is* an obligation – say because justice to his employer requires it – this is a moral consideration.

The absolute character of moral obligation is evident to us from consciousness. We experience it as binding unconditionally. When someone insists that a particular action is against his conscience, and we see that he is sincere, we experience that his decision must be respected, that it would be rationally repugnant to coerce him into doing what he believes to be wrong. This unconditional respect for a sincere conscience is based on the unconditional character of morality. If the man in question objected to acting on grounds of expediency or through stubbornness or selfishness, there might be justification for forcing his compliance. His stand could be harmful to the common good, and the government might rightly coerce his obedience.

Why is moral obligation unconditional? It is because moral acts are related in a special way to the ultimate end. They are proximately towards a fitting good, and ultimately towards *the* fitting good – God. An action which is merely useful for something beyond itself derives any goodness it has from the end to which it is directed. Likewise, a pleasant act, as such, lacks the character of morality. Only the fitting good has moral value – it alone is intrinsically worthy of choice. And the better something is, the more worthy of choice.

But all lesser goods derive from the supreme good, God. To act morally is to tend towards those ends that befit us, and ultimately towards that highest end in which our happiness consists. And one should act in that way because the object is good, not primarily because one hopes for satisfaction from it. The subjective happiness to be gained is a legitimate aspiration; but to make it the ultimate object willed is to subject the intrinsically fitting good to our personal satisfaction: which is hedonism. One who "served" God with the overriding motive of ensuring one's own enjoyment, in this life or the next, would be using God as a means, and would therefore be choosing himself, not God, as his highest good.

Just as the goodness of moral acts has its foundation in the divine nature, the unconditional character of moral obligation comes from the linkage between man's actions and the true ultimate end, God. We are bound to desire our last end – and therefore to desire those fitting goods bound up with the last end, and to reject evils repugnant to it.

The fundamental principle of morality. The basic moral precept is given by St Thomas as, "Good is to be done and pursued, and evil shunned."[15]

It is impossible to choose anything at all unless we see it as in some way good or attractive. That which presented no attractive features whatever to us would be simply unchoosable, just as something completely transparent would be unseeable. If I woke up in the morning and saw no attractiveness about anything, I would be powerless to act. All possible choices would be indifferent: remaining in bed, getting up and having breakfast, or reading a book, or going out, etc. So sheer indifference would cause me to remain where I was. The final result of my mental state, if no one intervened, would be death; and that prospect would be as indifferent as any other.

The absolutely primary concept regarding activity is the concept of good. And from this arises the first, or fundamental, practical principle: "Good is to be done and evil avoided." It is irreducible to any prior practical judgment, and is obtained analytically from the concept of good: the predicate "to be done" arises from the understanding of good.

The objection may be put: If we necessarily see that good is to be done, how can we do evil? The answer is that we are not suggesting that whenever goodness is seen in something, we are irresistibly drawn to it. As we saw when examining free will, the same thing can appear good under one aspect and bad under another, and this indeterminacy leaves room for freedom. What we are saying now is that the concept of good is of something attractive, that of evil of something repelling. Consequently, a thing cannot be chosen unless it is apprehended as good in some way. But a particular thing need not be chosen even then, because it falls short of complete goodness. Also, a choice is of an object as it is known, and knowledge is not infallible: we can mistakenly think something to be good which in reality is not so.

Of course, good and evil are metaphysical concepts, and are not confined to moral values. So the principle, "Good is to be done and evil avoided," can be taken in either a wide or a restricted sense. In the wide sense it is a metaphysical principle applicable to all the activity of all things. In the restricted sense the terms good and evil are used of moral values, and it is in this sense that the principle is the fundamental one in ethics. The good referred to here is the fitting good for man, without which morality would be impossible, because activity for the sake of pleasure does not constitute an action morally good.

Natural moral law. Criticisms of the natural moral law often show surprising misunderstandings. Some confuse it with physical law, and object that natural law defenders, to be consistent, would have to oppose shaving or damming a stream, since these actions impede nature. It should be made very clear that when we uphold the natural (moral) law, we are not referring to physical laws of the universe.

All moral values are about actions that ought to be done or those that ought to be avoided. The distinctive point about the natural moral law is that the actions belonging to it are fixed to be good or bad by the nature of man. For example, people are obliged to worship God, and it is an obligation based in human nature; but they have no inherent obligation to give him special worship on a particular day of the week. If they have the latter obligation, it does not arise from their nature but from another source.

Some acts are seen as *necessarily* good from man's nature, others as *necessarily* bad. Granted that man is constituted as he is, that he is fitted for society with others, that his last end is God, certain moral laws are necessarily right, e.g., that he should avoid gluttony, should contribute to the good of society, should love God. The natural moral law is an ordinance of how man should act, which arises necessarily from his nature adequately considered. That is, he must be seen in his relationships to the world and to God; to examine him as though he were an isolated and self-contained being would be like trying to understand the law of gravity by selecting one stone and isolating it from all the other things in the universe. The natural moral law is the unwritten law of human nature. Based in human nature, it becomes known to each of us insofar as we understand what we are, personally and socially.

Clearly, not all acts having moral value belong to natural morality. Some derive their force from positive law. In a country where traffic keeps to the left, we are morally obliged to obey that law. But whence did it derive? Certainly not from nature: no matter how carefully we study human nature, whether in the individual, in society, or in relation to God, we shall discover no hint of whether traffic should keep left or right – or whether all the streets should be one-way streets. This law gets its binding power from the authority of the law-giver. It is not natural but positive. It is not intrinsically necessary: the opposite could have been chosen. It binds because it is imposed, whereas natural morality is binding from itself. Yet this positive law is related to the natural moral law. The traffic regulation is intended to guard against accidents – and that is not something indifferent. We are bound by natural morality to take reasonable care not to injure or kill others.

Every positive law – that is, every law that binds from the authority of the law-giver, not from its own nature – is based in the natural moral law. For whence derives the obligation to obey a law-giver? A government official may be given authority by his section head, and he by the head of the department, and he by the minister, and he by the Prime Minister as representing the people. But if all authority was derived there would be no basis for authority: the nation would have no more right to make laws than an office-boy. The only alternative to anarchy is authority invested naturally in particular individuals or groups, and ultimately in God. Parents from nature, not from legislation, have authority over their young children; authority in political matters is naturally invested in civil society, and so on.

Further, a rational animal must be directed by laws that are reasonable, not arbitrary. But if all laws were positive, none would be reasonable. Positive traffic laws are reasonable when based on natural morality regarding the avoidance of injury and death. They would be unreasonable otherwise. A law that cars be equipped with seat belts is not unreasonable; a law that they be equipped with mouse traps would be.

A denial of the existence of natural morality is, implicitly, a denial of the reasonableness of law. To the question, "Why should I obey the laws?" the reply could only be, "Because the law-giver commands it," or "Because you'll be punished if you don't," or some other non-rational, and non-moral, answer.

3. Application of the natural moral law

Moral questions cannot be solved unless human nature is seen rightly. Common sense takes us part of the way, but a more penetrating vision is needed if an adequate moral system is to be worked out. We must be guided by true principles if we are to live in a fully human way. The following four points arise from what has gone before.

A. Each person is unique, and also a part of society. As a person he has an end transcending that of any social groups to which he belongs. He is, as it were, caught up into God's infinity by being directed to the infinite good (whether viewed philosophically, or in the light of his supernatural destiny). But as part of a whole, that is, as an individual, he is subject to others – to society. He has strict duties in this respect. The part is for the sake of the whole. But the whole is for the sake of the person.

B. The fitting good must be followed. Hence appears the sacredness of each person and of his conscience; hence his immense responsibility.

C. Man lives in an ordered universe, not a chaos; and can understand this order, as it relates to him, well enough to act reasonably. However, there may be great practical difficulties here from social conditioning, etc. Each of us should strive to rise above these to a clearer vision of the truth of things.

D. Natural morality is a blueprint of how we ought to act; not that all moral acts belong to it, but all are at least reduced to it. It is a foundation. The current confusion in morality is due to ignorance (sometimes guilty ignorance) of this foundation. Situation ethics is a symptom and an outcome of this ignorance.

One of the misapprehensions about the natural moral law visualizes it as a rigid system of law standing apart from the concrete happenings of life, and trying to force them into its own mould. This is far from the truth. Would anyone think of physical law in that fashion? The natural moral law governing rational beings is just as intimate to them as physical law to all corporeal things.

Conditions of a just war. This objection was put to me concerning my rejection of situation ethics: "The Catholic Church approves of situation ethics in at least one case, that of the conditions necessary for a just war." The objection must have been prompted by a radical misunderstanding of the meaning of the natural moral law. I would regard the case in point as an excellent example of the application of natural morality. The principles involved are universally valid, and are indispensable for acting rationally in the matter.

First, the decision to wage war on another country must be made by the government, not by private groups. Secondly, the cause must be just, which in turn involves various conditions: that the war is to combat a grave injustice; that the said injustice is at least as serious as the evils likely to result from the war; that there is reasonable hope of victory; that the injustice cannot be overcome by other means.

Every one of these principles belongs to natural morality. Why would anyone confuse them with situation ethics? I think because of the above-mentioned illusion about the natural moral law. The man who saw that the conditions for a just war are applicable to numberless complex situations, that their application requires an intensely practical appraisal of a bewildering variety of circumstances, assumed that *this* was not natural morality, which he associated with the abstract and remote. But the natural moral law does not stand apart from concrete situations: its principles are embedded, as it were, in those situations.

Of course, the realities are not always crystal clear; sometimes they are appallingly difficult to see. So we have to gather all the facts, assess them prudently, compare them, and make a balanced judgment. Moral decisions are not the field of a cold, computer-like intellect, but of a whole person in healthy contact with reality. Nevertheless, we must see the principles (at least in a practical way) if we are to make a true and stable judgment. If one doubts this, try making a decision about the justice of a war without employing unchanging principles. If you disagree about the principles just summarized, others must be substituted for them if a decision is to be reached. Or if you say that war is essentially unjust, you have introduced that doctrine as an alleged natural principle of human conduct.

Sexual morality. The anarchy which ensues in morality when natural principles are rejected is probably more manifest in sexual morality than anywhere else. The sexual drive is so powerful that judgment about right and wrong is very easily warped by it. Pre-marital sexual relations, adultery, divorce, contraception: passion can pervert reason into their acceptance. Hence the supreme importance of a right understanding in these matters through clearly seen principles. The points enumerated at the beginning of this section have great relevance here. Man is a person and a part of society; and both aspects are integral to sex and marriage. Today great emphasis is placed (and rightly) on the truth that marriage is a union of two persons; but the other aspect tends to be forgotten. Biologically, sex is for the propagation of the human race; and the sociological function of educating new citizens – within a lasting family unit – is vital. Sex and marriage must be seen in a social (not just mutual) context if they are to be seen rightly. A couple have an obligation to society, not simply to one another – which is a point situation ethics often forgets. If one couple, in certain circumstances, can have sexual relations outside of marriage, so can any other couple in similar circumstances; and this weakens the whole social fabric of marriage. In order to satisfy a private good, a wonderful social good has been assaulted. And human frailty being what it is, the attack will rapidly accelerate.

The nature of civil society. How should society be organized? Theories have been proposed ranging from rigid totalitarianism to anarchy; and from complete socialism to unrestrained capitalism. Doubt exists as to where politics ends and economics begins: what some condemn as government interference with the rights of private enterprise (in price control, for example) is praised by others as prudent control for the sake of the common good. Immense confusion surrounds the notion of competition. Most people say they believe moderate competition is good. But they are unable to draw any definite line. Some say collective price-fixing practices by industry should be outlawed; others only object to really flagrant instances. And if industry is not to agree to fix prices, has the government any right to do so? Should international trade be free or restricted?

What principles of credit control should be applied? Should wages be determined by Court arbitration, by collective bargaining between unions and employers, by supply and demand, or what? How is inflation caused, and how can it be avoided? Are economic recessions caused by excessive government control, or by insufficient government control? Is a compulsory health insurance scheme a good thing, or an infringement of individual liberty?

Confusion reigns, among people generally and among politicians and economists, concerning the nature of civil society: the nature of each sphere (economics, politics, etc.), and how they should be harmoniously coordinated.

Suppose doctors made no attempt to understand the human body, but sought, with the aid of statistics, to relieve symptoms, being satisfied provided the patient didn't complain too loudly or change his doctor. A good doctor is far removed from that attitude; he seeks to understand the nature of the human body and the laws of its healthy functioning. He knows that treatment in violation of those laws will lead to worse sickness, or to death. Many people, including economists and politicians, treat society like a quack dealing with the human body. They do not ask themselves whether there are underlying laws of the economic and political spheres, laws which must be respected if society is to be healthy.

I am not suggesting that everything in the social order should be done in an invariable way, regardless of circumstances, that whatever is right for one community will be right for all, that nature prescribes one precise solution for each situation. There is certainly room, and need, for diversity. But there are fundamental laws which must be seen and followed if society is to be healthy. Society is natural: it pertains to human nature to form communities with economic, political, recreative and cultural levels. And nature does not merely say that people should live in society, but gives (as regards its fundamentals) a blueprint of the kind of society they should implement.

Each one is an individual who is subject to society, and a person for whose sake society itself exists; each is entitled to the fruits of his labour, but not to what belongs to others; a government must exist and civil laws must be made, but only because the common good requires them; every citizen should have a say in the running of society, but it should be an informed say. We can so easily go astray at any of these points unless we have a clear vision of the road.

The notion of natural moral laws in the social realm – especially in economics – is immensely important, and tragically neglected. We cannot explore it here (a whole book would be needed for that), but a little reflection shows that natural morality, given its reality, must be relevant in this field. I am convinced that the economic confusion and political oppression of today cannot be overcome until we understand the natural laws according to which civil society should be run.

4.   Concerning subjectivism, consequentialism and pragmatism

The proposition that moral values are objective and unique is contested by many philosophers, psychologists and sociologists. Let us look at this position.

Objection. According to Bertrand Russell, disagreements about moral values are not about objective truths, but about differences of taste. If one person says oysters are good, while another says they are bad, there is nothing to argue about, because each is expressing his personal taste in regard to oysters. It is the same with moral values, although we tend to think otherwise when the matter seems to us to be more exalted than oysters. "The chief ground for adopting this view is the complete impossibility of finding any arguments to prove that this or that has intrinsic value."[16]

Reply. If one person says it is good to exterminate a race we do not approve of, while another says it is bad, we are fully aware that the question is more than a matter of taste. As for the alleged impossibility of showing that this or that has intrinsic value, we have already dealt with the existence and nature of moral value in section two, above.

Objection. The first argument given in section two for the existence of unique moral values was from our alleged consciousness of them. But if everyone, or even most, have this consciousness, how is it that we find such radical disagreements about morality? Look at the views of the Nazis compared with those most of us hold. Contrast the views of modern civilizations with those of primitive peoples – regarding cannibalism, etc. We would feel horror at the idea of eating our dead enemies, and even greater horror at the idea of eating our dead relatives. Yet these practices have been perfectly acceptable to some societies.

Again, reflect on the vicissitudes of ethical views throughout recorded history: polygamy, slavery, religious persecution, cruel punishments for minor felonies – all these have been regarded as virtuous, but they are now thought by most people to be vices. The data seem to force us to the conclusion that moral values are not objective and present to the consciousness of people generally, but subjective and differing according to the psychological condition of the individual and the historical circumstances of the society he grew up in .

Reply. The argument from the consciousness of an irreducible moral value in our actions does not imply that people will always agree about the rightness or wrongness of a particular kind of action. Two people may have a keen awareness of moral goodness and badness, yet hopelessly disagree about whether a certain religion, or political policy, or social custom, is good or bad. The character of moral goodness or badness is evident; the diagnosis of whether action A is in accordance with morality may be very difficult to make. There is the difficulty of seeing the principles to be applied. There is the further difficulty of applying them. And there are differences of opinion about matters of fact – about, say, whether a hostile nation is making long-term plans to attack us.

C. S. Lewis points out that our attitude regarding witchcraft contradicts that of people centuries ago because we differ from them about the facts. "It may be a great advance in knowledge not to believe in witches: there is no moral advance in not executing them when you do not think they are there."[17]

We must also remember that the presence of a particular situation or policy does not necessarily mean that people think it morally good. People often act badly, knowing they are doing so; while others weakly acquiesce in an evil state of affairs. It would be naïve to believe that slavery or Nazism proceed from the sincerely held belief that they are morally good.

After taking full account of the variations between different cultures and epochs, there remains a striking similarity between the moral standards of all peoples at every point in recorded history. The cardinal virtues of prudence, justice, temperance and fortitude were analysed and admired by the ancient Greeks before the modern civilizations were dreamed of. Ideals of self-sacrificing actions on behalf of others have always been held, although differences have existed as to whether our benevolence should be restricted to our own family and friends, or our fellow citizens, or whether it should be extended to the whole world. The notion that each people has its own morality in the way that each has its own language is simply a myth.

Subjectivity would destroy morality. Denial of the objectivity of morality implies that we can do what we like without guilt. Cowardice, treachery, murder, persecution of anyone who disagrees with us – all these would be morally neutral. This contention is strenuously repudiated by the overwhelming majority of subjectivists, and I do not suggest they see the implication of their position. All the same, it is logically inescapable.

To deny objectivity is to say that actions really have no moral value, that nothing is better or worse than anything else. This means that "morality is in the mind of the doer". An action can be said to be bad for me only in the sense that I think it to be bad. Most of us would say a person is mistaken who thinks it immoral to have a blood transfusion; we would say there is nothing objectively wrong with it. Now, the denial of objective moral values means that all allegedly bad actions are in the same category as blood transfusions: they are not really bad, but some people mistakenly believe they are.

From this it follows that only the ignorant can be moral agents. A person who is enlightened about blood transfusions, i.e., who knows they are not objectively bad, can receive a transfusion without scruple. Similarly, a person who knew that morality lacks objective validity would know that any action is as indifferent as any other. So he could do anything without scruple.

Consequentialism and pragmatism. Consequentialism sees the rightness or wrongness of actions determined by the consequences that flow from them, and with nothing intrinsically good or bad. Pragmatism has a consequentialist approach to ethics. As we saw in chapter four, pragmatism regards thought as a means of coping with problems, and not as attaining objective reality. For the pragmatist, there is no objective intelligible order.

Richard Rorty speaks of "descriptions of the world and of ourselves which are less useful and those which are more useful".[18] He goes on to say that pragmatists are vague as to what these are useful for or in what way "a better future" is better. They can say it is better because it contains more of what we see as good and less of what we see as bad. And they see good in terms of "variety and freedom" or of "growth". Rorty thinks we should be aware of the sensitivity of other people and see the solidarity that binds us together in a community. This mutual identification should be extended to everyone, regardless of race, religion, social status and other differences. There will be a shared hope for a better world, not only for all living now but also for future generations.

The pragmatist's position regarding ethics flows from the denial that things have definite natures and that an intelligible order exists. We have seen in earlier chapters why those tenets should be rejected.

The contention that we should seek pleasure and shun pain, both for ourselves and for others, cannot logically be a binding principle for pragmatism or consequentialism. Why should I avoid inflicting pain on people if I get pleasure from doing so, or if I will gain what I want by doing so? Pragmatism cannot refute this, for to do so requires acceptance of an objective moral order.

A consequentialist will try to assess cases on their merits, while denying unchanging principles. But concrete situations alone cannot yield moral answers; unchanging principles are always needed. An instance of this was given in the previous section, under the subheading **Conditions of a just war**. If we are confronted with a mass of facts, and have no unchanging principles we can apply, no firm decision can be reached. Everyone uses principles, including consequentialists, but we do not usually think explicitly about them, and so it is possible to imagine we can dispense with them.

It may be objected: "I believe in rules or principles, so long as they are relative and changeable; it is absolutes I reject." But this won't do. Unless we have a network of absolute principles, we have no way of judging definitely about any particular situation. We could never judge whether a certain war was just or unjust if the most basic rules we could apply were variable. It would no more be possible to judge a moral situation with changeable and relative rules than to measure a field with a tape that kept changing its size. In practice, everyone accepts unchanging principles – as when a consequentialist gives primacy to personality over property.

We all know how easy it is to pretend that a particular solution to a moral problem is the right one in the circumstances merely because it suits our selfish interests. Consequentialism lends itself to that pretence. And in the sociological sphere it is highly vulnerable to power politics, an inevitable result when principles are whittled away.

5. Final observations

It is clear from the above that our general philosophy shapes our conception of morality and our judgment as to whether this or that is the right thing to do. A clear example is the ethical position taken by Peter Singer. He denies the uniqueness of human beings, together with any destiny beyond the present life or any divine providence. He asserts a principle of equality, whereby the suffering or enjoyment of one being is counted equally with that of another.

"…Whether a being is or is not a member of our species is, of itself, no more relevant to the wrongness of killing it than whether it is or is not a member of our race."[19] The basic question is: Does this being feel pain? In the case of a human embryo before it can feel pain, "an abortion terminates an existence that is of no 'intrinsic' value at all."[20] A further distinction pertains to whether the being is a person. For Singer a person is a being having self-consciousness, in the sense of self-awareness and perception of past and future. He concludes that newborn babies and some intellectually disabled humans are not persons. So "…killing a disabled infant is not morally equivalent to killing a person. Very often it is not wrong at all."[21]

In accord with Singer's definition, non-human animals with self-consciousness, such as dogs or horses, are persons and therefore of equal status with human persons. To inflict a certain degree of pain on a horse is morally equivalent to inflicting that degree of pain on a human person – taking into account the being's awareness of what is happening and its apprehension of what is threatened.

Peter Singer makes a revealing observation at the beginning of his book *Practical Ethics*. "…this book contains no discussion of sexual morality. There are more important ethical issues to be considered."[22]

In conclusion, the current confusion on ethical issues flows from conflicting views and confusion about the nature of things. One result is a bracketing of truth: an attempt by society to resolve contentious issues without asking the question: What is the objective truth? Instead the appeal is to feeling, not reason. A position is ruled out if it is seen as judgmental or hurtful or insensitive or divisive or unhelpful.

This has gone so far that maintaining certain politically incorrect judgments publicly can lead to prosecution. If one claims that homosexual acts are intrinsically immoral, the claim is not rationally discussed by those who disagree; instead the proponent of the judgment is seen as hurting the feelings of homosexuals, or as stirring up hatred against them. And if the person putting the politically incorrect case is charged with a legal offence, the truth or otherwise of the statement will be dismissed as irrelevant.

[1]   Chapter ten, section one.
[2]   Cf. Aristotle, *Nicomachean Ethics*, I, 5; X, 7.
[3]   Chapter ten, section three.
[4]   *Confessions*, I, 1.
[5]   *Summa Theol.*, I-II, q. 62, a. 1.
[6]   Chapter eight, section four.
[7]   *Summa Theol.*, I, q. 89, a. 2.
[8]   St Thomas, *Contra Gentes*, III, 49.
[9]   Ibid., chapter 50.
[10] Ibid., chapter 57.
[11] *Summa Theol.*, I-II, q. 21, a. 1.
[12] Cf. I, q. 79, a. 11.
[13] Cf. *In II Sent.*, d. 24, q. 3, a. 3, *ad* 3.
[14] I-II, q. 91, a. 1.
[15] I-II, q. 94. a. 2.
[16] *Religion and Science* (1935), p. 238.
[17] *Mere Christianity* (1956 printing), book one, chapter two, last paragraph.
[18] *Philosophy and Social Hope* (1999), p. 27.
[19] Peter Singer, *Practical Ethics* (1993 edition), p. 150.
[20] Ibid., p. 151.
[21] Ibid., p. 191.
[22] Ibid., p. 2.

Chapter Eighteen

THE IMPORTANCE OF PHILOSOPHY

The thoughts of this final chapter arise from all that has gone before on the nature of philosophy, its conclusions and its relation to other subjects.

1. Philosophy is a foundation of human knowledge

All natural knowledge is ultimately resolved into philosophy. In chapter five, analysing common sense, we saw that it consists of judgments immediately based on experience, self-evident propositions and easy inferences from these. But common sense does not defend its conclusions, nor does it plumb them to their depths. Philosophy does this, making its exponent (if he philosophises truly) a person with a stronger and clearer common sense knowledge than he had previously. On the other hand, an erroneous philosophy leads to a corruption of common sense. Look at Berkeley's contention that the objects of the senses have no extra-mental existence. Or J. S. Mill's contention that the propositions of mathematics, e.g., that $7 \times 7 = 49$, are empirical generalizations which could sometimes be false.

Some people with a common sense understanding of the arguments for God's existence are severely shaken when confronted with agnostic counter-arguments they cannot answer. They may have been perfectly satisfied with the proof from design, and unable to conceive how anyone can fail to see its force. They did not realize that their mere common sense approach would leave them almost defenceless before the onslaughts of a sophisticated agnostic. He asks them how they know the supreme designer is also the creator of all things; how they can argue from a very finite arrangement to an infinite mind; how they can explain the imperfections of the world if the designer is perfect and all-powerful.

Philosophy guards against the erosion of common sense through the infiltration of error. The person of common sense, if subjected to scientism, to false philosophical doctrines, etc., will find the natural certainties slipping away. He may finish up doubting almost everything: the evidence of the senses, the validity of universal principles, the existence of objective morality, free will. Philosophy's task is to defend these natural certainties by showing the evidence for them and answering objections against them. This leads to a deepening of common sense itself.

Similarly in regard to the empirical sciences. Philosophy shows where they fit into human knowledge, their scope and general method. The distinction[1] between science of the observable (empirical science) and science of being (philosophy) is of the utmost importance if we are to avoid confusion. If all human knowledge was confined to the observable, great questions that have fascinated people down the centuries would be beyond us, and we would be bound to a shallow phenomenalism. The attempt to answer philosophical questions through empirical science (and the attempt is constantly being made) is doomed to failure. It is like a surgeon seeking the soul with his scalpel, or an astronomer searching for God with a telescope. A terrible deformation of knowledge ensues; science is faced with a task beyond its powers, compelled to work at problems for which it is not equipped.

One result is a scientistic conception of reality. Another is that science and technology are used to dominate man: some biologists, for example, are given to dogmatic pronouncements about how we should run our lives; even how we should be compelled to conform to supposed biological laws. They do not seem to realize that biology and other scientific disciplines are part (and by no means the principal part) of a larger whole, and must be viewed in the light of the totality. But if empirical science were the highest knowledge accessible to man, how could the absolutist claims of scientific domination be refuted?

Sacred theology cannot be developed without philosophy. The task of theology is to penetrate God's Revelation to mankind, understanding it ever more clearly and deeply, and defending it against attacks and misrepresentations. But Revelation is not something isolated from the rest of our knowledge. If the theologian cannot answer objections against the credibility of Christian doctrine, he leaves it defenceless and fails in his duty. Moreover, lacking a true philosophy he lacks the insight into the nature of things that is indispensable for a theological understanding of the articles of faith.

Education versus indoctrination. Without philosophy no one is fully educated. Education involves more than the accumulation of assorted facts, opinions and skills. One may be very well-read yet very poorly educated. The intellectually integrated person needs a sure and delicate logic, a broad synthetic outlook, a depth of understanding. Dealing with knowledge, we saw that the activity proper to living things is an activity that perfects the operant, making it *more* than it was previously. This is pre-eminently true of intellection and willing. But since the intellect is meant for truth and the will for goodness, a terrible distortion occurs when the one falls into error or the other pursues bad objects.

Many are preoccupied, some are even haunted, by the threat of indoctrination in society. Technology has brought about a new intensification of the means of communication. Powerful pressure groups manipulate the mass media. So much data are at our disposal that their evaluation becomes almost impossible. Ever increasing specialization results, leading to a narrowing of outlook, each specialist concentrating on his particular tree and having no opportunity to stand back and view the wood as a whole.

The basic distinction between education and indoctrination is that the former involves *seeing* the reasons, knowing *why*; whereas indoctrination involves accepting conclusions on non-rational grounds: from having them constantly impressed over a long period, or from external pressure, or from passion. The educated person's knowledge is firm because it is stabilized by the object known. The geometrician understands the premises and sees that the conclusions follow from them; the learner lacks that insight and accepts conclusions through faith in the teacher. The educated person is one who is in close contact with reality, who penetrates the meaning of things, whose judgments are fixed by reality itself.

A second characteristic of education is that it is a vital activity in which the one being educated is the principal agent of his own education. Every educated person is self-educated. Of course he has to learn from others; but he actively assimilates what he gains from others, allowing them to guide him, but not to dominate him. On the other hand, a person being indoctrinated is passively subject to the indoctrinator, who moulds him into the required shape.

Thirdly, education is for the sake of the person, for his perfection as a being of intelligence and will. Indoctrination, on the contrary, subjects the person to some special interest: that of a political or religious group, for example. At least that is its natural tendency, although a person guilty of indoctrinating others may not deliberately intend this.

Without philosophy, insight into the basic principles of all knowledge will be lacking, as will a reasoned understanding of the great truths about human nature and the way of life we should follow, the fundamental laws of civil society, the existence and nature of God. The true philosopher is the true radical. Etymologically, a radical is one who goes to the root of things. This disqualifies most of those who claim to be radicals. They remain on the surface, and remain tied to the society they claim to reject. Certainly they are in reaction against many aspects of contemporary civilization, but their very reactions are conditioned by that same society, and their lack of anything worthwhile with which to replace the status quo is due to a superficiality within them corresponding to the superficiality of the society they protest against.

Truly educated persons base their thought on the deepest, most solid principles. So any knowledge they gain of the physical sciences, the arts, history, etc., have for them an orientation and an intelligibility unobtainable otherwise.

2. Criticisms of philosophy

Let us conclude by looking at some commonly urged criticisms of philosophy, giving particular attention to those against Thomism.

Objection. Philosophy is too remote from reality. Linguistic analysts spend their time dissecting common-place sentences; existentialists get away from real existence and utter their own obscure thoughts in their own peculiar jargon – "The for-itself and the in-itself", "Man-in-the-world", etc.; Scholastics live in a universe peopled with abstractions like potencies, forms, essences. Philosophy is an academic discipline of no practical value whatever. It doesn't help people in the ordinary problems of their daily lives; nor does it help them find meaning in life. When a person turns to religion, for example, this is for reasons of the heart, not because of an intellectual conviction that a Prime Mover can be proved.

Reply. Philosophy searches out the deepest explanations; consequently it cannot be an easy subject, and many of its topics will appear obscure and academic to those unfamiliar with it. But if we were to reject it on that account, we would have to reject the positive sciences as well, because they are extremely difficult for the uninitiated.

I agree that some philosophers are excessively obscure and that others are excessively preoccupied with the analysis of language; but we should expose these faults where they occur, and not condemn all philosophy because of them. Philosophy has enormous practical value, but is situated at the root of practical affairs where it is at the same time crucial and very easily overlooked.

I strongly disagree with the implication that reason plays no part in religious conversion – or in the practice of religion. While supernatural faith is the principal thing here, it is not the only one; the total person is involved: and that includes the intellect and its natural reasoning processes. Reason removes obstacles to the reception of faith, which can be seen in the struggles of many converts in their progress towards Christianity, as they gradually overcome their intellectual difficulties.

St Augustine of Hippo is a good example. From grossly anthropomorphic imaginings about God he moved painfully but surely to a purer understanding, until "with the flash of one trembling glance it [his reason] arrived at THAT WHICH IS. And then I saw thy invisible things understood by the things which are made."[2] Philosophy can help elevate and purify our minds, making them more fit for the reception of supernatural truths.

Objection. Philosophers cannot agree about anything. Whatever conclusion you like to mention, some philosopher will be found who disputes it. And instead of giving their students surer knowledge, they give them greater doubts. Things have not improved in the half-century since Professor C. D. Broad commented that many philosophers are "individuals whose only function, on their own showing, is to cure a disease which they catch from each other and impart to their pupils."[3]

Reply. The confusion among philosophers is certainly distressing and disheartening. But it is a historical fact that Thomism has been a comprehensive and unified philosophy from the thirteenth century to the present time. Many disagreements occur among Thomists, but they are usually relatively minor and leave the substance of the philosophy unaffected. As I have already explained, I consider most of the fundamental differences of opinion among today's philosophers to be due to errors about the nature of knowledge – errors which, fortunately, are capable of a rational solution.

Objection. Thomism is tied to authority, and consequently is valueless as a philosophy. Thomas Aquinas did not reach his conclusions after an impartial investigation; he accepted them before he started his enquiry.

He was a saint who accepted on faith whatever the Catholic Church taught, and would not deliberately have let his reason deviate a fraction of an inch from that faith. Moreover, Rome has officially endorsed his philosophy. Most Popes for several centuries have explicitly approved it. This situation is repugnant to the genuine philosopher, who takes reason alone as guide, and sees it as a contradiction in terms to accept a philosophy on faith.

Reply. We have already insisted that reason is the only guide in philosophy, and that insofar as something is beyond reason it is beyond philosophy.

But we have also pointed out that all truths harmonize, that one cannot contradict another. An important corollary for a Catholic is that the teachings of his Church provide a confirmation of many philosophical conclusions. This does not mean he has to cease philosophising. For one thing, some philosophical problems have no light thrown on them by Revelation, and others are but dimly illuminated. However, even where faith gives a definite answer to a question that philosophy also studies, the believer can still philosophise with the same integrity as anyone else. He is interested in whether reason can solve the problem, and his evaluation of the evidence should not be swayed by the fact that his faith already provides an answer.

Somewhat similarly, a student of astronomy who begins to weigh the evidence for the Copernican theory is already convinced, on the authority of his teachers, parents, etc., that it is true; but this need not affect his judgment of the scientific evidence. St Thomas knew from the Bible that the universe had a beginning, but this did not compel him to say it can be proved from reason. Having weighed the case for and against, he concluded that philosophy cannot give the answer.

I realize that one may in fact jump to unwarranted conclusions in philosophising because of doctrines accepted through religious faith. But no one is justified in ignoring a philosopher on the *a priori* assumption that he must have distorted his reason because of his faith; if he claims to be speaking as a philosopher, he is entitled to a fair hearing.

Nor is it true that the religious believer is the only one subject to this danger. An eighteen-year-old who starts to think out his philosophy has already had eighteen years of sundry influences working in him. He may have had no religious education, but he has received some sort of education, and must have developed numerous opinions, prejudices, sympathies, antipathies. We learn from our social environment as spontaneously as we breathe air from our physical environment, and it would be ridiculous to claim that some thinkers (those lacking religious beliefs) can start philosophising unaffected by extraneous views and attitudes.

A crucial point is: how reliable are our beliefs? The beginner in science who has always accepted the Copernican system on faith will experience no difficulty on that score when he applies himself to judging the evidence. On the other hand, had he been brought up believing in the Ptolemaic system, he would be at a disadvantage: all his sympathies and his accustomed modes of thinking would incline him away from the true answer. A similar situation prevails between belief and philosophy. When one's early beliefs are in harmony with true philosophy, they will facilitate reasoning; when discordant from true philosophy they will hinder it. I am not speaking only of beliefs associated with religion, but of all views bearing on philosophy. Since people disagree about which beliefs are right, they will disagree about whether a particular set of beliefs will help or hinder one when engaged in philosophy. Is it a help or a hindrance to be brought up as a Marxist? Or a deconstructionist? Or an evangelical Protestant? Or a Catholic? Our answer will depend largely on our judgment of the truth or falsity of these positions.

Some will maintain that the person with the best chance of arriving at philosophic truth is the one who has been raised without definite beliefs, being left to work out the answers for himself when he is sufficiently mature. I think this view is about as sensible as a proposal that a child should be kept away from music so that he will be able to make his own impartial judgment about it when he is older. The likely result would be an inability to appreciate any music, or at any rate a drastically impaired ability to do so. When no attempt is made to enlighten a child's mind about fundamentals, he usually reaches adulthood with his aptitude in this area sadly atrophied. His mind is not broad and free; it is narrow and fixed – narrowed by the vagueness of his "educators" and fixed by the force of his passions and prejudices.

Pope Pius XII repeated the Catholic Church's settled position regarding the philosophy of which St Thomas is the greatest exponent. "There is much in the tenets of this philosophy which does not touch, either directly or indirectly, the provinces of faith and morals. All this the Church leaves open to free discussion among the learned. But this liberty cannot be claimed over a multitude of other points, and notably over the main principles it rests on, the main assertions it makes..."[4] This is a reasonable position to hold if one accepts the Catholic Faith. Those who do not may be cynical about the chances of a Catholic wholeheartedly assenting to the Church's teaching, yet maintaining his integrity as a philosopher. I can only invite them to judge Thomism on the rational evidence it can bring forward; the Thomist asks them for no more than this.

Objection. Imagine the ridicule a person would receive who advocated returning to thirteenth century physical science. Advances in knowledge have been so great that medieval science is of no more than historic interest; and this applies to the whole corpus of the sciences, not just particular areas. When we come to philosophy, however, we find people who accept a system that reached maturity seven hundred years ago, and is closely related to Greek speculation of the fourth century B.C. If the Thomist wants us to take him seriously, it is up to him to show why we should accept medieval philosophy while rejecting medieval science.

Reply. In chapter five, section one, the relationship between philosophy and common sense was discussed, and it was emphasized that philosophical conclusions depend entirely on self-evident principles and data directly experienced. And that is why philosophy can be reliable at a period when physical science is not. People find its basis already in their possession, whereas the natural sciences cannot be developed without a mass of specialized data and the use of instruments (microscopes, telescopes, etc.) which medieval scientists lacked.

The difference can be confirmed by reflecting on what would happen if someone today challenged modern science with medieval theories, and contrasting that with a Scholastic debating with a modern non-Scholastic philosopher. In the former case, the result would be laughable: the apologist of ancient ideas would be unable to present even the semblance of a strong thesis, and would be at a complete loss in criticizing today's science – his system, in addition to lacking the answers, would lack the framework for many of the questions. We owe scientists of antiquity and the Middle Ages admiration and respect; we should acknowledge their real achievements (which have mostly been assimilated by modern science); we can concede the faultiness of present-day science. But the disparity remains.

The position regarding the Scholastic and modern non-Scholastic philosopher is completely different. One may disagree with the Scholastic, but one cannot say he is at the kind of disadvantage suffered by the advocate of old physical science. His case has not been demolished by new discoveries; and the very arguments given against him, for the most part, are arguments that were known in ancient times. Even when a new school arises, say logical positivism, examination shows it to be grounded in ideas, e.g., empiricism, from the past.

Objection. Thomism is too exclusive. We need an ecumenical outlook in philosophy as in religion; and the philosopher should be more ready than most people to welcome truth no matter where it comes from. But Thomism stands like a fortress, intent on guarding its treasures and repelling attack.

Reply. This complaint suggests little real understanding of Thomism, which has assimilated truths from every available source. When philosophers contradict one another, it often happens that each has seen part of the truth; and when we turn to Thomism we find, time after time, that the complete view is contained there as in a synthesis standing between and above the opposing viewpoints.

For example, Thomism agrees with nominalism in rejecting the existence of universals as such, but with ultra-realism in accepting the natures present to the mind as universals. It agrees with empiricism that all our knowledge comes from sensation, but with rationalism in holding that the intellect knows far more than is contained in sensation. With materialism, it rejects Platonic and Cartesian theories that make man two substances, yet agrees with the dualists that man is spiritual as well as corporeal. In natural theology it avoids, by the concept of analogy, the extremes of anthropomorphism and agnosticism. In ethics it refuses to place the purpose of life in pleasure, yet does not swing to the austere extreme of Stoicism or Kantianism.

True philosophy must present a large and orderly view of reality, and must have all its different parts enlivened and unified by the same underlying principles. It must avoid exclusivism, and it must equally avoid eclecticism. It will lose its life if it becomes too mundane; but it will lose its reason if it becomes too poetical.

Thomism should be compared to a living thing, not to a fortress. Every living body preserves its life by rejecting what is harmful to it and assimilating what is health-giving. A philosophy, if it is to live, must reject errors and assimilate truths. A grave danger for Thomists today is that, under the guise of truth-seeking, they will allow serious errors to become part of their thought, and under the guise of broadening their horizons will turn to eclecticism instead of genuinely assimilating the insights of other thinkers.

Objection. Modern people cannot accept Thomism because their thought patterns are different. No matter how flawlessly you argue, they will remain unconvinced. This applies to young people particularly. Their thinking is concrete and emotive, not abstract and logical; and Thomism repels them as a cold, impersonal system remote from the urgent human problems facing us today.

Reply. Philosophy should be evaluated according to standards of truth and falsity, not according to whether it is popular or unpopular, or easy to grasp or difficult. However, while any philosophy is difficult, Thomism is not unusually so. It arises, as we have explained, from the common sense knowledge possessed by everyone; so we all start with the raw material we need. One who feels this philosophy to be cold and impersonal has not really understood it; and while we may wish sometimes for a more immediate emotional impact, we must remember the limitations of our human nature when exploring deep realities.

Young people today are quite capable of grasping and appreciating Thomism. If they say it is alien to their way of thinking, I suggest that they consider whether they are being blocked from the truth by influences from the sick civilization in which we are all immersed. We may feel comfortable if we tell ourselves, with an air of finality, that a particular way of philosophising is incompatible with modern thought patterns. But we should ask ourselves whether we are just being smug; and whether "thought patterns" is a euphemism for brainwashing.

A person who makes the effort to understand St Thomas' philosophy will find there a secure basis for thought and a unique enrichment of life.

[1]   Explained in chapter five, section four.
[2]   *Confessions*, book VII, section 17.
[3]   From a lecture delivered in the University of Oslo, March 1955. Published in *Clarity is not Enough*, edited by. H. D. Lewis (1963), p. 45.
[4]   Encyclical *Humani Generis* (1950), n. 30.

CHAPTER

```
                                          │its genesis ............................................... 1
                           │its genesis                        │to the Renaissance .......... 2
                           │and development    │its progress
              │rela-                                           │in modern times .............. 3
              │tively
              │to                           its present state ................................... 4
              │other knowledge ................................................................... 5
                                   │in general ...................................................... 6
                                   │sense knowledge ........................................... 7
                                   │intellectual knowledge ................................. 8
              │its principal
              │problem:
              │knowledge
                                                             │concerning
                                                             │idealism and
                                                             │empiricism ............ 9
                                   │consequences of the
                                   │doctrine of knowledge
                                                             │concerning the
                                                             │nature of man ...... 10
              │in
              │itself
              │classification of its parts ......................................................... 11
PHILO-
SOPHY│
                                          │first principles .............................. 12
                           │speculative
                           │philosophy │the nature of being ........................ 13
                                                        │his existence ............ 14
                                          │God          │his nature ................. 15
              │some
              │questions of

                                          │the philosophy of art   16
                           │practical philosophy
                                          │ethics ....................... 17
              │its importance ..................................................................................... 18
```

INDEX

Schlick, M., 74
Scholasticism, 42, 45, 89
Schopenhauer, A., 253
Science,
 as "certain knowledge through
 causes", 99
 logic is a science, 202
 speculative and practical
 sciences, 200-201
 empirical, 101-104, 320
  philosophy intrinsically
  independent of, 326
  is the study of phenomena,
  101-103
  and natural philosophy, 198
  cannot show the nature of
  knowledge, 163
 incompatible with idealism,
 157
Secondary qualities, 57, 126, 160
Seneca, 32
Sense knowledge, 123-131, 142,
143
Sexual morality, 309-310
Siger of Brabant, 38
Singer, P., 315-316
Socrates, 13-16
 condemnation and execution,
 16
 dialectical method, 15
 loved supreme goodness and
 beauty, 14-15
 sought definitions, 15
Solipsism, 158, 159, 162
Solomon, R. C., 85
Solzhenitsyn, A., 86
Sophists, 15

Soul,
 Anaximenes on, 10
 conflicting Greek views on,
 14, 19, 24
 Descartes on, 48
 Kant on, 65-66, 175
 Locke on, 54
 as form of the body, 39,
 187-189
 needs the body, 189-190
 immortality of human,
 173-175, 293
 spirituality of human, 173-174
 its knowledge after death,
 297-298
 and the Beatific Vision,
 299-300
 world-soul, 31, 33
Spinoza, B., 50, 100, 272
Stoicism, 31-32, 294
Suarezians, 228
Substance, 19, 188
 and accidents, 41, 214
 and primary matter, in
 Aristotle, 112
 cannot be affirmed by
 empiricism, 160
 confusion with quantity, 199
 denial of, and solipsism, 160
 meaning of, 23
 necessity of, 213-214
 Ayer and, 75
 Berkeley and, 56-57
 Hegel and, 67
 Hume and, 61
 Kant and, 64
 Locke and, 53-54

www.ingramcontent.com/pod-product-compliance
Lightning Source LLC
Chambersburg PA
CBHW052029090426
42739CB00010B/1841